"Every now and then a memoir is so well written that readers are able to find elements of their own life story in the chronicle of the writer's life. So it is with this eloquent, tender, witty memoir. Shifting artfully between the voice of a child and the perspective of an adult, John Grogan captures our hearts from start to finish."
—Doris Kearns Goodwin

"An extraordinary memoir of estrangement and reconciliation."
—*Booklist*

"With his telltale humor and poignant observations about life and our humanity, John Grogan delivers another emotional wallop here. *The Longest Trip Home* is a must-read for anyone who has questioned their faith, sought to understand their identity, and loved their family. In other words, everyone."
—Ann Hood, author of *Comfort: A Journey Through Grief* and *The Knitting Circle*

"Touching and inspiring. . . . *The Longest Trip Home* is an enjoyable story of growth and family from an incredibly gifted writer. Grogan makes the transitions between childhood, adolescence, and adulthood masterfully, weaving the threads of his life in a way that is both relatable and interesting to readers."
—*Buffalo News*

"Grogan is no lightweight. This is a serious story of how he painfully redefines his relationship with his parents and copes with their aging. But best of all, his stories of their unconditional love despite his abundant youthful mischief will evoke all the best parts of your childhood. This story is milk-and-cookies simple: pure and terrific."
—*Rocky Mountain News*

"Grogan is a gifted and engaging writer. His disciplined prose, winning way with anecdote, and knack for comedy serve him well. . . . Millions of people will identify with the progress of Grogan's boomer-era life with its familiar milestones."

—*Orlando Sentinel*

"You can see what Grogan means when he refers to his first book as a warm-up for this one. At its best, *Longest Trip Home* is tougher and truer than *Marley & Me*—an unflinching look at how parents and children can feel at once too close and too distant from one another."

—*Austin American-Statesman*

"A hilarious and touching memoir of his childhood in suburban Detroit. . . . In this tenderly told story, Grogan considers . . . the family he's made and the family that made him—and how to bridge the two."

—*Publishers Weekly* (starred review)

"Grogan's memoir of his journey for identity is akin to Barack Obama's *Dreams from My Father*."

—*Library Journal*

"This real-life coming-of-age story is a tender and touching tribute to parents Grogan loves and respects. Many anecdotes are hilarious. Some may well move readers to tears. . . . Readers will be grateful for this poignant treasure chest of moments that stuck for John Grogan—and to him for sharing them with us."

—BookReporter.com

"John Grogan is more like Marley than he might want to believe. An affable, unassuming rabble-rouser, the author who penned a bestseller about his goofy dog gets up to some hilarious antics of his own in a new coming-of-age memoir, *The Longest Trip Home*."

—*BookPage*

© SIGRID ESTRADA

About the Author

JOHN GROGAN grew up in Orchard Lake, Michigan, outside
Detroit, and earned degrees from Central Michigan and Ohio
State universities. He spent more than twenty years as an
award-winning newspaper journalist in Michigan, Florida, and
Pennsylvania, most recently as metropolitan columnist for the
Philadelphia Inquirer. He is also the former editor of Rodale's
Organic Gardening magazine. His first book, *Marley & Me,*
was a number-one international bestseller that was made into a
number-one major motion picture. John lives in a two-hundred-
year-old stone farmhouse in eastern Pennsylvania with his wife
and three children.

The Longest Trip Home

A MEMOIR

John Grogan

HARPER

NEW YORK • LONDON • TORONTO • SYDNEY

TO J.R., R.S., AND D.P., WHO TAUGHT ME EARLY ON
THE MEANING OF FRIENDSHIP

HARPER

A hardcover edition of this book was published in 2008 by William Morrow, an imprint of HarperCollins Publishers.

FIRST HARPER PAPERBACK PUBLISHED 2009.

Designed by Gretchen Achilles

Frontispiece photograph courtesy of the author.

Library of Congress Cataloging-in-Publication Data has been applied for.

ISBN 978-0-06-171330-9

09 10 11 12 13 OV/RRD 10 9 8 7 6 5 4 3 2 1

Contents

Preface

The call came on a school night in the autumn of 2002. Jenny was out, and I was fixing dinner for our three children, who were already at the table. I grabbed the phone on the third ring.

"John!" My father's voice boomed through the earpiece. He sounded exceptionally buoyant. At eighty-six, Dad was quite the physical specimen. Just as when he was a young man, he began each morning with calisthenics, including forty push-ups. He always loved the outdoors and still cut his own acre of grass, gardened, shoveled snow, and climbed on the roof to clean the gutters. Dad bustled up and down the stairs of his home with a teenager's vigor and routinely got by on six hours of sleep. His handwriting was as neat and controlled as on the day he went to work as a draftsman for General Motors in 1940, and he honed his mind each night by breezing through the crossword puzzle in the newspaper as he ate peanuts in his trademark way—with chopsticks so he wouldn't get his fingers greasy.

There was never enough time in each day for everything he wanted to get done, and fourteen years shy of becoming a centenarian, he joked that someday when life settled down, he would get to all that leisure reading on his list. "When I retire," he'd say.

"Hey, Dad," I said. "What's up?"

"Just checking in," he said. "How's everyone there?" I gave him quick updates on the kids, told him we were all fine. We chatted aimlessly for a few minutes as I carried the pasta and sauce to the table.

I placed my hand over the mouthpiece. "It's Grandpa," I whispered to the children and motioned to them to dig in.

"Everyone says hi," I told him.

"Say," he said, pausing just a little too long, "I need to talk to you about something."

"Is Mom okay?" I asked.

It was my mother we all worried about. Over the years she had grown weak and fragile. Her hips and lower back had deteriorated, rendering her all but immobile. And in recent years her memory had begun to slip. Dad had become her full-time caregiver, helping her bathe and dress, and doling out a daily regimen of medications that was comical in its quantity and complexity. Always the engineer, he kept track of them all with a meticulous flowchart. There were pills for her heart, for her diabetes, for her arthritis, for her aches, for what doctors said were the early stages of Alzheimer's disease. Despite Dad's characteristically upbeat tone, with every phone call I wondered if this would be the one with the bad news.

"Mom's fine," Dad said. "Mom's doing all right. It's me. I got a little bad news today."

"You did?" I asked, stepping out of the kitchen and away from the kids.

"It's the darnedest thing," he said. "I've been feeling a little run-down lately, but nothing worth mentioning. Just kind of tired."

"You have a lot on your plate, taking care of Mom and the house and everything."

"That's all I thought it was. But a few days ago I took Mother in to Dr. Bober for her regular checkup. The doctor took one look at me and asked, 'Are you feeling okay? You look washed out.' I told her I was a little worn down but otherwise fine, and she said, 'Well, let's get you tested just to make sure you're not anemic.'"

"And?"

"And the results came back, and sure enough, I'm anemic."

"So they give you iron or something, right?"

"They can treat the anemia, but there's more to it. The anemia is just a symptom of something a little more serious."

He hesitated a moment, and I could tell he was choosing his words carefully. "After my blood work came back, Dr. Bober said she wanted to rule out some other things and sent me in for more tests." He paused. "They show I have a kind of leukemia, and—"

"Leukemia?"

"Not the bad kind," he said quickly. "There's acute leukemia, which is what you think of when you say leukemia—the kind that can kill so quickly. I don't have that. I have something called chronic lymphocytic leukemia. It's just lying there in my bloodstream not doing anything. The doctors say it could sit there dormant for years."

"How many years?" I asked.

"Anywhere from a couple to ten or twenty," Dad said.

My mind raced to process everything I was hearing. "So that's good, right?" I asked. "It may just sit there for the rest of your life."

"That's what the doctor said: 'Go about your life, Richard, and forget about it.' I should try not to worry and they'd treat any symptoms, like the anemia, and monitor my blood every four months."

"How are you doing on the 'try not to worry' front?" I asked.

"So far pretty good," he said. "I just want to stay healthy so I can take care of Mother for as long as she needs me."

Standing phone to ear from three states away, I felt a swell of optimism. Dad always bounced back. He had bounced back from the heart attack he suffered shortly after retiring from General Motors and from prostate cancer after I was married. Dad, a man who greeted adversity with stoic determination, would bounce back from this, too. The sleeping cancer would simply be something to monitor as my father marched vigorously into his nineties, holding together the strands of the life he and my mother had spent more than a half century building together.

"It's really nothing," Dad assured me. "I'm going to follow doctors' orders and try to forget about it."

That's when I asked: "Dad, what can I do?"

"Not a thing," he insisted. "I'm fine. Really."

"Are you sure?" I asked.

"Absolutely," he said and then added the one request that was so deeply important to him, the one thing that seemed so simple and effortless, and yet the one I had such difficulty delivering to him.

"Just keep me in your prayers," he said.

PART ONE

Growing Up

Chapter 1

W ake up, little sleepyheads."

The voice drifted through the ether. "Wake up, wake up, boys. Today we leave on vacation." I opened one eye to see my mother leaning over my oldest brother's bed across the room. In her hand was the dreaded feather. "Time to get up, Timmy," she coaxed and danced the feather tip beneath his nostrils. Tim batted it away and tried to bury his face in the pillow, but this did nothing to deter Mom, who relished finding innovative ways to wake us each morning.

She sat on the edge of the bed and fell back on an old favorite. "Now, if you don't like Mary Kathleen McGurny just a little bit, keep a straight face," she chirped cheerily. I could see my brother, eyes still shut, lock his lips together, determined not to let her get the best of him this time. "Just a tiny bit? An eeny teeny bit?" she coaxed, and as she did she brushed the feather across his neck. He clamped his lips tight and squeezed his eyes shut. "Do I see a little smile? Oops, I think I see just a little one. You like her just a tiny bit, don't you?" Tim was twelve and loathed Mary Kathleen

McGurny as only a twelve-year-old boy could loathe a girl known for picking her nose so aggressively on the playground it would bleed, which was exactly why my mother had chosen her for the morning wake-up ritual. "Just a little?" she teased, flicking the feather across his cheek and into his ear until he could take it no more. Tim scrunched his face into a tortured grimace and then exploded in laughter. Not that he was amused. He jumped out of bed and stomped off to the bathroom.

One victory behind her, my mother and her feather moved to the next bed and my brother Michael, who was nine and equally repelled by a girl in his class. "Now, Mikey, if you don't like Alice Treewater just a smidgen, keep a straight face for me . . ." She kept at it until she broke his resolve. My sister, Marijo, the oldest of us four, no doubt had received the same treatment in her room before Mom had started on us boys. She always went oldest to youngest.

Then it was my turn. "Oh, Johnny boy," she called and danced the feather over my face. "Who do you like? Let me think, could it be Cindy Ann Selahowski?" I grimaced and burrowed my face into the mattress. "Keep a straight face for me if it isn't Cindy Ann Selahowski." Cindy Ann lived next door, and although I was only six and she five, she had already proposed marriage numerous times. My chin trembled as I fought to stay serious. "Is it Cindy Ann? I think it just might be," she said, darting the feather over my nostrils until I dissolved into involuntary giggles.

"Mom!" I protested as I jumped out of bed and into the cool dewy air wafting through the open window, carrying on it the scent of lilacs and fresh-cut grass.

"Get dressed and grab your beer cartons, boys," Mom announced. "We're going to Sainte Anne de Beaupré's today!" My beer carton sat at the foot of my bed, covered in leftover wallpaper, the poor man's version of a footlocker. Not that we were poor, but my parents could not resist the lure of a nickel saved. Each kid had one, and whenever we traveled, our sturdy cardboard cartons doubled as suitcases. Dad liked the way they stacked neatly in the back of the Chevrolet station wagon. Both of them loved that they were completely and utterly free.

Even in our very Catholic neighborhood, all the other families took normal summer vacations, visiting national monuments or amusement parks. Our family traveled to holy miracle sites. We visited shrines and chapels and monasteries. We lit candles and kneeled and prayed at the scenes of alleged divine interventions. The Basilica of Sainte-Anne-de-Beaupré, located on the Saint Lawrence River near Quebec, was one of the grandest miracle sites in all of North America, and it was just a seven-hour drive from our home outside Detroit. For weeks, Mom and Dad had regaled us with tales of the many miracles of healing that had happened there over the centuries, beginning in 1658 when a peasant working on the original church reported a complete cure of his rheumatism as he laid stones in the foundation. "The Lord works in mysterious ways," Dad liked to say.

When I got downstairs with my packed beer carton, Dad already had the tent trailer, in which we would sleep on our expedition, hooked to the back of the station wagon. Mom had sandwiches made, and soon we were off. Sainte-Anne-de-Beaupré did not disappoint. Carved of white stone and sporting twin spires that soared to the heavens, the basilica was the most graceful, imposing building I had ever seen. And inside was better yet: the walls of the main entrance were covered with crutches, canes, leg braces, bandages, and various other implements of infirmity too numerous to count that had been cast off by those Sainte Anne had chosen to cure.

All around us were disabled pilgrims who had come to pray for their own miracles. We lit candles, and then Mom and Dad led us into a pew, where we dropped to our knees and prayed to Sainte Anne, even though none of us had anything that needed fixing. "You need to ask to receive," Mom whispered, and I bowed my head and asked Sainte Anne to let me walk again if I ever lost the use of my legs. Outside, we climbed the hillside to make the Stations of the Cross, pausing to pray at each of the fourteen stops depicting an event in Jesus' final hours. The highlight of the visit was our climb up the twenty-eight steps that were said to be an exact replica of the steps Christ climbed to face Pontius Pilate before his crucifixion. But we didn't just climb the steps. We climbed them on our knees, pausing on each one to say half a Hail Mary aloud. We went in pairs, Mom and Dad first, followed by Marijo and Tim, and behind them, Michael and me. Step One: "Hail Mary, full of grace, the Lord is with thee; blessed art thou amongst women and blessed is the fruit of thy womb, Jesus." As we uttered the name of Jesus, we bowed our heads deeply. Step Two: "Holy Mary, mother of God, pray for us sinners, now and at the hour of our death, amen." Then we moved to the next step and started again. Over and over we recited the prayer as we slowly made our way to the top, Michael and I jabbing each other and crossing our eyes to see who could make the other laugh first.

On our way to the parking lot, we visited the gift shop, where I picked out a snow globe with Sainte Anne inside. Mom filled a bottle from a spigot behind the cathedral, figuring it had to be as holy as the water from Lourdes and other miracle sites. The parish priest would later bless it for her, and she would keep it in the linen closet and bring it out whenever we were sick with a particularly stubborn fever or sore throat or earache, touching the water to our foreheads or throats or ears and tracing a sign of the cross.

On the way home, Mom and Dad played the honeymoon game, which always delighted us kids no end. "Get down low, children, out of sight!" Mom coached and slid over in the seat up close to my father, resting her head on his shoulder and planting little kisses on his neck and cheek as he drove, both hands on the wheel and a quiet grin on his face. Dad wasn't one for displays of affection—he sent each of us off to bed at night not with a hug or a kiss but with a firm handshake—yet he seemed to enjoy the honeymoon game as much as the rest of us.

"Smooch smooch, Richie," Mom cooed.

We four kids lay in a heap on the backseat, looking up at them in lovebird mode and squealing at our clever subterfuge. Every passing motorist surely thought our parents were newlyweds on their honeymoon. Little did any of them know that the smooching couple already had four children hiding in the backseat and giggling with abandon. "Here comes another car," we'd scream in unison. "Kiss him again! Kiss him again!" And Mom would gladly comply.

Another successful family miracle trip was coming to an end. We had camped out in the crisp Canadian air, thrown rocks in Lake Ontario, eaten my mother's famous pork and beans cooked over an open fire, and prayed our way up twenty-eight steps on our knees. Life was safe and warm and good. I had parents who loved God and each other and us. I had two brothers and a sister to play and run and fight with. I had a house and toys and my own beer carton in which I could carry anything I wanted. Best of all, I had the comforting knowledge that if anything ever did go wrong, there was always Sainte Anne de Beaupré just a day's drive away, ready to use her miraculous healing powers to make everything right again. It was a dreamy, wondrous time.

Chapter 2

M y parents met in 1946, shortly after my father returned from four years on an aircraft carrier in the
South Pacific. A year to the day later, they were
married, and just weeks after that, expecting their first child.

Before they set off on the road to parenthood, though, they
made a pact that each of their offspring would be named after
either the Virgin Mary or her husband, Saint Joseph, who had
selflessly taken on all the responsibility of fatherhood without any
of the fun of procreation. Mary's sexless conception of Jesus was a
given in our household, with no room for debate. The Holy Spirit
had miraculously planted the seed of God's only begotten son into
the Blessed Mother's womb. Uncomplaining Saint Joseph took it
from there. Even as a little boy, I thought this terribly unfair.

My sister, the eldest, got the Daily Double of Catholic names.
My parents baptized her Mary Josephine, later shortened to
Marijo. Next came Timothy Joseph and Michael Joseph.

But before the boys there was another girl, one who didn't
make it. My parents baptized her Mary Ann, even though she

never took a single breath. The only one ever to see her, and then only for a few moments, was my father, who described her as perfect in every way, like a flawless porcelain doll. Hospitals administered anesthesia to women delivering in those days, and when my mother finally awoke, my father was waiting at her bedside searching for the words to tell her. He would never forget the look on her face in the instant she opened her eyes. She was radiant, a smile spreading on her lips, her eyes widening with joyous expectation. Then he squeezed her hand and said, "Ruthie, our baby's with the Lord now."

They cried and prayed and told themselves this was God's plan and there had to be a reason she was in heaven already before she ever had a chance to experience life on earth. Then they arranged for a Catholic burial, her tiny casket resting to this day between my grandparents' graves in Ann Arbor.

I came along in 1957. John Joseph. Mom and Dad were hoping I would be a Saint Patrick's Day baby. When I missed that date, they rooted for Saint Joseph's Day, which would have been fitting, given all our middle names. Late again. When I finally arrived on March 20, I had other bragging rights. I came into the world on the first day of spring.

Mom called me her little daffodil.

Right from the start, Mom's little daffodil was no wallflower. Maybe it was the Cap'n Crunch cereal I devoured in vast quantities each morning, so sugary it made my teeth tingle. Maybe it was simply being the youngest of four and doing what was necessary to hog as much of my parents' attention as possible. Whatever the reason, I was born with abundant energy and few tools for containing it. My earliest memories are of racing through the house like a miniature tornado, shrieking joyously at the top of my lungs. Sometimes Dad would simply swoop me off my feet and hold me off the ground, legs still pumping, until I calmed down enough that I wouldn't hurt myself. On one of my runabouts through the house, I grabbed Mom's broom and held it over my head like a knight with a lance. "Stop! Now!" Mom ordered. I did, but only after the broom struck the large glass globe hanging from the foyer ceiling, sending it showering down on me in a thousand shards.

That night at dinner, Dad pulled out his stopwatch and said, "Johnny, we're going to try a little test. I want you to sit perfectly still for one full minute."

"Not a word, not a wiggle," Mom added. It was clear they were convinced I could not do it.

The first try, I lasted twelve seconds. Then thirty. Eventually I made it to sixty seconds, sitting there, grinning and twisting my face up, thinking this new game was great fun. The instant Dad clicked off the stopwatch and said, "Why, I'll be doggoned, he did it," I shot out of my chair like a Saturn space rocket and orbited the living room several times, pinging off the furniture.

In kindergarten the teacher noted my need to practice self-restraint and helped by frequently sending me to the corner to sit alone. She called Mom to come get me only on special occasions, such as the day I used two of my fingers like a fork to poke a classmate in the eyes, just like Moe did to Curly in my favorite show of all time, *The Three Stooges*.

When we got home after that incident, Mom said to me as she did after so many of them: "Johnny, go get George."

Mom was a firm believer in the power of spankings to modify behavior, and George was her enforcer. Before George had a name, he was simply the laundry stick, a thin board about eighteen inches long and two inches wide that Mom used to poke the clothes down into the suds in the washing machine. "Johnny, go get the laundry stick," Mom would say, and I knew what was coming, a crack across the backside.

Then one evening, my father treated us to dinner at a fancy restaurant, and all four of us kids, giddy with excitement, would not settle down. Mom was too embarrassed to let the other diners overhear her threatening her children with a spanking, so from thin air she pulled two names. Looking at Marijo, she asked matter-of-factly, as if issuing pleasantries: "Would you like a little visit from Suzie when we get home?" And from her tone and the look in her eye, Marijo figured out right away that a visit from this Suzie person would not be pleasant.

Then she leveled her calm gaze at my brothers and me. "And boys, how would you like to meet my friend George?" Subtlety being lost on me, I screamed out, "Sure!" Then Mom added: "You remember George, don't you? My friend who lives in the laundry room?" Suddenly I didn't want to meet George anymore.

When we got home, she wrote the words on the stick in permanent marker where they remained for years, even as the soapy wash water faded them to gray: *George* on one side, *Suzie* on the other. From that day forward, the George-and-Suzie Spanking Stick was an effective part of Mom's arsenal. Usually a mere threat of a visit from George or Suzie was all that was needed to pull us back into line, but when punishment was required, Marijo always got her spanking on the Suzie side and the boys on the George side. The stick struck fear in the hearts of all four of us, even though Mom's whacks—and they always came from Mom, Dad not having the stomach for any type of corporal punishment—weren't much harder than love taps. That didn't stop me, however, from stuffing my pants with multiple copies of *National Geographic* to cushion the blow. I thought I was being outstandingly clever, but whenever Mom spotted a bulky load in my britches, she simply lowered her aim, to the back of my thighs.

Our neighborhood was known as Harbor Hills, though it really had neither. What it did have was a pair of gentle slopes on my street and a small man-made boat basin carved out by bulldozers between the two not-quite-hills.

The boat basin fed through a channel into Cass Lake, one of the largest inland bodies of water in metropolitan Detroit and unquestionably the biggest selling point of Harbor Hills, which consisted of three streets arranged in a sort of caste system in relation to the water. Only those fortunate enough to have waterfront lots could actually see the lake from their homes. These homes were large and glorious beyond description, and the people who lived in them were doctors and lawyers and business owners. Elsewhere in the neighborhood, on the landlocked lots, the dads tended to work in more middle-income professions. They were draftsmen and insurance agents and plumbers, and of course, automobile workers. Many, many of them, my father included, were gainfully employed by one of Detroit's Big Three—General Motors, Ford, or Chrysler. The farther away from the water you got in the neighborhood, the more modest the houses became.

But there was a great equalizer in Harbor Hills, and that was The Outlot.

The Outlot was a sort of grassy public space—not quite a park but more than a mowed field—covering a few acres right on the water. It surrounded the boat basin and was set aside by the developer for the exclusive use of the neighborhood. No matter how far back in the neighborhood you lived, you still had a piece of lake frontage to use as your own. There were big shade trees and picnic tables and, best of all, a small, stony beach with a raft and roped-off swimming area, where every kid in the neighborhood spent virtually every waking moment between Memorial Day and Labor Day. It was nothing fancy, but it was a beach, and that's all that mattered. The boat basin, universally known as The Lagoon, was lined with rickety wooden docks, and every house in the neighborhood was assigned one side of a dock. When you bought in Harbor Hills, you were getting more than just a suburban home on three-quarters of an acre. You were getting a waterfront lifestyle without the cost of a waterfront home—a place to swim and sunbathe and water-ski and picnic with the

cool lake breezes in your face. My parents never experienced anything close to this growing up during the Great Depression, and
like all good parents, they wanted more for their kids. They saved
for years to move us out of the city to this Shangri-la on the shore.
When you were lounging by the water on a perfect summer's day,
it was hard to believe the gray, belching auto plants of Pontiac
were just a ten-minute drive away.

In the summer, we swam and swam and swam. My brothers
and sister and I were soon true amphibians, as comfortable in the
water as out. This was a point of immense pride for my father,
a landlocked city kid who only learned to swim, and then not
well, when he joined the navy after Pearl Harbor. For my mother,
who never learned to swim at all, it was simply a mystery. But
summer wasn't the only season when we gathered in The Outlot.
In the winter, we shoveled the snow off The Lagoon and skated
until our legs ached and our toes were numb. We skated in the
daylight, and we skated at night, the ice illuminated by the glow
of rudimentary floodlights rigged to a nearby power pole. Sometimes one of the dads would build a warming fire next to the ice,
and we would huddle around it, all runny noses and rosy cheeks,
our breath rising in steamy clouds. In the spring and fall, the
kids of the neighborhood—and there were dozens of us—were
again down at the water, hanging out, goofing off, soaking our
shoes, throwing sand at each other, and skipping stones. Every
Easter there was a neighborhood egg hunt, and every Labor Day
the annual Harbor Hills picnic, the highlight of which was the
decorated bike parade. There were games and hot dogs and root
beer on tap and, best of all, coal-roasted corn on the cob dipped in
melted butter. The dads roasted the corn and ran the games; the
moms anchored the potluck and dessert tables.

But Cass Lake was only half of what lured my parents to
Harbor Hills. The other half, an even more powerful draw for
them, was Our Lady of Refuge. They believed fervently in their
duty to raise their children as devout Catholics. That meant not

only Mass every Sunday—a nonnegotiable—but Mass on as many weekdays as possible, too. It meant receiving the holy sacraments of confession and communion and confirmation. It meant evening rosaries and Stations of the Cross, altar-boy training and staying up for Midnight Mass on Christmas. It meant smudged foreheads on Ash Wednesday and a Catholic education from the knuckle-rapping, hair-tugging, ear-twisting Sisters of Saint Felix in their brown habits and starched white face boards. The nuns, Mom and Dad assured us, were building our character.

Our house was three doors from Our Lady of Refuge, and my mother could stand at the living-room window and watch us march across the backyards, not losing sight of us until we entered the back door of the school. They had worked hard and saved relentlessly to move here, but they never regretted a dime of the cost. This, they were convinced, was the perfect place to raise a family. Many of our neighbors were just like my parents, practicing Catholics drawn to the neighborhood's twin attractions.

The beach and the church were the two poles of our universe. All life, all activity seemed to gravitate around one or the other. We were either at the beach or at Our Lady of Refuge—in school or in church or waiting for confession or playing soccer or hardball on the athletic fields. Either that or we were on our bicycles riding between the two.

To say my parents were devout Catholics is like saying the sun runs a little hot. It defined who they were. They were Catholics first, and then Americans and spouses and parents. Right from the start, their relationship was forged in their mutual devotion to Jesus and the Blessed Mother. One of their earliest dates was Mass followed by a rosary. As a kid hearing my mother tell the story for the umpteenth time, I could only sit, mouth agape in something approaching mortification, thinking, *Oh my God, I have the squarest parents in the universe.*

For fun, my siblings and I would sometimes count the Virgin Marys in the house; at one point we were up to forty-two. They filled every room, and they were not alone. Commingling with them were various likenesses of Jesus, Joseph, John the Baptist, Francis of Assisi, and an assortment of other saints and angels. There were crucifixes everywhere you turned in our house, the anguished, dying son of God staring down at us from the cross as we ate breakfast, brushed our teeth, and watched television. There were priest-blessed candles and holy water and palm fronds. Rosaries were scattered about in ashtrays and candy bowls. It was like living in a religious supply store. We even had an emergency Holy Communion kit, consisting of an aged oak box lined in purple velvet containing a silver chalice, a silver platter to hold communion wafers, two candleholders, and a cross. I had no idea where it came from, but it looked official and could be pressed into service by visiting priests who might want to say Mass at our dining room table. This happened more often than one might think.

My mother was constantly inviting priests to the house, and once she got them there, inviting them to give a group blessing or lead a prayer or say Mass. The priests, knowing a home-cooked meal would follow, seldom refused. She was a gifted cook, and her promise of good food even managed to lure a couple of bishops. We kids treated them like rock stars, taking turns dropping to our knees and kissing the big rings on their hands. It helped that two of Mom's brothers were priests. Father Joe and Father Vin, as we all knew them, visited often and, especially in the summer months, brought priest friends along to relax and enjoy the beach. It seemed we had clergy in our house more days than not, and they became a natural part of our family dynamic. Having Father O'Flaherty or Brother McGhee or even Bishop Schuster at the dinner table with us was just the way it was.

Our family was many things, but first we were Catholics. Of all my parents' dreams for their four children, only one was immutable: that we grow up imbued with the faith—devout, lifelong, practicing Catholics.

Chapter 3

Despite my parents' best efforts, you could say my life as a good Catholic boy got off to a rocky start.

In the spring of 1964, I was preparing to celebrate my first confession. Or at least that's how the nuns put it—*celebrate*—as though we would be having a party with cake and balloons. To a Catholic school second grader, this was a watershed event, and the sisters at Our Lady of Refuge had been preparing my classmates and me for the holy sacrament for months. We had all been baptized as infants; that was our first holy sacrament, and thank God for that because, as Sister and my parents pointed out repeatedly and very matter-of-factly, baptized Catholics were the only ones getting into heaven. The Protestants, Jews, Muslims, and everybody else were heading straight for limbo, certainly better than hell but basically just an eternal waiting room outside heaven's gate.

Confession was our second sacrament, and its importance could not be overstated. This was the Lord's gift to us, our chance to purge the sins from our second-grade souls, to confess our transgressions—the pilfered candy and whispered swear words, the cruel taunts and creative lies—and seek God's forgiveness. It was a beautiful thing, the nuns assured us. We would receive our penance from the priest, who was just a breath shy of God himself and had his full authority to forgive. A few Hail Marys, a few Our Fathers—maybe even a half dozen of each if we had some doozies on our list—and all would be bygones. We would walk out of the dark confession box with a spring in our step and a lightness to our shoulders because we would no longer be carrying the burden of sin. At least not our own sins. We were all stuck with Original Sin, thanks to Adam and Eve and the way they caved in to temptation and ate the apple, but there wasn't anything we could do about that. It was kind of like being born with a genetic defect; you just had to deal with it. We could wipe out our own transgressions, though, and start over fresh. As with the bath Mom made my brothers and me take every Saturday night, lined up in a row in the tub, the old grime washed down the drain, leaving us clean and ready to start getting dirty all over again.

There was another important reason for the sacrament of confession. It was a necessary precursor to the even more important sacrament of Holy Communion, in which the priest—who, did I mention, was just a breath shy of God himself?—would take an ordinary piece of bread and through a miracle turn it into the body of Christ. Not a symbol of the body of Christ, but an actual piece of his flesh. We'd be eating Jesus! And not only that, but we would get to dress up like we were getting married as we did it, the girls in lacy white dresses with veils and pearl-beaded gloves, the boys in navy-blue suits and ties just like our dads wore. The miracle, the nuns told us, was called *transubstantiation*—the changing of bread and wine into the body and blood of Christ. We would know it was real the instant we swallowed a little piece of Jesus because we would feel his presence in us. He would fill us with a warm glow, a joy a thousand times greater than the joy of an ice cream sundae on a hot August day or the Detroit Tigers making it to the World Series (something that would actually happen a few years later and which we all considered a miracle in its own right). But first we had to scour the impurities from our tot-size temples to make way for the Lord.

Sins were broken down into two groups. There were the run-of-the-mill venial sins—swearing, tattling, disobeying, coveting thy neighbor's oxen. Then there were the biggies, the mortal sins. This would include, for instance, slaying your brother like Cain did to Abel or worshipping false idols over the Lord thy God. The nuns assured us that the priests were very experienced and had heard every sin imaginable, even the mortals, and we shouldn't feel ashamed to tell them anything. Besides, they assured us, it was totally confidential. The priests took a vow never to divulge your sins, even if you were a famous murderer the police were looking for. Not only was it confidential; the whole affair was completely anonymous. We got to kneel in a dark box and talk through a screen to the priest on the other side. We could see him, but he couldn't see us. It was brilliant. He wouldn't know who we were even if he did want to tell the police or, worse, our parents.

Confession would be great, the first important step on the road to being lifelong Catholics and our ticket to salvation. It was the key to unlock our temples so that when we ate Jesus' body and sipped his blood he'd feel right at home inside us.

There was only one problem. My little temple carried a dark, shameful secret—two of them, actually—and I knew God would not wipe them clean with a few recited prayers or even a few hundred.

The first had to do with Mrs. Selahowski next door, whose daughter Cindy Ann Selahowski was not shy about letting me know she intended to marry me someday. It was a prospect that made my blood run cold, which is why Mom loved to tease me about her. Mrs. Selahowski, on the other hand, held an entirely different allure. Young, thin, and blond, she was my first love. It began when I was a preschooler. I played at their house nearly every day, and whenever Mrs. S. would walk into their rumpus room, I would gaze in adoration. When I was still napping in the afternoons, my mother would often lie beside me and doze off herself. I remember watching her as she slept, her face just inches from mine, and thinking she was the most beautiful woman in the whole world. After Mrs. Selahowski came on my radar, I revised my assessment.

Fueling my desire was Mrs. Selahowski's obsession with having the deepest tan in all of Michigan. Every single day, beginning in late spring, she would be out in her backyard, stretched on a chaise longue worshipping the sun. She would bake out there for hours in a tiny two-piece bathing suit, her blond hair piled loosely atop her head, rhinestone-encrusted sunglasses shading her eyes, baby oil slathered over her golden body. When she would lie on her stomach, she often reached back and unfastened her bathing suit top, which I found wildly provocative. One false move, and her bosom—I pronounced the word *ba-zooms*—would be fully exposed. From my second-story bedroom window, I had the perfect vantage point, and I prayed fervently for the lawn sprinklers to come on and shock her onto her feet. For my birthday, I asked for a telescope. "Our little Galileo," I heard Mom tell Dad.

A schoolboy crush would have been one thing, but by the time second grade had rolled around I had clearly moved into the sinful land of lust. I was coveting my neighbor's wife—poor Mr. Selahowski, he was such a nice man—and wife coveting was on the list not just of mortal sins but of *grave* mortal sins. That alone made me terrified of the confessional and the wrath I knew awaited me. But it got worse.

Sister Mary Lawrence was my second-grade teacher. She was stern and no-nonsense, a tiny woman who, as best as I could tell, was barely into her twenties. She wore the somber brown, scratchy wool habit of her order. A veil covered her hair, and stiffly starched linen boxed in her forehead, ears, and neck so that only the center of her face showed. Obviously she was no Mrs. Sela-howski, but still kind of pretty. At least what I could see of her.

One day I was sitting in class lost in my thoughts, gazing at Sister in front of the chalkboard as she called on various students to stand and read aloud. The floor-length brown robes fascinated me, and I couldn't help wondering what she wore under them. Did she wear a bra and girdle like Mom? Or more of a flowing white nightgown getup like Florence Nightingale? Or frilly pet-ticoats like Miss Kitty on *Gunsmoke*? Pretty soon, without mean-ing to, I was undressing her. Not to be dirty, but just to see what was underneath. I pictured her alone in her room at the convent, tired at the end of the day, pulling off her veil, her hair tum-bling down, then slipping out of the habit, letting it drop to the floor. Sure enough, underneath was a flowing white gown that at once managed to be both impossibly modest and revealing. From there, it was just a small hop on the Mortal Sin Express to get her out of her undergarments. I was lost in the moment, totally enjoying Sister's nakedness, the droning voices of my classmates miles away.

That's when I heard my name.

My eyes moved from Sister's milky, naked torso to her face. She was fully clothed again, her face sandwiched between the mortarboards, and she was staring right at me.

"Well?" she asked. "Come on now. We haven't got all day."

"Uh," I responded.

"Begin where Michael left off."

I knew the drill. I was to stand beside my desk and read in a loud clear voice from my Catholic Reader until Sister said, "Thank you, take your seat." The only problem was, at that exact moment I happened to be sporting a full-blown, raging, miniature . . . situ-ation. I still was not sure what to call that thing that sometimes visited when I least expected it. I looked down at my lap and my navy-blue uniform pants were poking up like a pup tent. I still be-lieved in the literal power of prayer then, and I pulled out every big gun I could think of. *Please, dear Jesus, dear God the Father, dear Holy Spirit, please make it go away.* The tent pole held its ground. *All the angels and saints in heaven, please. Please! Don't make me stand up. Dear Blessed Mother, make her call someone else.*

"Uhhh," I said. I was stalling for time. *Please, Saint Christopher, Saint Francis, Saint Joseph the Carpenter.*

"Mr. Grogan, we are all waiting."

I lifted my book off my desk and fidgeted with the pages, pretending to find my place. *Dear Saints Peter and Paul, Saint Matthew, Saint Monica, please, please. All the poor souls in purgatory. Help!*

"Now, Mr. Grogan," Sister said in a voice that told me there would be no more stalling.

I took a deep breath and stood up, giving a sort of salute as I did. In an ill-conceived attempt to hide the evidence, I held the book as low as I could, my arms fully extended at belt level. But this served only to highlight my predicament. It looked like I was using the bulge in my trousers as a book rest. A couple of kids began to giggle. I soldiered on. "Soon they saw an animal jump out of the snow," I read aloud. "It was a gray rabbit. Hop hop, it went to the big tree." I held the book away from me to steal a glance at my crotch. Still standing tall. I searched my brain for anyone who might rescue me from this humiliation. *Please, dear Saint Aloysius. Saint John the Baptist. Saint Thomas? Please, saint . . . saint . . . Saint Someone. Saint Anyone! Make it go away.*

Then I remembered Sainte Anne de Beaupré. Of course! Sainte Anne! My old friend! Surely she would remember me from my pilgrimage. The Stations of the Cross, the holy water, all those stairs I climbed on my knees. Mom had said that if I asked, she would hear me. Besides, malfunctioning body parts were her specialty. *Dear Sainte Anne, please fix this. Fix it now. Fix it like you fixed all those broken people. Please, Sainte Anne, if you can make cripples walk and blind men see, I know you can make this thing go away.*

Not even she could help. "Soon an old mother rabbit and five baby rabbits came to eat," I read. More kids snickered. If Sister noticed my aroused state, she gave no sign. Finally she released me from my torture. "Take your seat, please," she said and called the next student. I sat, and when I looked down, it was gone.

In the weeks that followed, Sister continued to drill us about our sins and how we were to confess them. Over and over again we reviewed the protocol—pulling back the curtain and walking into the dark box, kneeling in front of the screen and waiting for Father to open the little door between us. Then we were to begin, "Forgive me, Father, for I have sinned . . ." Boy, had I ever. I had fantasized the most salacious thoughts imaginable. I had coveted not only Mr. Selahowski's wife, but Jesus' wife, too. We were taught the nuns were the brides of Christ, and they wore the wedding bands to prove it. I had gazed upon a dedicated servant of the Church, wife of Jesus, and stripped her bare with my eyes. I was in serious trouble. I steeled myself to tell the truth. As Sister had made clear, the worst sin of all would be to lie in the confessional because you would really be lying to God, and no one got away with that. I approached First Confession with all the joy of a condemned inmate making that last lonely walk to the gallows.

Our Lady of Refuge was a young parish, being built in phases. There were three buildings: a large, ominous brick convent where the nuns lived, a friendlier-looking rectory where the priests lived, and the school, serving first through eighth grades. The real church was still years off, eventually to be built on the soccer field. In the meantime, church was held in that part of the school designed to become the gymnasium. It was an austere cinder-block structure with industrial glass-block windows and a linoleum floor. In front was a rudimentary sanctuary, still in cinder block but with thick red carpeting to give it a regal air, and a marble altar bedecked in starched linens beneath a towering crucifix. Separating the sanctuary from the pews was a varnished oak railing fitted with red-velvet kneelers where the faithful lined up to receive Jesus' body and, on special occasions, a sip of his blood, too. Our house of worship was to the great cathedrals of Europe, and even to the just mildly magnificent churches of America, what a White Castle is to Morton's steak house. But to me it was grand, mysterious, and enticing beyond words, permeated with the smells of incense and beeswax.

This gym-turned-house-of-worship was where my first confession would take place. The church had a confessional built into each of the four corners, wired with red and green lights activated by weight-sensitive switches on the kneeler inside to let you know if it was empty or occupied by a confessing sinner. Because we had seventy children in the two second-grade classes, plus the public-school kids from the parish, the pastor had asked priests from the Catholic seminary across the road to help out.

Four showed up to help Father handle about a hundred kids. Every one of the priests had been to our house for dinner; every one of them knew me by name. To accommodate the fifth priest, a portable confessional was set up in a cloakroom off the vestibule. It was basically a folding divider with a grate to speak through, a kneeler on one side for the penitent and a chair on the other for the priest. The children were divided into five groups and assigned confessionals. I was in the group assigned to the portable unit. No problem. Through the open door of the cloakroom, I could see it was just as private as the permanent booths. Unless Father recognized my voice, he would never guess that the sex-crazed nun coveter on the other side of the screen was actually the son of Ruth and Richard Grogan, loyal and devout parishioners and two of his most energetic volunteers.

I was about twelfth in line. Each child ahead of me walked into the cloakroom, closed the door behind him, and emerged a few minutes later with a penance to say. As I waited my turn, I practiced my lines. *Forgive me, Father, for I have sinned. This is my first confession.* Breakfast roiled in my stomach. How could I admit what I had done? "Impure thoughts" did not begin to cover it. *Please, Saint Dominic Savio, childhood saint, don't let Father recognize my voice.*

I had hardened myself to the task at hand. I would march in and lay it all out so I could purify my temple for Jesus and start anew. No more lusting, no more leering, no more stiffies.

A chubby classmate named James Coombs was immediately ahead of me, and when he came out from his confession, he did something none of the other children had done. He closed the door to the cloakroom behind him. *Click.*

My turn. I walked up and tried the knob. I turned it back and forth. I rattled it. Nothing. *Dear God the Father, dear Jesus, dear Holy Spirit, all the angels and saints in heaven, please don't let it be locked.* I shook the door again, this time more forcefully. I shot Coombs a dirty look, and he shrugged his shoulders as if to say, *I didn't know.* Fear rose in my throat. Father was in there waiting, wondering what had become of the next penitent. I knocked the door against its frame. I hit it with my shoulder. Then it opened. There stood Father Schroeder, the pastor, looking down at me. "Ah, Johnny Grogan, come in, my son. We'll have to do something about that lock, won't we?"

Oh, dear God, let me die now.

He took his place behind the partition, and I knelt, seeing his silhouette through the screen, smelling his aftershave mixed with the churchy mustiness of the room. I briefly weighed the two options before me: eternal damnation or immediate shame and humiliation. There was only one thing to do.

"Forgive me, Father, for I have sinned," I said. "This is my first confession."

Then I lied my ass off.

Father Schroeder had a positive ID on me; he was friends with my parents and over at our house practically every week for dinner or lunch or just to say hello. I could tell the truth, confessing the shameful secret that at the ripe age of seven I was already a sexual deviant. I could come clean and face what seemed near-certain condemnation, humiliation, and excoriation by my parents, the nuns, and the principal, all of whom Father would surely tell after he was done screaming at me in the confessional so that all my classmates would hear, too. Or I could simply . . . fudge a little. Actually, it would not be so much a lie as a small sin of omission. I would just leave a few things out.

"I fought with my brothers twelve times," I confessed through the screen. "I disobeyed my parents six times. I lied to Sister about my homework two times."

"Anything else, my son."

"Not really, Father."

"Go ahead," he coaxed. "There must be something more."

Oh God, he knew. He knew I was holding back. I had to give him something, anything. Anything but the truth. I started making things up.

"Well, I stole a radio."

"A radio, you say?"

"Yes, Father."

"You must return it, my son."

"I can't, Father."

"But you must."

"I threw it in the lake, Father."

"Good Lord, Johnny, what possessed you?"

"I didn't want anyone to know. And I . . ." My mind raced for a transgression that would at once be salacious enough to satisfy him without humiliating me. "I looked at naked ladies in *National Geographic*." I could see his silhouette nod as though he had heard this one before. I searched for a number. "Sixty-seven times."

"Sixty-seven?" Father asked. "Did you say sixty-seven?"

"Maybe sixty-eight, Father. I kind of lost count."

I filled out my list with age-appropriate misdeeds. "I lied to my parents ten times; used the Lord's name in vain nine times; read my sister's journal three times." Finally, the priest seemed satisfied.

"Anything else, my son?"

"That about does it, Father."

He mumbled absolution, blessed me, and gave me my penance—three Hail Marys and three Our Fathers. I bounded from the cloakroom with a mix of relief and dread.

My first confession. My chance to scrub my soul clean and return to the good graces of the Lord. And I had lied. Lied to Father and lied to God. What was worse, I knew there would be no going back now. I would have to lie in confession for the rest of my life. Because how could I ever confess to lying in the sacrament of penance, and my first time no less? There was no choice now but to take these sins to the grave with me, and I knew what that meant.

I was seven years old and already doomed to an eternity in hell. Even the Protestants and Jews and Muslims would fare better than that.

Chapter 4

———

Growing up in Harbor Hills, I had two nearby playmates, but I never considered them friends. Next door was Cindy Ann Selahowski, the girl who was blind to my crush on her mother. In the house behind us was a crusty-eyed boy named Lawrence who was still calling for his mother to wipe his behind when he was seven years old. As casual playmates, they were fine. What I did not have was a best friend.

Then in 1966, when I was nine, a new family moved in on the next street. A family the likes of which I had never before known. The parents spoke in clipped brogues and constantly walked around with mugs of milky tea in their hands. The father, who worked at one of the General Motors factories, had immigrated to the United States from Wales as a young man; the mother was from Ireland. Their accents were as strong as the day they stepped onto American soil. They were the Cullens, Bevan and Claire, colorful and opinionated—and blessed, if you could call it that, with six sons. The second oldest, Tommy, was my age.

Shortly after they moved in, I wandered over to check out the new kid and found him and his five brothers working in the yard with wheelbarrows, shovels, and rakes. In the driveway were towering piles of wood chips, dumped there for free by the power company. One wheelbarrow at a time, the Cullen boys were spreading the mulch around the one-acre property. Their home had gone up on a lot that was nearly pure sand, and Mr. Cullen was nothing if not thrifty and inventive. With six mouths to feed on a blue-collar paycheck, he did not have disposable income to pay a landscaping company to lay down topsoil and sod. And so he struck a deal with the workers who trimmed tree branches away from the electric lines. They agreed to drop their trimmings for free at his house; it saved them the longer drive to the dump and tipping fees. You could call Mr. Cullen a pioneer organic gardener. From the old country, he brought the generational wisdom that plant matter— branches, leaves, bark, grass clippings—would eventually break down into humus, the foundation of rich soil and a healthy lawn. What he lacked in money, he made up for in time and energy— and free child labor. He was a tightly wound bundle of muscles with enough confidence to fill a stadium, and his plan was to cover the entire sandy property with six inches of mulch, give it a year to break down into loam, till it under, and plant his grass seed.

Truck after truck pulled up that summer with huge steaming piles of debris. On that first visit, I said a few words to Tommy, then just stood watching as he hurried back to work before he got scolded. Mr. Cullen, working beside his boys, eventually noticed me. He paused, wiped the sweat from his brow, and shouted out in his heavy brogue, "Well, what are you waitin' for, mon? Get your hands out of your pockets and grab a shovel!"

It was, I would learn over the years, Mr. Cullen's pet peeve and signature command. Hands in pockets could do no work; they were idle and useless, the sign of a slouch. On an almost hourly basis, he would yell out at someone—a son, a neighborhood kid, the scouts he would oversee as scoutmaster—"Get your hands out of your pockets, mon!"

On that first day, not knowing what else to do and unwilling to turn my back on his commanding presence, I did just what he ordered. I pulled my hands out of my pockets, grabbed a shovel, and began slinging mulch. There was something satisfying about the work, even if blisters quickly rose on my soft palms, and I returned day after day to help. Soon I was eating peanut butter sandwiches with the other boys at the long table in the Cullen kitchen. And soon Tommy and I were fast friends, as our parents would become, as well. The Cullens, like most of the families in the neighborhood, were Catholic and active in the parish. Like the Grogan kids, all six Cullen boys were enrolled at Refuge.

Tommy and I sweated together making the Cullen lawn, but mostly we played. That first summer, Mr. Cullen and my dad took us out and let us choose our first bicycles. Tommy and I settled on the identical model, the Schwinn Typhoon. It was big and heavy, with fat balloon tires and handlebars solid enough to carry a passenger. Tommy picked out a metallic red Typhoon. I went with metallic blue. We had our wheels, we had our freedom. Harbor Hills, every square inch of it, was our turf.

Tommy and I bombed up and down the neighborhood streets, coasted no-hands down the little not-quite-hills, and stood on our pedals to huff up the other side. We rode to the school to shoot baskets. Rode through people's backyards.

We had only one restriction on our summer wanderings: no leaving the neighborhood. Despite the ironclad edict, soon after Tommy and I brought home our Typhoons we did just that. The bikes gave us mobility we had not known, and the temptation was too great. I felt like Adam with the apple. About a half mile from our house, along busy Orchard Lake Road, was a small shopping plaza with a supermarket, a pharmacy, a pizza parlor, a chicken take-out place, and knickknack shops. Our first trip to the plaza seemed terribly daring. Our hearts pounding, we peered at every passing car, fearing one of the neighbors would spot us and call our parents. But no one did, and soon the plaza became our second home. We would hang out there for hours, buying candy bars and sodas with the money we had made by cashing in returnable bottles we found along the way. A small order of fries was 32 cents with tax at the chicken joint, and we would each cough up 16 cents to split an order, which we would drown in ketchup and eat sitting on the sidewalk.

We swiped books of matches from the pizza parlor and would have wars in the parking lot, flicking lit matches at each other. We hung out at the record store and were soon hooked on Paul Revere and the Raiders, the Rolling Stones, the Beach Boys, and most of all, the Beatles.

Mostly, though, we rode to The Outlot to swim and hang out. Mr. Cullen brought a no-nonsense, tough-love sensibility to his sons. Girls might need warm water to wash up in the morning, but cold water worked just fine for men. Suntan lotion was for softies. So were beach towels. Real men air-dried, and that's what Tommy did every day after we swam, goose bumps rising on his skin. Soon I stopped bringing my towel, too.

It was at The Outlot, when we pulled off our shirts to jump in the water, that the one big difference between us became obvious. I was chubby, pale, and bespectacled, with a blubbery spare tire hanging over my suit and little breasts that actually had a sag to them. Tommy was just the opposite, lean and muscular, not an inch of spare flesh to pinch. The sun turned his skin a deep bronze and his blond hair to a silvery white. I envied his Adonis looks.

One day Tommy and I swam out to the wooden raft anchored in our swim area where a group of neighborhood girls our age sunbathed. In an attempt to show off, I took a running leap and dove into the water. When I climbed back on the raft, the girls encouraged me to dive again. I obliged them, and they asked again. And again. They were tanned and skinny, all legs and giggles, and they seemed fascinated by my running dive. I was basking in their attention until Tommy finally dove in after me and bobbed up, his face inches from mine. "Don't dive anymore," he whispered. "They're all just laughing at you."

That night after I took off my glasses and climbed into bed, I prayed to all the saints and angels in heaven, to God the Father, God the Son, and God the Holy Spirit, to make me less fat and more tan. Less clumsy and more athletic. More like Tommy, a boy the girls admired rather than ridiculed.

Near the end of fourth grade, as spring was poised to burst into summer, Dad and Mr. Cullen drove Tommy and me far out into the country to a farm where each of us could pick out a free puppy. For months I had been pestering my parents for a dog, promising to feed and care for it, insisting I would not shun my responsibilities once the novelty wore off. Our family had always had cats, first Lulu and later Felix. Cats were fine, but I wanted a dog. After months of deflecting me, Mom and Dad gave in. I think it was mostly Dad convincing Mom that a boy and a dog were meant to go together. As a child, Dad had had Fritz the German shepherd, who was his loyal companion into adulthood, bringing laughter and joy into a childhood that wasn't always easy. At the farm, the fathers told us to take our time and choose carefully because these pups would most likely be with us for the rest of our boyhoods.

Tommy chose a black-and-tan mutt he named Toffee, and I brought home Shaun, a golden, long-haired dog of unknown ancestry with a white blaze on his chest. I thought he was the most beautiful creature I had ever seen. Tommy and I sat side by side in the backseat of the station wagon, holding our puppies on our laps, letting them clamber over us and lick our faces. Soon they were tagging along with us everywhere we went. Within weeks, Toffee was struck and killed by a car, but Shaun would be at my side through the rest of my childhood—and I kept my end of the promise, feeding and caring for him every day until I left home for college.

It was 1967. While Tommy and I began another endless summer, my parents' comfortable world was exploding around them. The Vietnam War was escalating, and my cousins Joey and Vince had both shipped out to fight, while my other cousins joined thousands of students in antiwar protests on the campus of the University of Michigan, my father's alma mater. The Apollo space program, which hoped to put the first man on the moon, was reeling from a launchpad fire earlier that year that killed three astronauts, and America's cities were tinderboxes of racial tension, ready to erupt in even deadlier flames.

My sister, Marijo, had abandoned her pleated skirts and sweater sets for muslin smocks, bell-bottoms, and round wire-framed glasses, and began bringing home college boys with long hair, flowing beards, and names like Strike and Freedom, whom my parents greeted at the door with nervous smiles and awkward small talk. Tim, sixteen and enrolled at an all-boy Catholic high school, was lashing out against my parents' orderly world. He would sit silently simmering through Sunday Mass, refusing to participate. He was fighting hard to grow his own hair out that summer, and my parents were fighting back with everything they had, convinced that long hair was a stepping-stone on the path to drugs, sex, and this new, loud, and radically unnerving music they did not understand. The strain began to show on my parents' faces.

One afternoon I walked in from the beach to find Mom sobbing inconsolably in the living room. My swimming suit was still dripping as I put my arm around her.

"What's the matter, Mom?" I asked.

"It's Tim," she blurted out. "I've lost him."

"No you didn't," I insisted. "He's not lost. I just saw him. He's down at the beach. I just saw him there."

She bawled all the harder. "You don't understand. I've lost him, I've lost him." I rubbed her back a little, finally realizing it was his heart and soul she felt slipping from her. "It's gonna be okay, Mom," I said.

She dried her eyes on her apron and gave me a brave smile. "That's what I keep asking our Lord for," she said. "Now go get out of that wet suit, and I'll make you a snack."

That year the Animals released "When I Was Young," a song that Tommy and I adopted as our anthem. One verse in particular captured our ten-year-old preoccupations. It began: "I smoked my first cigarette at ten, and for girls I had a bad yen." School had been out for just a few days when Tommy and I decided it was time to fulfill the prophecy. I don't recall whose idea it was, but together we hatched a plot to buy our first pack of cigarettes.

We had been fascinated by the idea of smoking for months. The teenagers down at the beach, at least the cool ones, all smoked when no parents were around. It was clear that the short path to acceptance was to have a cigarette hanging from your lips. My uncle Father Joe was a devout priest. He also loved his Scotch, his Lucky Strikes, and the horse races, habits my parents tolerated but did not share. Mom and Dad knew that most smokers got hooked as teens, as Father Joe had, and told me they would buy me a gold watch for my twenty-first birthday if I stayed away from cigarettes until then. But the promise of gold could not compete with the promise of coolness. After one of Father Joe's weekly visits, I snitched a snubbed-out, half-smoked Lucky from the ashtray, and Tommy and I raced into the woods on the edge of the neighborhood to try it out. He held the match to it while I puffed. Then I handed it to him and he puffed. Our eyes watered, our noses ran, and we coughed uncontrollably. Two puffs each and we had had enough. But rather than be deterred, we settled on a simple truth: filterless Lucky Strikes might work for Father Joe, but we needed to get our hands on something smoother, something with a filter. The older kids all seemed to gravitate toward Marlboros, and they never seemed to cough or wheeze. That's what we needed, a pack of Marlboros.

The plan was hatched. The shopping plaza where we hung out had cigarettes, but only over the counter. We needed a vending machine safe from prying eyes, and we both knew what that meant: a road trip to Sylvan Lanes bowling alley. It was a good five miles away, but we knew it had a cigarette machine in the outer lobby, separated from the bowling lanes by glass doors. We set out on a hot June morning, pedaling through the back streets of the neighboring town of Keego Harbor until we got to the next village beyond that. We parked our bikes around the corner from the bowling alley, out of sight, and approached the door. We knew from the older kids that a pack of cigarettes cost 35 cents, and Tommy had brought a quarter and I a dime.

"I'll keep a lookout," I volunteered.

"Why do you get to be the lookout?" he asked.

Because I was petrified, that's why. I just said, "You're faster than I am," and Tommy seemed to see my logic because he grasped the coins in his fist and boldly strolled down the sidewalk and through the smoked-glass doors. He was in there forever, and I tried to look nonchalant as I kept my eye on the parking lot for grown-ups. It was early and all was quiet. Finally he burst out of the doors and came sprinting toward me. That was all the signal I needed to take off at full throttle. By the time Tommy caught me, I was around the corner and swinging my leg over the bar of my Typhoon.

"Stop! Stop!" he hissed. "I don't have them." He held up the dime. "I got the quarter in, but then one of the workers spotted me." Tommy had spent all that time in there studying the league schedules on the wall, trying to summon the nerve to drop in the dime and pull the lever. "Here," he said, pressing the coin in my palm. "Your turn."

My pride trumped my fear. I couldn't refuse the assign-

ment without unmasking myself as a total jelly ball of coward-
ice. Inside, I perused the bulletin boards and gumball machine,
all the while sneaking glances through the interior doors at the
workers. When they seemed suitably distracted, I sidled over to
the cigarette machine and yawned with great effect, stretching
lazily and patting my mouth. *Look at me! See how relaxed and at
home I am here in the outer lobby of Sylvan Lanes. Just another
ho-hum day. Not nervous at all. Bored, actually.* Directly in front
of me loomed the money slot. All I needed to do was reach out,
slip in the dime, and pull the Marlboro lever. I rubbed the dime
in my fingers, summoning my nerve. That's when I heard a metallic clink and watched helplessly as the coin rolled across the
floor. I was on my hands and knees, butt up in the air, peering
under the machine when I heard the door swing open. I looked
up, and there stood a man. In uniform. A very large man in uniform. My heart stopped. *Dear Jesus, Dear Holy Spirit, Dear God
the Father* . . . A full second passed, and I could see him trying to
process why a child would be sprawled on the floor beneath the
vending machine. I smiled weakly. Then I realized his was the
uniform of a deliveryman. He pushed a dolly loaded with beer
past me and disappeared inside. What if he reported me to the
manager? I wasn't about to stick around to find out.

Back outside, I explained our dilemma to Tommy, and we spent
the better part of a half hour strategizing about what to do next.
Twenty-five cents of our money sat in the machine and ten cents
beneath it. The only prospect worse than getting caught would be
someone coming along to buy cigarettes and getting our quarter.
There was no turning back now. This time we would go in together.
Tommy volunteered to dive for the dime; I would watch the doors
and stand ready to pull the lever once he got the coin in the slot.

Inside, the plan went like clockwork. Tommy quickly located
the dime deep beneath the machine, scrambled to his feet, and
without looking back, shoved it in the slot. "Pull! Pull!" he ordered.

I froze with fear. "Pull!" he yelled.

I lunged in the general direction of the Marlboro lever and pulled. With a loud, happy burp, the machine dropped a pack of cigarettes down the chute and into the tray. I grabbed the pack and was about to dash out the door when I saw my mistake. Tommy saw it, too. "Oh no," he said as if he had just witnessed a horrible accident.

I wasn't holding the manly red-and-white packaging of Marlboro. I had accidentally pulled the lever for a low-tar, low-nicotine cigarette recently put on the market to address health concerns. Tommy could not have looked more mortified had a decomposing body part spilled out at us.

"True Blues?" he gasped. "True Blues! Oh God, girl ciggies." It was a fate of unspeakable shame. I stared at them as if, through the sheer force of concentration, I might be able to transform them into Marlboros, like the priests transformed bread into the body of Christ. We both stood there for a moment longer before the precariousness of our situation sank in. We were standing in a public lobby holding evidence of criminal wrongdoing.

"Crotch 'em!" Tommy barked, and I shoved them down the front of my shorts inside my underwear. We bolted out the doors and sprinted to our getaway vehicles. "Don't run! Don't run!" I insisted even as I raced as fast as my legs would carry me. We grabbed our bikes, got a running start, then hopped aboard with one foot as we swung the other leg over the seat. It was our well-practiced power takeoff, and it was the quickest way to go from zero to a full-throttle fifteen miles per hour. We pedaled off in a standing position, pumping furiously with everything we had. When we finally looked over our shoulders several blocks later, no one was following. We had pulled it off. So what if I had chosen the most unapologetically wimpy cigarette known to mankind? We had our smokes, our entrance to cool-kid, grown-up behavior. Tommy and I settled back on our seats and rode through the neighborhoods side by side, no hands, whooping and laughing as we went. Ours were the joyful cries of victory. "True Blues," he said, still in disbelief but now with more amusement than disdain. "Fucking True Blues."

"Fucking yeah," I said. And we laughed some more.

Across Erie Drive from my house was a vacant lot covered in high weeds. At the back of the lot, a rickety wooden stairway led down the steep bank to Cass Lake and a narrow sand beach. Someday, another fancy doctor's house would rise there, but for now it was an absentee landowner's investment—and Tommy's and my personal clubhouse. It was totally private and totally ours. Right near the water's edge was a large tree with a hollow in the trunk, perfect for stashing all sorts of boyhood contraband. Over the years, that hollow would safely and dryly hide copies of girlie magazines, purloined adult beverages, and bags of marijuana. On this day, it became the tabernacle for our first pack of cigarettes.

Tommy and I rode directly there from the bowling alley, ditched our bikes out of sight in the weeds, and made our way down to the water's edge. There we ripped off the cellophane, tore open the foil, and each placed one of the long, skinny cigarettes between our lips. Tommy lit his own and then held out the match and lit mine. We puffed and coughed, puffed and coughed. Our eyes watered, our heads spun. Honestly, it wasn't much better than Father Joe's half-smoked Lucky Strike, but we persevered in the pursuit of cool. We each finished one cigarette, then passed a third between us.

The moment was so heady, it seemed only natural to try out the new vocabulary we had learned that school year.

"Fuck!" Tommy shouted at the top of his lungs. "Fuuuuuck!"

"Shit!" I shouted. "Shiiiiit!"

"Goddamn!" he yelled.

"Motherfucker!" I added.

"Son of a bitch!"

"Bastard!"

We went on like this, passing the cigarette between us and happily screaming out every filthy word we could think of, our voices carrying over the water to nowhere. Part of us wanted to get them out of us, flush them from our souls, because we knew they were bad and wrong and sins to be confessed. Part of us thrilled at the rebelliousness of it. It was our way of letting the Sisters of Saint Felix, the priests of Our Lady of Refuge, and our very Catholic parents know they had not won the indoctrination battle quite yet. Not by a long shot.

After we had buried the butts, we rubbed cedar boughs between our hands to mask the smell. Crossing the street to my house, we marched single file through the kitchen, right past my mother at her primary battle station, the kitchen sink, proceeded up the stairs past the matching statues of Saint Joseph and the Virgin Mary and into the bathroom. There we locked the door and squeezed gobs of toothpaste into our mouths, squishing and laughing and jabbing each other. We emerged moments later, reeking of nicotine, cedar, and Crest, and marched right past Mom again. If she noticed anything suspicious, she never let on.

Chapter 5

A few weeks later, in July of 1967, we awoke to a pall of smoke hanging over the horizon. The city of Detroit was on fire. All three television networks were covering the riots live, and my family and I circled the television, mesmerized. The scenes were shocking. It was a war zone, just like in the movies, except this was real and it was taking place just thirty minutes down the John Lodge Expressway, in the city where I was born. Entire blocks were ablaze, burned-out cars smoldered, firefighters were taking gunfire from snipers on rooftops, the police were pinned down in their precinct houses. Terrified residents scrambled for cover, and angry mobs looted and torched store after store. Soon National Guard soldiers in armored vehicles would rumble down Cass Avenue, and eventually troops from the 82nd Airborne, too. Detroit had long been a tinderbox of inequality and racial animosity, and the night before, a single spark—a police raid on an after-hours drinking club—had set it off.

As we watched the mayhem unfold, the telephone rang. It was

Father Vin, my mother's younger brother, who was the pastor of Saint Catherine's, an inner-city parish once proud home to Polish and Italian immigrants arriving in this country to work in the auto plants but now steeply in decline. He needed help. He had thirty-five people, mostly women and children, crammed into the rectory with him. When the rioting erupted the night before, they began streaming to his front door in search of safety. He and his parishioners had spent the night huddled on the floor with the lights off, crawling from room to room on hands and knees, afraid a stray bullet could pierce a window at any moment. He was now working the phones, seeking places for the families to ride out the storm.

Mom hung up and said to us, "We're going to have some company for a few days, kids." This did not surprise any of us. My parents were nothing if not do-gooders. Part of their Catholic faith was to help others less fortunate, and they threw themselves into various acts of charity with the zealousness of missionaries. Mom, it seemed, was always baking casseroles or collecting used clothing for families down on their luck, and Dad was constantly dragging us kids along to visit shut-ins and the like. One of my earliest memories was of accompanying my father to a tuberculosis sanitarium to deliver magazines to the patients, something he did once a month every month for years.

On more than one occasion, my parents took in sick or convalescing people who had no one else to look after them. One of them was a parish priest who lived with us for weeks, commandeering my sister's bedroom as he recovered from back surgery. They both volunteered for every imaginable duty at Our Lady of Refuge, from changing the altar linens to leading rosary groups, and my father gave gallons of his blood to the Red Cross. "When you're at the end of your life," Dad liked to say, "it won't be what you received that matters, but what you gave." Father Vin knew that if he asked, they would say yes.

An hour later, his black Chevrolet pulled into our driveway, crammed with children. The effect was almost comical, with heads and limbs and torsos poking out in all directions. How he fit them all in there, I didn't know, but one by one they untangled themselves and stepped out, seven of them, ranging in age from eight to fifteen, each grasping a paper sack containing meager belongings. They stood silently in the driveway, staring at us like we were aliens, and in a sense I suppose we were to them. Even before their neighborhood began to burn, they could only imagine a place like this, with its big, sprawling houses and parklike lawns, towering shade trees, and a lake and beach just down the street. Marijo, Tim, Mike, and I stared back with the same puzzled, slightly suspicious looks. We could not have been more dumbfounded had a flying saucer landed in our driveway and deposited a band of Martians. The children came from two families. They were clearly very poor and very dirty, dressed in ill-fitting hand-me-downs. The new arrivals had a streetwise, mess-with-me-at-your-own-peril toughness about them, even the younger ones. With our cigarettes and swear words, Tommy Cullen and I thought we were tough. In that instant I grasped the undeniable truth. We weren't tough at all. We were sheltered suburban kids trying to act tough. These kids were the real thing. Until that day I'd had only the vaguest notion that places like Detroit, with its festering poverty and hopelessness, existed. My whole world was Harbor Hills, with its summer schedule of swimming and horseback-riding lessons and stolen puffs on cigarettes. We considered ourselves solidly middle class—just one car and an antiquated black-and-white television, after all—but I could tell from these kids' faces that they saw us as impossibly privileged. It was as though they had just parachuted into the Land of Oz.

My mother broke the silence. "All right, everyone into swim-suits and down to the lake. It's too hot not to be swimming!" She directed all the boys into the garage to change, and all the girls upstairs. Only later did I learn her hidden agenda: she wanted the opportunity to launder their clothing and underwear without embarrassing them.

Down at the beach, the city kids eyed the water warily. Suddenly they didn't look so tough. They looked afraid. What to me was a source of endless, effortless fun, to them was a deadly threat. Not one of them knew how to swim. Fortunately, our stretch of Cass Lake had a gradual drop-off. You could wade for yards and still not be up to your armpits, and even in the deepest part of the swim area the water was barely over a ten-year-old's head. Soon we were all frolicking in the shallows, splashing each other, whooping and laughing. Shaun pranced among us, jumping and barking. In the water, the sun glistening on our wet skin, the differences of class and privilege washed away and we were all just kids on a hot summer day.

Ours was a three-bedroom house, with my sister having the smallest bedroom to herself and my brothers and I sharing a larger room. When we got back from the beach, my mother had turned the boys' bedroom into a dormitory for the visiting girls. That evening, when my father arrived home from work, he set up the tent trailer we used for summer camping trips in the backyard, and this became the boys' domain.

For five days and nights, as the riot raged unabated, eventually claiming forty-three lives, the children stayed with us, and gradually, cautiously, we became friends. One boy, Leo, was my age, and we took to each other. We swam and rode bikes and sneaked down to the shopping plaza to hang out. Tommy and I led him to the hollow tree where we stashed our True Blues. Leo knew all about smoking, including how to inhale. He showed us how to suck the smoke deep into our lungs, hold it for a few seconds, and then exhale it through our nostrils. Not only did this give us something unfathomably cool to show off in front of the older kids at the beach, but the head-spinning, stomach-churning rush was like nothing I had experienced before.

Leo, it turned out, had another talent I could only dream of.

The kid could draw like no one I had ever met. Right before my eyes, he cranked out amazingly accurate renderings of any comic book or cartoon character I would toss at him. Superman, Batman, Flash Gordon, Captain America—he could do them all. From the Sunday comics, he would copy exact replicas of Nancy and Beetle Bailey and Dagwood. I, on the other hand, could barely make stick figures, and I swooned over his talent, especially after learning he had nurtured it on his own, with no help from any adult. I became his loyal groupie and he my artistic mentor. "It's easy," I remember him saying. "You just look at the lines and do the same thing." With his tutoring, I managed to produce rudimentary versions of the Peanuts characters, and Leo was kind enough to say things like "See, I told you. You just need to look at the lines."

While we were swimming, smoking, and sketching, Mom was working. She went into full dorm-mother overdrive that week, reeling out towering platters of tuna-salad sandwiches for lunch and oversize trays of lasagna and hot dog casserole for dinner.

Each meal, of course, began as all meals in our house did, with a prayer. Dad if he was home (Mom if he wasn't) would ask for quiet and then bless himself, touching his fingertips to his forehead, then his chest, then each shoulder as he said, "In the name of the Father, the Son, and the Holy Spirit." We did the same, dropping our eyes to the empty plates before us and mumbling along with the prayer hammered into us from earliest memory: "Bless us, O Lord, and these thy gifts, which we are about to receive from thy bounty through Christ, our Lord, amen." I had no idea what those words meant, and no curiosity to learn, either, but I happily rattled them off, knowing that no food would reach my plate until I did. It was just what we did in our home, one of the small prices of admission. Some kids had to take off their shoes at the front door; we had to pray before the first bite.

I passed most meal prayers with a singular mission: to make my brothers laugh. In one of my proudest moments, I caught Michael's eye just after he had sneaked a big swig of milk. When the prayer began, he froze, holding the milk in his mouth. I made my most moronic face, crossing my eyes, and just as we reached the words "and these thy gifts," Michael exploded in hysterics, milk spraying from both nostrils. And he, not I, was the one who got in trouble. Life didn't get any better than that.

One of my favorite parts of our house was the screened-in porch just off the kitchen. We did not have air-conditioning, and all summer our family pretty much lived out there, eating our meals at a glass table and sitting around late into the night in the dark listening to Mom spin stories about growing up as one of nine children being raised by a widow in the Great Depression. Her stories were tapestries filled with colorful characters—Uncle Bert the bootlegger and Aunt Lulu with the enormous bosom and the aged Mrs. Fink next door who was the target of endless childhood pranks. In one of Mom's favorite stories, she described how she once called Mrs. Fink and pretended to be from the phone company. "We're going to be blowing the dust out of your phone lines," she said in her most grown-up voice. "You're going to want to spread newspapers on the floor because they haven't been cleaned in quite some time and it could cause quite a mess." And then she and her brothers and sisters watched through the window with delight as poor Mrs. Fink did just that.

My mom never lost that juvenile sense of humor. Every day was an opportunity for another prank, and I came to believe that one of her primary reasons for having children was to have a steady supply of subjects to torture. She would hold a pin in her lips and then pucker up for a kiss, pricking whichever one of us took the bait. She told us she could do magic, and if we would look up the sleeve of an old winter coat she had, we would see all the stars in the universe. When she finally coaxed a victim to put his head inside the coat and peer up the sleeve, she'd mumble some made-up magic incantation and then ask, "Do you see the stars yet?" When the victim, from under the coat, said no, still no stars, she'd add, "How about now?" and pour a glass of water down the sleeve and into the person's face. This delighted her no end. Of course, it worked only once per victim, and soon we were in on the conspiracy, luring various friends, classmates, and neighbors into her lair. My quiet father would just nod his head and smile patiently at his wife's antics.

With the seven Detroit kids in our house, my mother was delighted to have a new audience to subject to her tales and tricks, and she held court each evening after dinner. Before the week was over, every kid got a face full of water down the sleeve of that old coat, and every kid got a pinprick kiss. At first they didn't know what to make of this nutty woman, but soon they were all calling her Aunt Ruthie and treating her like their own mother.

Some nights, as darkness fell, we roasted marshmallows over dying coals in the backyard and lay in the dewy grass, staring up at the stars that our visitors had not even known existed, so obliterated were they by the city lights where they lived. And then Aunt Ruthie would bark the order for bath time—the girls one night, the boys the next—not letting anyone escape until she had inspected their feet and necks to make sure they had been properly scoured.

By the end of the week, when Father Vin returned in his Chevrolet to collect the children and return them to the smoldering ruins of their neighborhood, we were all tight friends. More than that, really. We had become like cousins. Everyone hugged and promised to stay in touch. Leo presented me with a full-color portfolio of action heroes. I gave him my lucky rabbit's foot, which I figured he needed more than I did.

"Everybody in the car," Father Vin ordered, and my mother handed each of them a paper grocery bag filled with clean, folded clothes she'd collected for them, and gave each of them a long hug and a kiss, this time without any pins. Father Vin's good deed had an unintended cruel edge to it. He had dropped these seven children of the inner city into the magical Land of Oz, a place of lakes and parks and star-studded skies, and allowed them to stay just long enough to realize what wonders lay beyond their grasp. They saw my life—they had to—as a fairy tale, a tantalizing dream from which they would soon awaken. The greater lesson was mine to take. Despite our differences of place and privilege, we were all just kids. Kids who loved goofing off and hated wearing shoes. Kids who forgot manners and found mischief. We said the same prayers to the same God, yet God had not blessed us the same. Even then, I found it unfair. What I learned in school, about all men being created equal, might be true. But I had discovered that all children did not grow up equal. Never again could I pretend the playing field was level, that all kids got the same shot at life's boundless possibilities.

"Thanks for teaching me to dog-paddle," Leo shouted out the window as Father Vin backed down the driveway.

"Thanks for the drawings," I shouted back.

I waved as the car disappeared down Erie Drive, the children's happy faces peering back through the rear window. For a year or so, we kept our promise to stay in touch. And then, after Father Vin's transfer to another parish in another city, we lost track of each other forever.

Chapter 6

My parents had a lot of dreams for their four children, but none so all-consuming as the dream that one of us might someday heed the call to a religious vocation. If they could choose between having one of us become, say, a Nobel Prize–winning scientist or a parish priest, there was no question they'd pick the priest every time. As Dad frequently reminded us, a priest was God's embodiment on earth. Priests did his work and were endowed with his infallible moral judgment. My mother held the same belief and was indescribably proud to have two brothers who wore the Roman collar. She herself came close to entering the convent after high school before realizing her true calling was as a mother and baker of the world's most outrageously moist oatmeal cookies.

Growing up, my brother Michael came closest to fulfilling their dream. While other kids were playing cowboys and Indians or astronauts and race-car drivers, Mike was down in the basement playing priest. Mom sewed him vestments out of scraps of corduroy and satin, and hemmed and starched old sheets to serve as altar linens. An antique dresser from her childhood was drafted into service as an altar. Covered in Mom's linens and other churchly accoutrements, it looked impressively official, and Mike behaved accordingly. With great solemnity, he donned his vestments and proffered blessings to any who would stand still for them. He said Mass—reciting the entire liturgy verbatim in Latin—and gave long, impassioned sermons. He consecrated cubes of bread and glasses of grape juice and sometimes drafted me into the role of altar boy as he distributed pretend Holy Communion.

Michael led rosaries and wafted incense through the air. He made himself available to hear confessions, though as far as I know got no takers. When we brought home Dickie Bird and Lady Bird, a pair of parakeets, Michael bestowed on them the sacrament of marriage. After all, we were hoping they would start a family. And when Dickie turned up dead on the floor of the cage one morning, the young priest in training invited the neighbors in for what turned into a two-hour high funeral Mass, including a forty-minute eulogy. Dickie was one great parakeet, and yes, we all loved him dearly, but even I was impressed that anyone could find forty minutes' worth of things to say about a bird. I spent the whole service admiring the tanned shoulders of Mrs. Selahowski in her sleeveless sundress.

What some parents might have found alarming, Mom and Dad found boundlessly endearing, and they nurtured my brother's budding vocation with enthusiasm. Mom armed him with candlesticks, hymnals, a crucifix, and an old pewter goblet to hold the grape juice. Dad faithfully captured my brother's priestly reenactments on 8-millimeter home movies. Their son might have been only twelve, but he was already on the road to the priesthood. It was everything they'd ever dreamed.

I was another story. While Michael was saying Mass in the basement, I had found a different calling. My father was a longtime photo buff, and he subscribed to *Popular Photography*. The magazine itself was quite boring, made even more so by the fact that Dad tore off and discarded the covers because they often featured pouty-lipped models sporting come-hither looks. But the tiny classified advertisements in the back grabbed my attention. One after another featured ads for photography courses. The ads promised that you, too, could lead the exciting life of a professional model photographer. And to illustrate just how exciting that life could be, many of the ads featured tiny thumbnail photos of that most exciting possibility of all: topless women. Topless women smiling into the camera, pouting into the camera, ignoring the camera. Some frolicked in the surf; some lounged on park benches or reclined in convertibles. Some were in bikini bottoms, others in nighties that had mysteriously slipped off their shoulders and fallen around their waists. One, I remember, was dressed for a horseback ride. She wore knee-high boots, riding pants, and a hat; she even carried a crop. The only things missing were her blouse and bra. It was impossibly provocative, this concept that women might set out on any given day having breezily forgotten a few essential items of clothing, leaving their wondrous milky bazooms fully, gloriously exposed. I holed up next to the furnace for hours with those magazines, studying the various pairs of breasts with the intensity of an anatomist. My God, it was better than the underwear section of the Sears catalog. Better even than *National Geographic*.

While my brother was memorizing the Eucharistic prayer, I was memorizing as many breasts as I could fix my eyes on. Once Tommy Cullen moved into the neighborhood, he joined me at the Altar of the Voluptuous Bosom. We both worshipped with the fervor of new converts and passed countless lazy afternoons discussing the relative merits of various boob sizes and shapes. We debated large and droopy versus small and pert. We became discerning connoisseurs of the female nipple and areola. We noted the effects a swim in chilly water could have on them and the way they could glow iridescent in candlelight. Breasts became our business. If ogling them was a sin—and I knew it surely was—it certainly did not feel like one. I conveniently purged it from my confession list along with all the others.

Perhaps it was because Dad's photo magazine collection was becoming a little too thumb worn, or because Michael was showing an interest in photography and beginning to read some of the articles, but one day Mom and Dad called the two of us into the kitchen. On the table were a few issues of *Popular Photography,* the covers duly removed.

"This is a great magazine with a lot of informative articles about photography," Dad began. "But sometimes it runs photos that we do not approve of. Photos of ladies without many clothes on." I gazed up at him with the biggest doe eyes I could muster as if the thought of half-naked women had never occurred to me and, now that he had brought it up, was truly horrifying. "We would be very disappointed if we found out either of you were looking at them," he said.

"It's natural for boys to be curious about the opposite sex," Mom chimed in. "Do you have any questions? Is there anything you want to ask us?"

I did have one burning question. I knew girls did not have penises like boys, but from there, things got murky. One boy at school had told me, quite knowingly, that they had miniature versions of wieners. Another that they had tunnels. A third said he had seen his sister and could swear on the Bible there was nothing there at all. I was ten years old and still anatomically clueless. I wanted an up close, personal view of female parts, but I wasn't about to ask Mom for it.

"Any questions at all?" Mom beckoned. Michael and I both shook our heads furiously no.

"These doggone advertisers," Dad lamented. "Why do they have to go and spoil a perfectly good magazine?"

"We don't want you to think there's anything dirty about the human body," Mom interjected. "There's not. The human body is beautiful. It's God's creation, and it is truly a thing of beauty." I must have nodded my agreement with a bit too much enthusiasm because she quickly added: "But promise me you won't ever look at those pictures."

"I promise," Michael said, and from the way he said the words, I knew the young priest in training meant them.

"I promise, too," I repeated.

Beneath the table, inside my PF Flyers, my toes remained firmly crossed.

In the autumn after Detroit went up in flames, Tommy and I signed up to be altar boys. In both our houses, all the sons were expected to serve at Mass, no questions asked. It was not an elective like soccer or karate. My sister, on the other hand, was off the hook because girls weren't allowed. At first I considered this terribly unfair, not because I was a budding feminist outraged that the Church would treat my sister and any other girl as somehow unworthy to grace the altar, but because she got a free pass and I didn't. My outrage disappeared the instant I learned of one of the great secret perks of altar service: free booze. Tommy and I had heard the rumors, supported by credible eyewitness accounts, that altar boys got to sneak swigs of the leftover sacramental wine. Our parents were ecstatic at our decision to join the altar corps, and now, with the promise of daily morning cocktails, so were we.

The rumors proved true. On our first Mass as servers, Tommy and I were paired with two older boys who knew the ropes. They helped us select our outfits from a closet in a room off the sanctuary. The altar-boy uniform consisted of two parts: a floor-length black cassock that buttoned down the front; and a short white linen gown of sorts, called a surplice, that slipped over the cassock and gave altar boys their classic black-and-white look. So dressed, we resembled miniature priests, although close up you could see that the cassocks and surplices had a lot of miles on them. Most were covered in wax spills, and nearly every garment had at least one burn hole from a misadventure with a candle or incense ember.

Tommy quickly located a cassock that fit him perfectly. For me, the job was more challenging. The cassocks that were the correct length were too tight around the middle. When I found one that buttoned comfortably around my stomach, it bunched around my feet and dragged on the floor, an accident waiting to happen. Finally I found one I could live with—a little tight at the waist but also just a few inches long at my feet. It would have to do.

The older boys walked us through our duties, which began with lighting the altar candles. Then they led us into a small closet in the sacristy where Father donned his vestments. Inside were shelves lined with crystal cruets, a sink, and a refrigerator filled with jugs of altar wine. Our job was to fill one cruet with wine and a second with water—the essential ingredients for the priest to perform the miracle of transubstantiation. We placed both on the altar. At the appropriate time, the priest would motion for two of us to approach with the cruets. As he recited the Eucharistic prayers, he would reach over for the wine and pour some into his chalice, then for the water, which he would add to the wine in proportions that said a lot about the priest's tolerance for an alcoholic drink first thing in the morning. A teetotaler priest would use mostly water with a splash of wine, but most would use nearly all wine with just a drop or two of water.

As we filled the cruets in the closet under the older boys' direction, we got our first hint of the rewards to come. "We're lucky this morning, boys," one of the veteran servers said. "We've got Father Donohue. Two-Drop Donohue. He barely touches the wine." Tommy and I looked at each other, trying to figure out what Father Donohue's altar-wine habits had to do with us. Then the other boy said with a wink, "The less for Father, the more for us."

My first Mass as an altar boy was uneventful. The older boys

handled the important duties, and Tommy and I mostly concentrated on trying to look solemn. I genuflected a lot, mumbled
through the prayers I never quite memorized, and got to ring
a brass bell when Father raised the communion wafer toward
heaven, and again when he lifted his chalice of wine. There was
an art to bell ringing, and somehow I made both events sound
like five-alarm fires.

Our mentors were right. Father Donohue placed barely a
drop of wine in his chalice. After communion, he wrapped up the
service with the words "The Mass is over. Go in peace to love and
serve the Lord," and we formed a procession down the center aisle.
One of the older boys led the way, carrying a large crucifix. The
next followed with the Bible. Then came Tommy and me, immediately in front of Father, each brandishing a large beeswax candle
on a floor-length brass holder. This was a challenging maneuver.
The candles on their stands resembled flaming javelins and were
nearly as tall as we were. The tip of each candle was fitted with a
brass ring that created a reservoir, preventing the hot liquid wax
from running down the sides. The trick was to make it down the
aisle without spilling any of the pooled wax. Tommy and I gripped
our candles with sweaty palms and crept down the aisle as if we
were wired with explosives. Both of us made it without incident,
and I said a little prayer of thanksgiving for not having tripped
on my too-long gown.

Back in the sacristy behind the altar, Father hung up his vestments and departed for the rectory, leaving us boys to finish up.
We blew out the candles, straightened the linens, and returned
the pair of cruets to the closet where they were to be emptied,
rinsed, and dried. One of the older boys immediately uncorked
the wine cruet and took a swig, then handed it to his friend, who
took another swig. "Here's to Two-Drop Donohue," he toasted as
he handed the cruet to me. I held it in my hands, knowing this
had to be a major-league mortal sin, chugging the same holy wine
Father turned into the blood of Christ.

"Go ahead," one of the boys said. "They don't care. Honest."

Who was I to argue? We were just emptying the cruets as instructed, weren't we? And to waste was a sin. I placed the cruet to my lips and poured in a mouthful. It was sticky and sweet and musky. When I swallowed, I felt an unpleasant burn, followed by an odd, comforting warmth that spread through my body. I handed the cruet to Tommy as I stifled a cough. We went one more round, and then the cruet was empty. I dutifully rinsed and dried it and replaced it on the shelf, my feet and fingertips tingling. As I hung my cassock and surplice up, I noticed that my eye-hand coordination was just slightly off.

Outside the church, my parents waited, their faces beaming. They had sat in the front pew for their youngest son's debut as an altar boy. "We're very proud of you, son," Dad said. "You're doing the Lord's work."

I smiled glassily and turned my head to divert my breath from him.

"Just next time," he counseled, "go a little easier on the bells."

Chapter 7

Besides being zealous Catholics, my parents were famously frugal. They never did manage to shake the imprint of growing up hand to mouth during the Depression, and even though they now lived in a spacious new house in a desirable subdivision on a lake, they carried with them the habits they grew up with. Mom cut paper napkins in half. She made her cup of tea in the morning and set the tea bag by the stove to dry for another use. Dad hung paper towels over the edge of the sink to dry for a second and sometimes third use. He had it down to an art form: the first use would involve a task that required a fresh towel, such as wiping a dish; the next use would be less critical, such as cleaning up a spill on the floor; from there the multitasking towel would move to the garage where Dad would use it to check the oil dipstick on the car.

His desire to find maximum utility applied to all things. He used oversize junk-mail envelopes to organize his important papers, each meticulously labeled in his draftsman's hand. After washing the car, he would shout through the house, "I've got a nice bucket of sudsy water down here! Anyone need some good sudsy water? Perfectly good still!" As far as I know, Dad never got a single taker for his slightly used soapy water, but that didn't discourage him from going through the same ritual the next time. "Who needs soapy water? Got a nice clean bucket down here!"

Neither of them could bring themselves to throw anything out. If a lamp or appliance broke, Dad would store it away in the basement as a potential source of parts for a future repair. In the kitchen, we had what surely remains the world's largest collection of washed-out mayonnaise jars and margarine tubs. My mother came home one day, immensely pleased with herself for scoring an unbelievable price on a set of nesting dessert bowls. Then I saw why they were such a bargain: each was emblazoned with the Delta Airlines logo. "See," Mom said proudly, "they don't quite nestle. The airline wouldn't take them." For years, I ate my ice cream while dreaming of flying Delta to far-off places.

Instead of replacing our broken toaster, Dad figured out all it needed was a sturdy piece of masking tape to hold down the lever. When the bread was fully toasted, the unit would make a horrible grating sound and begin vibrating frantically across the counter as it strained against the tape to pop up. That was our clue to leap for the toaster and rip off the tape before smoke started pouring out. More times than not, we were too late, but Dad always had the same response, even as he scraped the carbon off the toast's surface: "I like it on the dark side." We kept that old toaster for years, and the only maintenance it required was a new piece of tape every month or two.

One of the more visible signs of my parents' frugality was our lawn mower. In Harbor Hills, the yards were large and required a substantial machine to keep them manicured. Most of the wealthier neighbors with lake frontage hired lawn services; the rest of us cut our own grass. The first thing nearly every home owner did upon moving to Harbor Hills was to purchase a gleaming new riding mower with a padded seat. Dad would not even consider such an extravagance; instead he found a used walk-behind mower that was already an antique. By the time I was in grade school, the Gravely had taken on the rusty sheen of a museum piece with its old-fashioned round mowing deck, jutting oak handgrips, and faded red paint. The muffler was barely functioning, and the engine's roar drowned out all other sounds within a hundred yards. Occasionally it would backfire with the velocity of a shotgun, and I could watch the neighbors flinch as if taking sniper fire. The Gravely looked and sounded like it belonged in a scene from *The Grapes of Wrath,* before the Okies leave the Dust Bowl for California. But Dad pronounced it "perfectly adequate for our needs" and scoffed at the modern riding mowers, which he pointed out no man could ride without resembling a circus clown. Besides, he claimed to enjoy the workout he got trotting along behind the Gravely as it roared across our acre of grass in a cloud of blue smoke. For all its faded glory, it ran reliably, and Dad, an adept engine tinkerer, ensured that it stayed that way, repacking bearings and rebuilding the carburetor as needed.

Grass-cutting was a weekly father-son event. As Dad cut with the Gravely, my older brother Tim trimmed with a push mower, and Mike and I coiled hoses, picked up sticks, and raked clippings. More than my brothers, I gravitated toward yard work, and I tagged along with Dad as he completed various chores, whether it was planting marigolds or fertilizing the rhododendrons or trimming the hedges, something he did using a complex system of stakes and strings to assure symmetrical perfection. I was his helper, his tool fetcher, his grunt laborer, and I loved being out there with him.

If Mom was the family talker and storyteller, Dad was the listener. He was introspective bordering on taciturn and not much for aimless chitchat. But there was something about physical labor that brought out his talkative side. Working side by side, our hands in the dirt, he would freely share tips and techniques with me, always looking for opportunities to teach a little lesson, the lessons I imagine his father had taught him. At the workbench, it might be the importance of sanding with the grain or measuring twice before making a cut. In the garden, he would point out the complex social structure of an ant colony and the nifty way nature turned old grass clippings and leaves into rich plant food. It was on one of these work excursions that Dad finally worked up his courage to deliver my one and only sex-education lesson.

We were finished mowing and had just planted petunias around the oak tree. He directed me to drag a hose over to water them, but when the hose proved too short, he asked me to bring another length from the garage. Then it was time to connect the two hoses.

"John, hand me the female end, will you?" Dad said.

I stared dumbfounded at the two ends of the hose. I had no idea what he was talking about. "The what?" I asked.

"The female end," he said, a hint of exasperation in his voice, as if to add: *You're not going to make me explain how male and female parts go together, are you?*

I picked up both ends and stared at them. By this stage of my life—age twelve—I had moved on from the tiny boob shots of *Popular Photography* to the flawless women of *Playboy,* compliments of Marty Wolkoff, a classmate who lived one neighborhood over and whose father subscribed. I even got brief glimpses during a Boy Scout campout of Pat Wendell's big brother's "library," which was a worn leather satchel containing a well-thumbed collection of pornography showing men in a fully aroused state and women positioned as if posing for a gynecologists' convention. Thanks to these visual aids, I finally had a clear concept of male and female anatomy (though I was still unclear how exactly they went together). But looking at the ends of the garden hose, I could see no correlation whatsoever to anything I had seen in those magazines. I stood there gripping the hose ends with a look on my face that I suppose was not unlike the look my dog Shaun might have struck if given the task of figuring out an algebraic equation.

"Here," my father said with a weary sigh, grabbing each hose end away from me. "This is the male end," and he held up the end with the brass threads showing. "And this is the female." He jammed the male into the female and began twisting the threads together. "The male screws into the female like this," he said, then paused before adding: "Just like in nature."

Suddenly I saw what he was getting at. Just like in nature . . . *Ewwwww.*

"Got it?" he said.

I nodded up and down, my mouth agape. If I appeared awestruck, it was not over this anatomical breakthrough but over my father's choice of props. It occurred to me that never before had any father pressed into service a garden hose to demonstrate the act of sexual intercourse. Not birds and bees. Not mating wolves. Not oak trees and acorns. The two ends of a rubber hose. Only my dad.

"I got it," I said.

"Good. Now let's get back to work."

With that, my sexual education was officially over. Dad had fulfilled his fatherly duty, one he no doubt had fretted over for months before delivering. He never came anywhere near the topic with me again.

Other kids, especially those with older brothers, were more than happy to fill in the details. With the help of the Playboy Advisor and Penthouse Forum, and the wildly candid *The Happy Hooker,* which Tommy and I pooled our money to buy, and which featured among its many colorful stories a memorable encounter with a German shepherd, I was slowly piecing together the nuts and bolts of sex. I saw how the parts fit together, and why. It was all nature's way of assuring that the human race would carry on.

What puzzled me, though, was why, if sex was so natural and

so necessary, it was also so bad. If God was the creator of all things, and God was infallible and could do no wrong, then why did the priests and the nuns and my parents and Tommy's parents and every other adult I knew treat this aspect of God's handiwork as unspeakably embarrassing? It didn't make sense. My mother could look at a rosebush in bloom and say, "See, Johnny, that rose is proof of our Lord. There is no other possible explanation for something so perfect and beautiful." But when it came to swelling penises, lubricating vaginas, and mating urges so intense they could blind both men and women to even the need for food, God's perfect handiwork seemed a little, well, less perfect. I suppose that's why the Blessed Virgin Mother got a special pass from all the heavy breathing and unpleasantries of coitus.

For Lent that year, Mom and Dad urged each of us kids to give up something special, something that would be a true hardship and honor the ultimate sacrifice Christ made when he died on the cross to save our souls. Lent began in late winter with one of my favorite holy days, Ash Wednesday, during which we got to walk around all day with a sooty smudge on our foreheads that made us look like junior firefighters. It continued for six weeks and was intended to be a time of personal reflection leading up to Easter. My parents told us to give it some thought and find a meaningful act. For instance, giving up creamed spinach wouldn't be much of a sacrifice, nor would giving up something so specific you probably wouldn't encounter it anyway. You couldn't give up, say, lemon meringue pie and simply switch to apple or pumpkin. Likewise, on the charitable acts front, you couldn't promise to do something you were supposed to do anyway, like take out the trash or complete homework. You couldn't vow to brush your teeth every morning. It had to be a real sacrifice, something that took effort. Something that was a struggle to fulfill.

I thought and thought before landing on the perfect Lenten sacrifice. It would be the ultimate challenge for a twelve-year-old boy who had recently discovered that uniquely satisfying, solitary pleasure one could enjoy while locked in the bathroom with a copy of *Popular Photography* or *The Happy Hooker*.

I would give up that one thing I had recently come to enjoy most in life, the thing that at once was a source of profound pleasure and profound guilt because I knew it was a sin, and a sin I committed on a daily, sometimes hourly, basis.

My sacrifice was not a joke; it was not a lark. I was deadly serious. On the bookshelf in my parents' bedroom I had found a Catholic primer on human sexuality and read all about the sin of masturbation, or "self-pollution," as the book called it. Self-pollution was a depraved sin, a weakness of the flesh. It was a surrender to lust and a selfish act, too, because every time one self-polluted was a time he was not sharing the sacred seed with the sacred womb, as God intended. For the record, I was primed and ready to share every last sacred seed in my arsenal with whatever womb waggled my way. I was dying to share. But I was not so delusional as to pretend it was going to happen any time soon, if ever.

Tommy and I both had girlfriends now. His was Karen Mc-Kinney, a sandy blonde who always seemed to sport a sunburned nose, even in winter. Mine was Barbie Barlow, who had bright brown eyes that actually twinkled when she smiled, and budding hints of breasts beneath her plaid school jumper. The only thing was, Karen and Barbie didn't have the slightest clue they were our girlfriends. We jostled with them on the playground, pulled evil pranks on them, and pretended we more or less detested them. But each afternoon down at the beach with our cigarettes, Tommy and I would gush at length about their many virtues and what we would do with our goddesses if we ever, hypothetically, got up the nerve to let them know we liked them.

No, I wasn't too worried about the selfish part of my sin. I would happily share my seed if I could. In the meantime, I figured, there were plenty more where they came from. I was self-polluting at a furious pace, despite the Catholic remorse that followed each explosive release. I had allowed myself to become a virtual landfill of self-pollution. My temple was so dirtied by my actions, the Lord would never choose to fill it with his spirit. I was convinced what I was doing was horribly wrong, a serious transgression against God that would only increase the already near-certain likelihood that I would spend eternity burning. When Mom and Dad asked what I had decided to give up for Lent, I told them it was private. They were always respectful of their children's privacy, and this was no exception. They asked no questions. "Just try your hardest," Dad said. "If you do that, and in your heart you know you did the very best you could do, then that's all we ask. That's good enough for us."

The first day of Lent went quite well. In anticipation of my cold turkey abstinence plan, I had gone on a self-pollution bender the previous evening. I passed Day One with only a few passing impure thoughts. Day Two was not so easy. I had caught a glimpse of Barbie Barlow's underpants on the playground as she climbed the monkey bars—so close, so out of reach—and recounting the glorious moment in exquisite detail later for Tommy only heightened the tension. Barbie Barlow in pink panties; I could think of nothing else. By the time I got home from school on Day Three, I was crazed with hormonal lust. *Please, dear Jesus, dear God the Father, dear Holy Spirit, give me strength.* I really wanted to keep my promise, but not even they could infuse me with the necessary willpower. Less than thirty-six hours into my six-week vow of abstinence, I caved in to desire. I wasn't proud of myself. *A onetime lapse,* I promised, and marked the calendar above my bed with a small *X* to mark my fall. I vowed not to let it happen again. But as the weeks progressed, I marked *X* after *X*. My calendar became a minefield of *X*s, littering the days of the week and providing a shameful road map of my sinful secret life.

"How are you doing with your Lenten resolution?" Dad asked a couple of weeks into it.

"I'm sure trying," I said with a jauntiness I hoped would leave room for optimistic interpretation.

"That's all we ask, son," he answered and left it at that.

Chapter 8

The seven days leading up to Easter are known as Holy Week, and it was the year's most sacred and important time in our Catholic household, bigger even than Christmas. This was the week, we were taught, when Jesus laid down his life for our sins. In the words we recited each Sunday at Mass, it was the week when "he suffered under Pontius Pilate, was crucified, died, and was buried. He descended into hell, and on the third day he arose again, in fulfillment of the scriptures, and ascended into heaven to sit at the right hand of the Father." It's not every day someone covers so much ground in a single week, and our family celebrated each step of the way. It began with Palm Sunday, the day Jesus and his disciples had arrived in Jerusalem nearly two thousand years earlier, and wrapped up a week later with Easter Sunday, marking the day when Christians believe Jesus rose from the dead. In the middle was Holy Thursday, marking Jesus' last supper with his disciples, and Good Friday, which I always thought was egregiously misnamed considering that the only begotten son of God was hanged from a crucifix to die that day.

For some reason, my mother got it into her head that our family should celebrate Holy Thursday the way the Lord celebrated it nearly two thousand years earlier—with a traditional Jewish Passover dinner. Mom didn't know much about Judaism other than it wasn't Catholicism and that meant it was not the one true faith. But she knew Jesus had been a Jew and had spent his final meal on earth celebrating Passover. If it was good enough for Jesus, it was good enough for the Grogans.

Our neighborhood was so Catholic it could have qualified as an official outpost of the Vatican. There were a few Protestant families, and then there were the Kabcenells, who lived down the street from us, right across from the convent. To my knowledge, they were the only Jews for miles around. Mom and Mrs. Kabcenell were neighborly but danced around the topic of their faiths. They both seemed to think some things were best left unexplored.

But this Lent Mom went on a Passover crusade, and she wanted to get it just right. She laid out her plan to Mrs. Kabcenell, who was more than happy to sign on as Mom's Seder mentor. The two of them were on the phone for hours, Mom furiously jotting down Passover pointers and Kabcenell family recipes for matzo ball soup and *charoset,* a salad of spiced apples and chopped nuts. Naturally, the more they spoke, the less mysterious the other's religion seemed.

When Mom announced at dinner one day that we'd be celebrating Passover on Holy Thursday, I was thrilled. "We get to drink wine! We get to drink wine!" I squealed. The Kabcenells had a son my age. I had told him all about the fringe drinking benefits of being an altar boy, and he had told me all about the intoxicating virtues of Mogen David and Manischewitz.

On that Thursday before Easter, Mom called us to the table, and we found it laid out with an assortment of unfamiliar dishes. Dad took his seat at the head of the table. As the youngest child, I had the honor of asking the question to start things off.

"What is the meaning of this night, Father?" I read off a card my mother had handed me, being careful not to glance at my brothers. I knew they would be wanting payback for all the times I had made them laugh when they were supposed to be solemn.

Dad took his cue and read from a borrowed Haggadah, a Jewish prayer book that told the story of the Israelites' flight from slavery in Egypt. We ate unleavened matzo, and Dad explained how the Jews, in their haste, did not have time to let their bread rise. We dipped parsley in salt water, and sampled horseradish, which he said symbolized suffering and tears. My mouth stuffed with sawdust-dry crumbs and my eyes watering from the horse-radish, I decided those Catholic fish sticks we ate every Friday during Lent weren't so bad after all.

We ate hard-boiled eggs, which he told us stood for spring and renewal. The apple mixture was a reminder of the mortar the Jewish slaves used to build pyramids, and I had to admit Mom's version had the consistency of concrete. The wine was the highlight, even if it did remind me of grape cough syrup. The Catholics, I decided, definitely had an edge when it came to the quaffability of their sacramental alcoholic beverages.

"Sip, don't gulp," my father admonished. He had no idea that my training as an altar boy had taught me otherwise.

The Seder behind us, Mom brought out a roasted shank of lamb, a reminder of the first Passover sacrifice. "Hey, this is just like our Catholic lamb!" I said. It was dawning on me that Catho-lics and Jews were not that different after all. Something else was dawning on me as well. I am certain it wasn't the message my mother hoped I would take from our Passover celebration, but sitting there as my parents tried to connect the Judeo and Chris-tian traditions, I suddenly realized: there was no one true faith and no one chosen people. Not us, not the Kabcenells, not anyone. Heaven was not a paradise reserved for the exclusive use of any one religion. The Lord could not be that unfair. There could be either one God who loved everybody the same, or no God at all.

Whatever Mom's motivation, she succeeded in bridging at least one gap: she and Mrs. Kabcenell remained close friends for years to come, and the Passover Seder became an annual event in our house.

If there was one day out of the year on which even the most wayward Catholic dragged himself into church, it was Easter Sunday. The services were always packed, and Father added extra Masses to handle the crowds. Every altar boy was pressed into duty, and I was assigned the eleven o'clock Mass. It was a mob scene. Every pew was crammed. People stood three deep along the side and rear walls. The choir loft overflowed and so did the glass-encased cry room, filled with mothers and noisy babies. Dozens of white lilies lined the altar, filling the church with an overpowering, nearly narcotic fragrance. All the mothers and daughters came decked out in their new spring dresses, and there was real excitement in the air. I felt like I was at a rock concert—and I was onstage with the main act.

During communion, the congregants filed forward, pew by pew, to the altar rail. My job was to stand next to the priest and balance a gold plate beneath each chin as Father pressed a host on the parishioner's tongue. Just in case Father fumbled the host, which happened at least once per Mass, I was there to catch it. Or at least try. If I was lucky and caught it on the plate, Father could simply pick it up and carry on. But more times than not, it missed and fell to the ground, in which case Father would have to bend down, retrieve it, and swallow it himself.

Some priests were so skilled they could deftly pop a host on the tongue without making any flesh-to-flesh contact and almost never fumbling. But most of them, in their caution not to drop Christ's body and risk a sacrilege, ended up touching the recipient's lip or tongue, then doing it again for the next person in line, and the next. Standing beside him, I could actually see Father's thumb and fingertips wet with saliva. The number of germs spread in communion lines should have triggered a four-alarm public-health alert, but no one seemed to mind. What was a little shared spit among true believers who were all going to heaven anyway? Besides, it was hard to imagine the son of God would come into your body and then let you catch a disease simply because Father's host-dispensing skills weren't up to par. If Jesus could multiply fishes and loaves and raise the dead, he could certainly make sure no one contracted strep throat from the communion line.

I was holding the gold plate for Father when my eyes wandered down the altar rail. There, making her way toward me, was the lovely, budding-breasted Barbie Barlow. She was in a wispy pastel dress with a matching ribbon in her hair. It was the first time I had seen her in anything other than her blue plaid school uniform, which resembled something that would be issued at a women's penitentiary. I nearly gasped out loud. She looked beautiful, ethereal, as if it were Barbie who was meant to ascend to heaven on that spring day. She seemed to float toward me in the communion line, and soon she would be kneeling right before me. I sucked in my stomach and stood taller. So what if my cassock pinched around the middle and bunched at my feet; I never felt prouder to be in the uniform of the altar corps. When it was her turn, Barbie knelt in front of the priest and lowered her eyes. I slipped the gold plate beneath her chin and watched, mesmerized, as her lips parted and her tongue slipped out to accept the host. She swallowed, blessed herself, and just as she was stepping away, glanced at me and smiled. It was only a little grin—the kind one classmate might slip another in recognition—but her eyes had that twinkle, and I felt my heart stutter. The ascension-worthy Barbie Barlow had bestowed her beatific smile upon me. My eyes followed her as she returned to her pew and knelt again, still grinning my way. I nearly dropped the gold plate.

As Mass concluded, the other altar boys and I formed our

usual procession. I carefully lifted one of the big floor-length candles from its stand and took my place behind the boy carrying the Bible. Father proclaimed the Mass over, blessed everyone, and told them to go in peace to love and serve the Lord. That was the cue for the organist, who launched into the recessional hymn, and the congregation began to sing. It was the big finale of the biggest service of the year, and Father joined us in line for our grand parade down the center aisle. I scanned the crowd, and there was Barbie holding a hymnal, looking right at me with those twinkling eyes. I sneaked a small smile back and gripped my giant candle in its long brass holder, wielding it like a knight with a lance. Father gave a sign, and we stepped forward, down the steps. As we marched toward the rear of church, I stared straight ahead with my manliest expression. How could she *not* be impressed? I stole another quick glance. She was still looking, still twinkling.

That's when it happened. It started with a barely noticeable tug on my cassock. In the next instant, the tug became a pull and the pull a sharp yank. The toe of my shoe had gotten tangled in the hem dragging on the floor. I steadied the candle in front of me, the flame flickering inches from my face, and tried to free my foot. A little shake would do it, I was sure. The trapped foot was in midstep; I just needed to kick the material clear before my foot hit the ground and all would be well. I was confident I could recover without so much as a misstep. But as my foot made contact with the floor, I could feel the cassock heaving down hard at my shoulders. It felt like someone had reached up from a hole in the floor and grabbed ahold. I heard my voice rise above the organ music: "Whoaaaa!" I made one last, valiant maneuver, shooting out my other foot to regain my balance. In that split second, I paused to marvel at my ability to keep my oversize candle with its voluminous pool of hot liquid wax stable through my crisis. I stumbled forward on the pinned fabric, and my free foot did the only thing it could do. It made a giant, graceful arc as if kicking a football. What it kicked, though, was the bottom of the brass candlestick. My hands gripped the stick in the middle, making an efficient fulcrum point. As the bottom flew forward, the top jerked back. Simple physics.

Scalding wax showered down on me, coating my hair and forehead, searing my skin. Wax ran over my eyebrows and into my lashes. It felt like someone had pressed a hot iron to my face. I heard my scream, as if from outside myself: *Yeow!* But the worst part, the very worst part, even worse than the scorching pain of bubbling wax on my skin, was my glasses. I was blind without them, and they were doused in wax, rendering them opaque. With a rip of fabric, I felt my foot break free, and I quickly regained my balance. But now I could not see a thing. I began to weave and swerve blindly down the aisle, caroming off the other altar boys and the ends of the pews. I heard Father's whispered voice behind me: "For the love of God!" I peered desperately into the opaqueness of my lenses and found a small break in the coating through which I could see. It was like looking through a keyhole stuffed with spiderwebs. The first thing I did was get my bearings. I was back on track, heading straight down the aisle. The next thing I did was find Barbie in the crowd. Maybe her head had been down as she prayed. Maybe she had her nose in her songbook. Maybe she hadn't noticed a thing.

When I finally located her, right there beside her parents, she was staring directly at me. The sweet, twinkly smile from a few moments earlier was gone, replaced by a big, openmouthed grin. Barbie was laughing. The whole congregation, it seemed, was laughing. The other altar boys were laughing. I think even Father was laughing. Who could blame them? I looked like a blind escapee from the wax museum.

I peered through my waxy glasses at the shoulders of the boy in front of me and plowed ahead, past Barbie, past my parents, who were not laughing but grimacing, past everyone, and out the rear doors. Later, back in the sacristy, I ran hot water over my glasses and combed as much wax out of my hair and eyebrows as I could. The other altar boys chortled at my public humiliation but in the end took pity and let me have the entire cruet of wine to myself. I accepted gratefully.

Chapter 9

The Detroit riots had scared everyone and cracked the resolve of many families living in the city, pushing them to sell their homes at fire-sale prices and flee to the suburbs. One of those families moved into a new contractor house kitty-corner to ours on June 6, 1968—the day after Senator Robert Kennedy was shot and killed at the Ambassador Hotel in Los Angeles. My family sat glued to the television that day, but I mostly looked out the living-room window at the moving van across the backyards, depositing the new family in our midst. Even from a distance, I could see there were five children, and the oldest looked just about my age.

His name was Ronald, and he was the world's biggest Detroit Tigers fan, wearing his team letter jacket everywhere and usually carrying a souvenir program in his back pocket. On his first day in the neighborhood, as everyone else in the nation reeled in shock over the second Kennedy assassination in five years, Tommy and I wandered over to give the new kid our Harbor Hills Welcome Wagon treatment.

The boy barely came up to my shoulder and was skinny and pale with freckles all over his face; his toes pointed inward like a pigeon's and his knees knocked together. Tommy walked right up to him and without saying a word slammed him hard in the chest with both palms, knocking him to the ground. Then we ridiculed his Tigers jacket and stomped on his souvenir program. I felt a little bad about it, but Tommy was convinced it was important to establish the neighborhood pecking order right up front. When Ronald did not cry or run away, we decided he was worthy.

Tommy, who exhibited an early knack for ironic observation, quickly rechristened him Rock. Of course, Rock looked more like a twig than anything so unyielding as stone, which made the nickname all the more delicious. It stuck, and we welcomed him into our Secret Society of Smokers, Swearers, and Sacramental Wine Swiggers. Soon our constant twosome was a threesome.

The following summer, the Sacorellis moved in directly behind the Cullens. Mr. and Mrs. Sacorelli had arrived from Italy as teenagers and brought a lot of the old country with them. He spoke in fulsomely accented English that reminded me of the man in the spaghetti-sauce commercials. Mrs. Sacorelli spoke no English at all, did not drive, and seldom ventured farther than ten feet from her kitchen stove. She lived to cook, and amazing smells of tomatoes, garlic, and veal filled the house and wafted across the neighborhood day and night. The Sacorellis made their own pasta, rolling the dough out on the kitchen table with floured hands. They stuffed their own sausages and hung them from the rafters in the basement to cure. They pressed grapes in a hand-cranked contraption that looked like a torture device, and kept oak casks of homemade wine below the hanging meats. Unlike the rest of us kids in the neighborhood, the six Sacorelli kids did not have to filch their booze. Before each meal, one of them was dispatched to the basement to pour a pitcher for the table and the whole family to share.

Right in the middle of the Sacorelli pack was Anthony, a rosy-cheeked cherub our age whose giant brown eyes brought every girl in the neighborhood to her knees. Tommy, Rock, and I did a quick assessment—let's see, magnet for the opposite sex, check; a mom who would feed us vast quantities of delicious food but couldn't understand anything we said, double check; *and* an unlimited source of free, untraceable booze. "You're in, Sack," Tommy proclaimed, and then we were four.

Actually, we were five if you counted Shaun, my dog, who accompanied us everywhere—to The Outlot and the basketball courts, to the smoking tree and each other's houses. He was so naturally well behaved, the whole family nicknamed him Saint Shaun. He tagged along without a leash, came whenever I whistled, and happily pulled me through the neighborhood on my bike. Some school days he showed up unannounced at the playground during recess and joined our soccer games. He spent hours at the beach with us, diving off the dock and reemerging with giant rocks in his mouth. He even raced along as we rode our bikes down to the shopping plaza for candy and French fries, waiting patiently outside for us to reemerge, his eyes fixed on whatever door I had entered.

Shaun was a fixture in the neighborhood and was mostly well received. Those were more tolerant days, and the neighbors hardly seemed to notice that a dog, especially one as well mannered as he, was running unleashed through their yards and across the community beach. Only one person complained, and that was Old Man Pemberton. He had been retired for as long as anyone could remember and was as ancient as the Great Pyramid at Giza. Mr. Pemberton's property abutted The Outlot and looked out over The Lagoon, and he spent hours every day fussing about, hand-pulling dandelions from his grass, sculpting his hedges, watering flower baskets, and touching up the trim on his house. He scrubbed his driveway with soapy water and used a blowtorch to incinerate weeds that dared show their heads above the white pebbles surrounding his mailbox. The place, with its giant picture windows looking out over the boat basin and the lake beyond, belonged in a magazine. It was perfect in all ways but one: it shared an unfenced property line with The Outlot. His emerald lawn blended seamlessly into the common property, and this drove Mr. Pemberton insane. As families walked through The Outlot to their boats or the beach, they invariably cut across the lower corner of his yard, causing him to glare and sputter. If the offenders were kids, he would shout out, "You're on private property!" Eventually he painted a sign with a giant arrow and drove it into the ground on his property line, directing trespassers to stay on the other side. Every kid in the neighborhood promptly and gleefully ignored it. So did Shaun.

Mr. Pemberton appointed himself the enforcer of neighborhood rules and was constantly scolding children for every imaginable infraction. "This isn't a playground," he'd yell. "No shouting! No jumping on the docks! No throwing sand! No glass containers allowed!" If teenagers were down at the beach after dark—and there was no better place to take a girl and a six-pack than the beach late at night—he would turn on the powerful spotlights mounted to the eaves of his house and dial the police. My free-running dog was a particular irritant to him. "Pets must be leashed at all times!" he would bark. "No dogs allowed on the beach!" "Yes, Mr. Pemberton," I would mumble, and the next day Shaun would be right back there beside me, swimming and sniffing and diving.

Of course, when Tommy, Rock, Sack, and I got together and felt the collective itch for wrongdoing that boys of a certain age are powerless to resist, Mr. Pemberton was almost always our target of choice. With four houses among us, our parents seldom knew exactly where we were. We could be howling around the neighborhood till midnight, and the Cullens would think we were all at the Sacorellis', the Sacorellis would be sure we were at the Grogans', and so on. It was a beautiful arrangement. Some nights we camped out in a tent in one of our backyards, and these nights were best of all, especially if we knew neighborhood girls were also sleeping out. All four of our houses were roughly in a row—mine backed up to Rock's, Tommy's was across the street from Rock's, and Sack's was behind Tommy's—and we could watch as each house went dark for the night. That was our cue to get up and wander around. Our top destination was the party store on the corner where we could buy loads of candy and where Tommy perfected the art of walking out with bottles of Boone's Farm shoved down the crotch of his shorts. He did this while the rest of us created a diversion at the cash register, usually involving fumbled change or fizzing sodas. How he got away with it, I never understood, the theft was so obvious. The bottle filled the front of his shorts with a lusty exuberance that gave him the look of the most generously endowed thirteen-year-old on earth. With cocktails secured, we would lie on our backs in a field of tall grass, safely hidden from headlights, puffing our Marlboros and passing the bottle of wine. About halfway through the bottle, one of us would usually seize on yet another brilliant scheme to pimp Old Man Pemberton.

We put dog feces in his mailbox and poured motor oil on his driveway. We collected trash from houses up and down the street and spread it across his front yard. One of our better schemes was to tiptoe to the side of his house where he stored his canoe and hoist it into the branches of a nearby tree.

There were so many kids in the neighborhood, all of them avowed antagonists of the Pembertons, that the old man didn't know where to begin. We were all suspects, and the older teens, who had the most reason to despise him, were the biggest suspects of all.

Dad had his own vague suspicions, even if he couldn't prove them. "Go easy on Mr. Pemberton," he would counsel. "Show respect and give him his space. Someday you'll be old and you'll understand." Dad was big on the Golden Rule and recited it often. "Remember, John, do unto others as you'd have them do unto you."

Mr. Cullen was less diplomatic. One afternoon he lined us up in the driveway, pushed his face up to ours, and said, "Get your hands outta your pockets, mon, and listen up. If I ever find out you've been messing with Mr. Pemberton or anyone else in this neighborhood, I'm going to ride your bloody ass to Singapore and back. Do you understand me, boys?" We looked at the ground and nodded. We understood perfectly.

But then came the Fourth of July and the big fireworks celebration at Pine Lake Country Club.

It was a private, pricey club with a spectacular golf course nestled along Pine Lake, the next lake over from ours and an easy bike ride away. Like many kids in the neighborhood, Tommy, Sack, and I worked as caddies there, schlepping golf bags on our shoulders and handing nine irons and drivers to the golfers. (Rock, if I recall, tried it once and never went back.) We earned four dollars for eighteen holes, and usually got a 50-cent tip. Sometimes we could squeeze in two rounds a day—sweaty, tiring work but not bad money when you could buy a loaded eight-inch pizza at the Village Inn for $1.79. Being a caddy had other privileges. If you didn't mind dodging sprinklers and lawn mowers, you could golf for free on Mondays. You could always bum a cigarette and hear obscene jokes at the caddy shack. And every July Fourth, caddies were allowed to hang out in the employee parking lot of the country club for an up close view of the fireworks display. A very up close view. The club members were in their lounge chairs on the fairways where they could watch the pyrotechnics explode over the water. But we got to watch from a vantage point just yards from the launchpad, in a roped-off corner of the parking lot. The workers would drop a charge, mortar-style, into a steel tube, light the fuse, and jump back. *Boom!* Up it would streak into the sky above the water, blossoming into a rainbow of screaming colors and whistling streamers. Two other boys from our class at Refuge were caddies, too, and they joined up with us. One we called Doggie on account of the woebegone expression perpetually engraved on his face, even when he was laughing. Doggie looked like he had basset hound in his gene line. The other boy we all knew as Poison for his ability to traipse through poison ivy without getting so much as an itch. He was an adopted kid with a wild streak that made Tommy and the rest of us look like angels. Poison kept count of the number of bottles of Boone's Farm he stole from local stores, and one day proudly proclaimed himself an ace, having surpassed one hundred.

The six of us crowded around the launch site with the other caddies, mouths agape as the pyrotechnic rockets soared skyward yards from our faces. It was like being ringside at Cape Canaveral for a space launch. That's when we noticed the open crates of fireworks sitting just inside the rope line, unguarded.

Over and over, workers filed over to the crates, grabbed a rocket or two, and filed back to the launchpad a dozen yards away. I'm not sure how we got the idea, or if we even discussed it. I can't even remember which of us bent over the rope and reached into the crate. I just know it wasn't me. And I know I thought it was a *very* bad idea. If an M-80 could blow off Kevin McConnell's thumb and two fingers, as one with a faulty fuse had done a few years earlier, what could one of these babies do? But in the next instant there we were, scurrying along the edge of the parking lot in the dark, cutting in and out of the pine trees—in possession of a four-foot-long, ready-to-fire missile. "Jesus Christ! Jesus Christ!" I hissed as I raced to keep up. "Oh my God! Jesus Christ!" We cut through the back of the golf course, jumped fences, and made our way through a series of backyards and woods, avoiding all roads. The rocket was heavy and we took turns carrying it in teams of two. When we got to the field of tall grass where we liked to drink wine, we lay down out of sight with our prize and caught our breath. No one was following us; apparently no one had even noticed. As our fear of capture ebbed, we became drunk on the endless possibilities for our newly acquired arsenal. Just holding it in our hands was a narcotic. You could almost feel the pent-up power pulsing beneath its skin, ready to be unleashed at the place and time of our choosing. We hashed out several scenarios but in the end all agreed there was no time like the present, and no audience more fitting, more deserving, and certainly more likely to respond in a memorable way than Old Man Pemberton.

The plot was brilliant, pure genius. It would be hilarious, spectacular, epic. The prank to end all pranks. The escapade of a lifetime. After this caper, we could retire as mischief-makers, knowing our world-class reputations would be secure. We were going to launch a one-rocket fireworks show in Mr. Pemberton's front yard. Directly in front of those big picture windows. The ones we knew he sat behind in the dark, watching for teenage miscreants sneaking down to the water's edge with their beer and blankets. He wanted something to see? We'd give him something to see.

We had studied the workers at the country club. Launching looked simple. You dropped the rocket in a tube, lit the fuse, and stood back. Virtually foolproof. We hoisted our contraband and made our way through the fields and across Commerce Road to Harbor Hills, stopping on the way to pick out a length of clay sewer pipe, about six inches across and three feet long, from a construction site. It would make a perfect launch tube.

A few minutes later, we lay on our stomachs beneath a gnarly apple tree in The Outlot. From this vantage point we could study the Pemberton house, all dark and quiet. Our destination was a clump of shrubs in the Pembertons' front yard, behind which we could hide as we prepared our missile for launch. Two by two, we made the dash. No lights came on.

Doggie and Tommy began kicking up the sod with their heels, digging a shallow hole, and Poison ground the sewer pipe into it, working it down into the dirt until it stood upright on its own. We checked the alignment and pronounced it just about perfect, with just enough arc to get the firework directly over the house before it exploded, its display showering down directly in front of the picture windows. Sack and I slid the rocket into the tube. Then we all looked at each other. Who was going to light the fuse? Who was willing to take responsibility for this stunt of the century? It wasn't going to be me. I was happy to be the coward and was the first to back away. So did Sack and Rock and Doggie. Finally, Tommy grabbed the matches out of Poison's hand. "I'll do it," he said.

His hand was trembling as he lit the match and held it to the fuse, which protruded from just below the missile's nose. For a second nothing happened, and I thought, with some relief, that we had a dud. I was just starting to exhale when the fuse caught, just like a sparkler, and began burning toward the rocket. Tommy jumped back with the rest of us, but as he did, he bumped the tube. Now it was no longer pointing skyward with just the perfect arc to bring the light show directly overhead. Now it was pointing directly at the Pembertons' roof.

"Holy shit!" Tommy cried.

"Holy shit!" we all echoed.

Without another word, Tommy dashed forward, grabbed the clay tube in both hands, the sparkling fuse lighting his face, and tugged it back into position. The fuse was two-thirds gone. He let go and the tube again slumped down. There were just a few seconds left. Tommy straightened it again and this time pushed it down into the dirt with all his strength. Then he dove back with us and lay on his stomach. That's when we saw that Tommy's best had not been good enough. The tube had again shifted, this time pointing even lower than before. It was pointing so low, in fact, that it looked like the rocket might plow into the lawn a few yards ahead of us.

We held our ears. I said a prayer. With a deafening boom and blinding flash, the firework screamed off in a near horizontal position. It skimmed over Mr. Pemberton's perfect lawn and nipped a shrub, gaining elevation as it went. We stared frozen, holding our breath as it zeroed in on the front of the house, spiraling directly toward those giant plate-glass windows. The rocket's total journey could not have lasted more than a second or two, but it unfolded before us in slow motion. I could picture Mr. Pemberton lurching back in his chair in the window. I could see the terror on his face, the dawning realization that he was going to die. *Dear God, what have we done?* I thought.

Blam! The firework slammed into the brick wall, right between the two windows. Another three feet in either direction and it would have crashed through the glass and into the house. It disintegrated into the bricks with a loud blast, followed by a series of shrieking, burning streamers flying in all directions. Bursts of multicolored sparks sprayed outward, catching the grass on fire. The explosions kept coming. In plumes of green and red and blue and blinding white. Whirling, whistling flares corkscrewed out and skipped across the lawn. Glowing balls of fire catapulted in all directions.

And then it was over. We all lay there for a moment, staring at the pall of smoke hanging a few feet above the ground. "Fuck!" someone whispered. Then Poison was on his feet and sprinting toward the beach like I had never seen anyone run before. The rest of us bolted after him.

"Holy shit! Holy shit!" Tommy kept saying.

Dear Jesus, dear God the Father, dear Holy Spirit, I prayed silently. *Don't let us have killed Mr. Pemberton. Don't let his house burn down. Please, don't let him die. Please, don't let us get caught.*

We waded into the lake and, hugging the shoreline, made our way up the beach, not stopping until we reached the vacant lot where the smoking tree stood. No doubt the police were in the neighborhood by now. We crept up the bluff and peered over the edge at the street. All dark and quiet. Silently we crawled through the empty field and were almost to my street when we heard a car engine. "Down!" Tommy hissed, and we lay flat in the weeds, our breath ragged and nervous, so loud I was certain it would give us away. First a pair of headlights swept over us, then a spotlight. The police cruiser continued down the street, raking each lawn with its powerful beam. After it was out of sight, we scurried across the street and divided up without a word, each heading to his own home.

Inside, Dad was still up.

"How were the fireworks?" he asked.

"Great," I said. "Incredible."

"Well, good," he said. And with that, I walked upstairs, washed my face and hands, and turned in for the night.

The next morning I paced nervously around the house, acting as nonchalant as possible but dying to find out just how much damage we had done. I watched my parents carefully, but they showed no signs of knowing anything. Each time the phone rang I jumped, but they were all false alarms. Finally I put on my trunks and announced I was heading down for a swim.

"Okay, honey," Mom said. "I'll have lunch ready when you get back."

Down at The Outlot I concentrated on not staring over at the Pembertons' house. Only a guilty man would show up the next morning to gawk. I could not stare. I must not gaze. The briefest momentary glance was all I dare risk. After all, I just happened to be strolling by on my way for a refreshing morning dip. I looked up at the trees, marveled at the blue sky, paused to admire the water. Then, as subtly as I knew how, I let my head drift in the direction of the Pemberton property, and that's when I saw it. The brick wall where the firework hit was charred black. The hedge below was burned lifeless. The eves and awnings were scorched, and the lawn was marred with trails of blackened, seared grass. There in the midst of the carnage was Mr. Pemberton, raking up the debris as best he could. Just as I looked at him he looked at me, and what I saw staring back was not steely defiance or suspicious accusation, but defeat. He was a broken man. In his watery eyes, I saw only a question: "Why?

Why would you kids do this to us?" I didn't have an answer. I looked away and continued down to the beach, being careful to stay on the outside of Mr. Pemberton's arrow sign. I wanted to turn back and apologize, to tell him we never meant for it to turn out this way. Instead, I kept walking and did not look back.

After my swim, I cut through the neighbors' yards so I wouldn't have to face the old man again. By the time I arrived home, Dad knew about the fireworks at the Pembertons. He had heard from Mr. Cullen, who had heard from Mr. Sacorelli, who had heard from another neighbor. The news was all over Harbor Hills.

"Do you know anything about this?" Dad asked.

"No, Dad."

"You don't know anything about this?" he said.

"Not a thing, Dad."

He studied my face. "I better not find out that you did, do you understand?"

"You won't, Dad," I promised.

That night I lay on top of the sheets in the July heat, the crickets' symphony drifting through the screened windows, and squeezed my eyes shut. "Dear Jesus, dear God the Father, dear Holy Spirit," I whispered. "Tell Mr. Pemberton I'm sorry. Tell him we didn't mean it. Tell him it wasn't as cruel as it seems. It was just a dumb idea. And thanks for not letting it turn out any worse."

Chapter 10

The nuns at Our Lady of Refuge were renowned for their cruelty. With the relish of medieval torture masters, they imposed a strict discipline that relied on physical pain and the constant threat that it could be visited on anyone at any moment for any reason. Corporal punishment was an important part of the Catholic education experience, and the tool of choice was the twelve-inch steel-lined ruler, which every nun carried at all times like every police officer carries a gun. Small and compact, it allowed Sister to make her way among our desks, delivering welt-raising blows without warning other than the brief shrill whistling sound the ruler made as it rushed through the air in the instant before impact. The knuckles were a favorite target, followed by the forearms, kneecaps, thighs, and occasionally the back of the head. Passing notes? *Whack!* Chewing gum? *Whack!* Staring absently out the window? *Whack!* Holding your pencil wrong? *Whack, whack, whack!*

For the bigger discipline jobs, the nuns brought out the heavy armaments—stout wooden yardsticks and the even more deadly rubber-tipped pointers. Punishment was styled after the public flogging of old and involved both pain and humiliation. The guilty student was ordered to the front of the class to assume the position: back to the class, feet spread, palms pressed on the blackboard. He—I can't remember a girl ever being up there—would be forced to wait while Sister fetched her yardstick. She always took her time. The waiting was torture. One sharp, withering whack across the back of the thighs, and it was over. But the worst part was yet to come—the public humiliation of turning to face the class. Some boys cried, some merely blinked back tears; the strongest managed to stay dry-eyed or even smirk defiantly. But there was one thing no one could hide, and that was the wet, clammy palm prints left behind on the blackboard. They served as a sort of corporal-punishment fear detector. You might be able to fake a brave face, but the sweaty palm prints told the truth. The class would roar with laughter, and Sister would chortle with approval. *Look how smart the smart aleck looks now, class.*

The nuns had other tricks, too. Over the years, I had my ears twisted, hair yanked, and face slapped. One nun, with a major leaguer's accuracy, wound up and hurled a chalk eraser across the room, nailing a student on the forehead. In seventh grade, I spent hours decorating an old cigar box to hold my pencils and pens. I was working at my desk with it open beside me when the perpetually angry Sister Mary Edward, for reasons I never determined, slapped it to the floor, sending the contents flying. "Now pick it up," she sneered and walked away, leaving me to crawl on my hands and knees among the desks as my classmates snickered. This kind of treatment was nothing new. My mother remembered—with great humor, for some reason—a nun at her Catholic school forcing her younger brother to eat a dead fly he had been caught playing with. Forcing an insect carcass down the throat of a second grader—now, there's the Christian spirit! Nuns and abuse just seemed to go hand in hand.

The only thing was, none of us considered it abuse, least of all our parents, who had the same basic response to every reported atrocity: "Well, if Sister decided you deserved to be hung by your thumbs while she flogged you with a cat-o'-nine-tails, then Sister must have had a good reason." The nuns were not quite as infallible as priests, but they were close. If they chose to smack or ridicule us, we obviously got what was coming to us.

I became convinced that the only real joy in the nuns' austere, lonely lives was the terrified yelps of small children. There was one exception at Our Lady of Refuge, and that was Sister Nancy Marie. She was young, mid- to late twenties, and plain but with a beatific smile and shiny complexion that combined to give her a preternatural glow. Unlike the older, more conservative nuns with their scratchy habits and starched face boards, she dressed in a knee-length skirt with a blouse and jacket. Except for a crucifix around her neck and a small veil on her head, which allowed a shock of hair to tumble onto her forehead, she barely even looked like a nun.

All the students loved Sister Nancy Marie. She was one of the original "What Would Jesus Do?" disciples, and took seriously her vows to act like Christ. No matter how serious your transgression—forgotten homework, chatting in class, playground fisticuffs—she would never strike, never scold, never even raise her voice. Her response to almost any situation was to fix those earnest brown eyes on you, clasp her hands together, and say, "Now, let's see how we can resolve this." In her vocation, she was a lamb among embittered wolves.

I suppose we should have gone easy on her.

Sister Nancy Marie was the religious-education instructor, and it was her job to infuse us with the wonders of our faith. It was in her nature to win our hearts with sweetness, and she sometimes managed to make religion seem fun. One of her innovations was to let us choose popular songs by our favorite bands to play during Mass. We would bring in our record albums and listen to the lyrics of Simon and Garfunkel or Bob Dylan or The Doors, discussing any themes that might apply. Most of the songs were complete stretches, but she gave us latitude. I remember playing The Beatles' "A Day in the Life," from *Sgt. Pepper's Lonely Hearts Club Band,* at one student Mass. At another, I suggested "Tired of Waiting for You" by The Kinks, and Sister approved it. What this song of boy-girl longing had to do with religion, I didn't know, but Sister Nancy Marie was game. She was always looking for ways to blur the line between the secular and the spiritual, to demonstrate that God could and should be integrated into every part of our lives. It would be up to Tommy, with wholehearted encouragement from me, to determine Sister Nancy Marie's limits.

We had no cafeteria at Refuge and ate lunch at our desks. One day in seventh grade, Sister Nancy Marie announced a new idea: Record Day, at which we could bring in albums to play during the lunch hour. When Record Day arrived, she rolled in the record player on its cart, plugged it in, and invited us to take turns playing our favorite songs while we ate our sandwiches. "Listen carefully to the lyrics," she beckoned. "Contemplate what the artist is saying. What is his message? How does it touch your lives?" And then she left the room. Sister Nancy Marie operated on trust. No need to stand over her students with a club. Treat them like adults, and they will act like adults. One girl stepped forward and put on "Where Have All the Flowers Gone?" Another dropped the needle on Peter, Paul, and Mary's version of "Blowin' in the Wind." A third offered The Byrds' rendition of "Mr. Tambourine Man." Then Tommy stood up. He, too, had brought a favorite album, carried inconspicuously into school between his books. The album was by The Fugs—and The Fugs definitely were not what Sister Nancy Marie had in mind for contemplative lunchtime listening.

They were the raunchiest, most indecent band I had ever

heard. Some critics would later hail them as the original punk band, bravely paving the way for the Ramones and the Sex Pistols and all the others to follow. But on this day, they were just one thing to Tommy and me: the biggest Catholic-school no-no we could imagine. One song opened in a yodeling voice, sustaining an obscenity. Another had the catchy title "Boobs A Lot." A third sang the praises of marijuana and cunnilingus.

But the coup de grâce, the album's pièce de résistance, was track three, a song called "Supergirl." Unlike relationship songs by the Beatles or Monkees or Stones, this one did not waste time on holding hands or gazing dreamily into eyes or even spending the night together. It got right to the point in the opening line.

I'm not sure whose idea it was to play "Supergirl" in class. My memory is that it began as an abstract hypothetical. *Just imagine the look on old Nancy Marie's face if "Supergirl" ever came on.* From there, it was elevated to an idea. *What if we sneaked Supergirl on? My God, how hilarious would that be?* And from an idea it graduated to a dare. And if there was one thing I already knew about Tommy, it was never to challenge him to do anything you did not want to see him try.

Tommy carried his record to the front of the room and peeked out the door into the empty hallway. All clear. He pulled the vinyl disk from its cardboard sleeve and placed it on the spinning turntable. As always, I was rapidly losing my nerve. *Don't do it, Tommy,* I telegraphed. *It's not too late. Don't do it.* Leaning over for a better view, he balanced the needle over the vinyl.

"Now, boys and girls," he called out in a high voice that was his imitation of Sister Nancy Marie. "I want you to contemplate what the artist is saying. Listen to the words. How do they touch your lives?" He hesitated for a moment, then expertly dropped the needle onto the empty band between tracks two and three.

Tommy reached for the volume knob and cranked it as high as it would go. Amplified pops, hisses, and crackles filled the classroom. He raced back to his seat, and the song began, first with clashing guitar chords and then with the opening lyrics. At full volume, the music was badly distorted. But the words remained perfectly understandable. They boomed through the room and out the open door. And this is what they said:

"I want a girl who can fuck like an angel."

The F-word stood above the rest, and screamed down the hallway like a fireball, filling every corner, crack, nook, and cranny of Our Lady of Refuge. It was so loud, I wondered if Mom could hear it back home in our kitchen four doors away. *"I want a girl who can FUUUUUUCK like an angel."*

The second verse began: "I want a girl who can—" The class never found out what. Sister Nancy Marie, her face as red as I have ever seen a human face, sprinted into the room. She was running so fast her veil actually flew out straight behind her, like a flag in a stiff wind. She dove at the record player, arced her arm like a tennis pro executing a perfect backstroke, swung it around, and smacked the needle with all her strength. It skidded across the vinyl with the sound of ripping fabric. Then the room went silent. She picked up the album in both hands, raised it over her head, not unlike the way the priest raised the host to heaven during the consecration, and brought it down hard on the side of the cart. The Fugs shattered into a hundred pieces. She threw the chunk still in her hands to the floor and stomped on it. She was screaming and shaking, her face now a deep crimson. The crucifix had flung around her neck and somehow ended up behind her, hanging between her shoulders. She stopped, bowed her head, and stood there silently for a few seconds, eyes closed, breathing heavily. Then she reached around and retrieved her crucifix, raising it to her lips and kissing it as she blessed herself. Her voice was calm again. "No one is leaving this classroom until I know who did this," she said. "This . . . this . . ."—and her voice rose again—"this . . . disgusting . . . filth."

I glanced over at Tommy; he was as white as chalk. Then I saw why. On the desk in front of him in plain view sat the Fugs album cover. It was the one part of our brilliant plan we had over-looked. There was no hiding it now. He folded his hands over it, and we both stared straight ahead. Within seconds, Tommy was busted. Sister ordered him to the principal's office. Not long after, I was summoned, too. As a co-conspirator with advanced knowl-edge of the crime, I was in nearly as much trouble.

The principal, Sister Mary Noel, segregated us, Tommy in her office and me in the tiny nurse's station across the hall. She dealt with him first, as I waited with clammy palms. Finally the door opened and in she walked. I was expecting her to be angry, but she mostly looked sad.

"Mr. Grogan, tell me this," she began, and I braced for an in-terrogation on the Fugs conspiracy. But her questions had noth-ing to do with it. "What are you going to be in this life?" she asked. "Are you going to be a tree that spreads its roots deep and reaches proudly to the sky? Or are you going to be a weed that bends in any breeze and never grows to its full potential?" I stared blankly at her. *What in God's name is she talking about?*

"You come from solid stock, John Grogan. Your parents planted an acorn that has the potential to grow into a mighty oak. But you choose to mingle in the weeds instead of growing strong. You could be a leader in the forest, standing tall above all the other trees. The weeds never amount to anything. They don't take root and are quickly overshadowed by the other trees. Is that what you want?"

Sister Noel pushed her face close to mine. "What are you going to be? A solid oak? Or a common weed wallowing in the ditch?" I sat silently. Frankly, I didn't want to be either. I liked being a boy just fine. And if being an oak tree meant turning my back on Tommy—and it was dawning on me that that was what Sister was getting at—I'd take my chances as a weed. Tommy was my best friend; we'd grow together side by side.

"An oak or a weed?" Sister repeated. "Only you can decide."

She told me she was going to let me sit there to think about the choice before me, and on her way out the door she turned back and said it one more time: "An oak or a weed?"

Our parents were called, and that night at home I tried to put the best spin on the day's events. The incident confirmed my parents' opinion of rock music as an evil, perverted influence on their children's lives. A couple of years earlier, I had pranced through the house singing the words to the Rolling Stones song "Let's Spend the Night Together," and my shocked mother confiscated the album, saying, "The sacred union of a man and a woman should never be trivialized. Our Lord blesses it only within the sacrament of marriage."

The Fugs made those lyrics seem quaint by comparison. I feigned innocence, telling them it was Tommy's idea and I had no clue what was on that album or that he planned to put it on and turn up the volume. I had been wrongly ensnared, I insisted, because he was my best friend, a case of guilt by association. I felt a little bad blaming it all on him, but I knew my parents would never confront Mr. and Mrs. Cullen about it. And besides, I was pretty sure that at that exact moment he was blaming it all on me. We had covered for each other this way before. That's what best friends were for. My parents looked at me skeptically and said what they always said, that they believed me and that I deserved whatever punishment the good sisters saw fit to impose.

Tommy and I spent the next week reporting to the convent each day after school. For bringing The Fugs and the F-word into the halls of Our Lady of Refuge, there would be no beatings or knuckle-raps or twisted ears. For this offense, we were ordered to do something we had never heard of any other student being ordered to do—enter the private, mysterious residence of the Sisters of Saint Felix to work on our hands and knees.

The convent was made of brick, large and imposing, and inside it was dark and smelled of fried food and floor wax. There was a chapel lit only by votive candles in red glass canisters where the nuns prayed, and small, cell-like rooms where they slept. Tommy and I were put to work scrubbing the baseboards and washing walls on all three floors. It really wasn't so bad, and when we were done each evening, the sisters led us into the kitchen and gave us each a glass of milk and a dish of whatever they were having for dinner. I remember lots of boiled meats and vegetables.

One afternoon as we scooted along the second-floor hallway on our knees with our buckets and scrub brushes, Tommy and I heard the soft click of a latch. A door opened in front of us, and out stepped one of the ancient nuns. But something was not right, and soon I saw what: her habit and headdress were missing, replaced by a floral housecoat and slippers. What shocked us most was to see her without her veil and face boards. She had cropped gray hair. Her face was wrinkled and saggy, fuller and softer than it looked wedged into her headgear. We stared up at her. She was no longer the harsh, humorless authority figure from school, but simply an old and tired lady. It took her a moment to notice us, and when she did, she hurried past without a word and disappeared down the hall.

"Whoa! Did you see that?" Tommy asked.

"Whoa!" I said.

As we worked, Tommy and I snooped around, peering into closets and down staircases and listening to the smothering silence. A favorite rumor around school was that the nuns maintained a secret tunnel beneath the playground connecting the convent to the rectory, allowing late-night liaisons with the priests. Tommy and I set out to prove its existence once and for all, but what we discovered instead was a place so oppressive, it felt like a black hole from which not even sunlight could escape. There were no sounds in there. No laughter or music or chatting voices. Only the hushed whispers of prayer and the creaks of rubber-soled shoes on linoleum.

It hardly seemed equitable. Across the soccer field, the priests lived in a house much like any in the neighborhood, large and breezy and comfortable. They had a housekeeper and cook, a color television and stereo, thick woven rugs, a regulation pool table, a wine cellar, and a well-stocked bar from which they could enjoy a cocktail at the end of the day.

But here in the convent, there were none of those comforts. The sisters had taken vows of poverty, and they lived in utter austerity. Their only recreation, as far as I could see, were the evening walks they took in pairs around the neighborhood. No wonder they were always so grim. My stint scrubbing the convent had opened my eyes to these alien creatures in brown wool who ruled their students without mercy. They weren't beasts or ogres. They were women. Women who had given their lives to God and the Church. From what I could tell, many of them were lonely and isolated and demoralized. Even then I had to ask, If God is really up there calling the shots, and if he is all great and all merciful as we were taught, why would he treat these women who had sacrificed their lives in his service so harshly? Why would he treat his male servants so much better? To my parents, this was just the way it was. Men and women answered God's call in different ways. To them, the priests deserved adulation and creature comforts, and the nuns were happy in their simple lives of deprivation. I wasn't buying it. The nuns, I decided, needed their own advocate, their own patron saint, someone like Saint Joan of Arc not afraid to fight for what she believed. But then look what happened to that strong woman. We learned all about her in school. Burned at the stake as a heretic.

Sister Nancy Marie, as we knew she would, eventually forgave us our trespasses. Just as Jesus would have done, she returned to her cheery ways and earnest looks. Neither Tommy nor

I ever did replace that Fugs album. The truth was, the only thing it had going for it were the dirty words. We liked to think we sacrificed it for the greater glory of our cause—to let the nuns know the battle was not over, and we would grow into whatever kind of trees we wanted. We were pretty sure The Fugs, if they ever found out, would have approved.

Chapter 11

My parents were the trusting sort, even when I gave them every reason not to be. The evidence against me could be overwhelming, as it was in the Fugs incident, but if I pleaded my innocence earnestly enough they usually bought the story, no matter how far-fetched. Or at least they pretended to. When, on a scout campout, Dad caught a group of us inside a tent smoking, I told him an unnamed older boy from a neighboring campsite had given us two cigarettes to try, and "a few of us"—the clear inference being that I was not one of them—had lit them up. It was a transparent lie. All he had to do was smell my breath or fingers to catch me. But Dad accepted my account. Just as he had accepted the story that the *Penthouse* he found hidden in the culvert under our driveway must have been stashed there by unknown neighbor kids. Dad wasn't dumb; he wasn't naive. He wanted to believe what he wanted to believe—that his son, a good Catholic boy who received Holy Communion every Sunday and confessed his sins once a month, would not let him down. He and Mom always seemed to give me the benefit of the doubt.

Usually I did not deserve their blind trust, but there was one time I ended up wrongly accused, and from that day forward I never again took their faith in me for granted.

The smoking tree down by the water, in addition to being my gang's gathering spot for cigarettes, swearing, and stolen Boone's Farm, was a place I went often by myself. On these solo trips, I did nothing more delinquent than sit and stare across the water and daydream. Early on, my father had instilled in me a deep love of nature and the outdoors, and I could sit for hours in the woods fantasizing about wilderness survival. When I was in Boy Scouts, Dad regularly took me into the woods, where he taught me how to use the sun as a compass, fashion a lean-to from pine boughs, and forage edible plants from the forest floor. I read everything I could find on the topic and knew how to splint a broken leg with a tree branch, weave vines into rope, and brew tea from staghorn sumac. Fire-making was a particular point of pride for me. I learned how to find dry kindling even in the soggiest conditions, arrange sticks so the air could wick through them, and nurse the feeblest flame to life. I practiced until I never needed more than one match. I built my fires responsibly, always careful to fully extinguish them before leaving.

On a chilly fall day after school at the start of eighth grade, I whistled for Shaun and the two of us headed down to the smoking tree. Shaun chased ducks into the water and fetched rocks off the bottom, and I decided to build a small fire. I peeled a few shavings of papery bark off a white birch for my tinder, gathered a variety of kindling and dry sticks, positioned them into a tepee, and lit the bark. One match and a few soft puffs on the flame, and I had a cheery little blaze to sit beside as I dreamed of surviving in the Yukon with nothing but a jackknife and flint and steel. As the sun set over the lake, I let the little fire die, then stirred the embers into the sand. Twenty feet away was a neighbor's wood dock, out of the water and piled in sections against the bluff for the winter. Beneath it were some charred driftwood and a mess of spent matches from what looked like a long-ago attempt at a campfire. I thought nothing of it other than to disdain whoever needed to use so many matches to start one blaze.

I whistled for Shaun and then, just for the sheer joy of being a boy outdoors with his dog on a crisp fall evening, began to run. I raced up the bluff and sprinted across the field back home as if a bear were on my tail. It was the running that must have caught Mr. Simpson's eye. He lived next to the vacant lot, and he was second only to Old Man Pemberton as the grouchiest grown-up in the neighborhood. He had shooed my friends and me off the vacant lot more than once.

I was home only a few minutes, washing up for dinner, when the doorbell rang. I opened the door, and it was Mr. Simpson. He asked to speak to my father. Dad came and invited him inside, but something I could not make out was mumbled, and Dad stepped out on the porch and shut the door behind him. The two men stood in the cold talking for several minutes, and when Dad came in he had a look that told me there was a problem.

"Were you down at the water across the street just now?" he asked.

"Yes," I told him. "I took Shaun for a swim."

"Were you messing around with matches?"

Dad knew my skill as a one-match fire-maker. I was surprised at his choice of words. I told him about making the little fire and sitting beside it before burying it in sand and heading home.

"Did you run away for some reason?" he asked.

I began to see where the questions were leading. How do you explain sprinting wildly from a fire for no reason other than to feel the wind in your face and your heart beat against your ribs? "I just felt like running," I said.

Then he came out with it: "Mr. Simpson thinks you tried to set his dock on fire. He saw you running away, and when he went down, he found combustibles piled up and burned matches, and warm coals nearby. You were the only one down there."

"Dad," I said.

"This is serious, John. He wants to call the police."

"Dad, I didn't do it. I saw those matches, too. It wasn't me."

It sounded as lame as all my other lies. Yes, I was down there with matches. Yes, I had lit a fire. Yes, there were dying coals in the sand nearby. Yes, I had sprinted manically from the scene. But no, I had nothing to do with it. "Dad, honest, I didn't—"

He stopped me in midsentence. "I know you didn't," he said. "I'll talk to him." Then he added the words that meant so much: "I believe you."

Over the years I had given him so many reasons not to believe. Now for the first time I needed him to, and he did. He had taken my version over the version of a grown-up. I wanted to throw myself in his arms, to hug him, and to reassure him that this time his faith was not misplaced. But being a Grogan man, I did as Grogan men were expected to do. And Grogan men didn't hug, they didn't kiss, and they never said, "I love you." I jabbed my hand toward him, and he grasped it in his and shook it vigorously. The robust Grogan handshake.

"Now, let's go eat," Dad said.

Eighth grade drifted by, and as graduation approached, every one of my friends gushed about heading to the state-of-the-art public high school recently built a few miles down Orchard Lake Road. It had a swimming pool, tennis courts, a groomed running track, a sunny courtyard, and an acoustically tuned performing arts auditorium. Our tax dollars at work, and everyone was going. Tommy and Rock and Sack and Doggie and all the cute girls from the neighborhood. Everyone, that is, except me.

My parents enrolled me at Brother Rice, an all-boys Catholic high school in Birmingham, a half-hour drive away in one of Detroit's wealthiest suburbs. The kids who attended Brother Rice were the same kids whose parents owned memberships at the country club where I caddied. Tim and Mike had gone there, and both told hair-raising stories of the sadistic disciplinary techniques of the Irish Christian Brothers who ran the place, tactics that made those of the Sisters of Saint Felix sound quaint by comparison. Tim hated all four of his years there; he bristled at the authority, at the wealth and hypocrisy, at the religious doctrine crammed down his throat. Michael, who years earlier had abandoned his priestly aspirations but still loved everything Catholic, felt at home there. As for me, I didn't want to be separated from my friends, but I accepted Brother Rice as a given. It was where the Grogan sons were meant to go, just as the Grogan daughter was meant to attend Marian, the all-girls Catholic high school separated from the boys' school by a drainage moat. Marijo and Tim were now both attending Catholic colleges, and Mike was on his way to one in the fall. We were preordained for Catholic education. It was the one thing on which my frugal parents did not mind spending their savings.

Shortly after dousing myself in hot wax, I had hung up my cassock for good and retired from the altar-boy corps. That did not mean I had a choice about attending Mass. In our home, Mass fell in the same category as breathing. Each Sunday morning began the same way: Mom waking us with that feather of hers and saying, "Get up, lazybones, time for Mass."

Nearly every Sunday, Dad served on the altar beside the priest. He was a lay minister, which meant that he read scripture and intentions for the sick, announced hymns, and led the congregation in liturgical responses. He even got to distribute communion from the altar rail, right alongside the priest. Dad took his duties seriously, and he genuflected reverentially every time he passed in front of the Blessed Sacrament. He bowed his head deeply in prayer and sang at the top of his lungs. Unlike Mom, who couldn't hold a tune if the Pope himself requested it,

Dad had a good voice and wasn't shy about using it. He sang and recited prayers with his eyes closed, something he could do because he had every hymn lyric and every prayer fully committed to memory. When the priest raised the communion host skyward at the moment of consecration, Dad would bow deeply and press a fist to his heart as if he had just witnessed something so magnificent it was blinding. It's hard to describe his bearing on the altar without making him sound sanctimonious. And some thought he was, including one condescending priest who, it came back to us, had sneeringly dubbed him Holy Richard. But he wasn't; he was merely caught up in the rapture of his faith. He was the exact same way when no one was watching. Dad was a nighthawk, always the last to bed, and sometimes I would get up late at night to use the bathroom and peek into my parents' bedroom to find him on his knees lost in silent prayer, his head buried in the covers of the bed inches from his sleeping wife. His devotion was no act.

Neither was my mother's. She was physically incapable of receiving Holy Communion without bursting into tears. I don't mean tearing up a little; I mean bawling. It was as predictable as the sunrise. She would file up to the altar rail, hands folded, eyes respectfully down, but looking just fine. If she recognized someone in line, she would smile, even wink. Then she would swallow the host, and by the time she was back in the pew and on her knees, the tears would be streaming down her cheeks like she had just been informed her entire family was lost at sea. Everyone knelt after communion; that was expected. But Mom knelt in a pose of utter surrender, her face buried in her hands resting on the back of the pew in front of her, fat tears falling to the floor. The Lord was inside her now; she was helpless to resist.

Communion would end, and the priest would work through his ritualistic chalice cleaning as the congregation continued to kneel. When he was finished, he would announce, "Let us stand." And everyone would stand. Everyone except Mom, who would

THE LONGEST TRIP HOME · 101

remain in her kneeling position, head down, face buried, snorting and sniffling away, lost in her communion with Christ. When I was little, I found great amusement in Mom's boo-hooing, but as I grew older the last thing I wanted was to stand out in a crowd. I just wanted her to get up when everyone else got up, and to try to keep the waterworks to a minimum. Sometimes she stayed there with her head down right through the recessional hymn, and even as the church emptied around her. It was an amazing thing to watch. She was totally swept away, oblivious to anything around her. I marveled at how something so simple—swallowing a small wheat wafer—could bring such an emotional reaction. I tried to share it. I would swallow the host and squeeze my eyes shut and try to feel Christ inside me. But I felt nothing, nothing but a low burn in my stomach, the host's reminder that I had fasted and was hungry for breakfast. Why, I wondered, was I not able to experience the same blissful magic? Maybe I was doing something wrong. I concentrated with all my might, burying my head in my hands like she did and beckoning the Lord into my soul. Still nothing. If he ever visited, he certainly was stealthy about it. I didn't waste any energy worrying about it, and soon I learned the art of daydreaming while appearing to be deep in prayer.

When Tim was home from college, it never occurred to me why he always chose to attend a service other than the one my parents attended. Then one Sunday shortly after I graduated from Our Lady of Refuge I tagged along with him and found out. As we walked over, he asked, "Are you going in or coming with me?" At first I didn't know what he meant, and then it struck me: He wasn't going to Mass. He never went to Mass. Tim, I found out that day, had stopped attending years earlier, at least whenever he could get away with it, carefully covering his tracks to keep it from our parents. He knew it would crush them.

Part of his cover was to swing by the church and peer in the doors just as the service was starting. He had learned that Dad always asked what priest was on the altar, not as a way of check-ing up on his kids but because he was genuinely curious. He fol-lowed the priests like a gambler follows racehorses. By getting a positive ID, Tim could nonchalantly answer, "Father Schroeder," or whoever it happened to be.

"We need to spot the priest, then we've got an hour to kill," Tim said. "I usually go over to Saint Mary's and walk around."

Saint Mary's was a Catholic prep school, college, and semi-nary directly across Commerce Road from our neighborhood. Its primary purpose was to train future priests. It might sound coun-terintuitive, skipping Mass to hang around a Catholic seminary, but the grounds of Saint Mary's were breathtaking; it was one of the most serene places on the planet. Situated on a bluff overlook-ing Orchard Lake, a smaller, more bucolic twin to Cass Lake, the campus long ago had housed a military academy and was studded with castlelike brick buildings and oak trees that had stood there since before the Civil War. Tim and I strolled the shady paths and sat in the grass looking out over the water. With his slightly longish hair and quirky taste in clothes, Tim was impossibly cool in my estimation, and I was honored that he had trusted me with his secret. Getting caught skipping Mass, we both knew, would be tantamount to an act of family treason.

It was one of those perfect summer days that made all the lousy Michigan weather worth it. The marvels of nature were everywhere—in the sun on our faces, the breeze in our hair, the birds surrounding us with song. Tim squinted across the water, its rippled surface dazzled with a million shards of sunlight, and said, "Now this is my kind of religious experience." His words took me aback. It had not before occurred to me that there could be any religious experience other than the one drilled into us at home and church and school. I thought about that for a few sec-onds and decided it was my kind, too. From that day forward, whenever he was home from college, Tim and I sneaked off each Sunday morning to spend an hour communing with nature—and each other. Brother to brother. We jokingly christened our new faith the Church of Tim and John. I didn't realize it at the time, but that summer was a turning point for me—the point at which I stopped trying to feel the same religious fervor as my parents. I rarely skipped Mass without my brother, but from then on I attended in body only, reciting the words from memory while my mind roamed to the far corners of the planet.

That September, Tommy and all the others started at West Bloomfield, and I headed off to Brother Rice. My friends were now free to wear jeans and T-shirts and grow out their hair; I reported to school each morning in dress shirt, navy slacks, tie, and loafers.

I settled into my new routine without complaint, going from class to class and sitting quietly during study hall, staying beneath the brothers' radar. I became friendly with a few boys, but it wasn't the same as with Tommy, Rock, or Sack. My new classmates had all grown up together at Saint Regis, the Catholic elementary school next to Brother Rice. They were clubby, and I was a stranger peering in from the periphery.

In the opening weeks of the school year, the old gang would still convene each afternoon down at the beach or at the smoking tree or behind the football field at Saint Mary's. They told me all about their new world and the cast of characters that inhabited it—the desirable girls and cool older kids and druggies who showed up high every day. In great detail, they described various romantic pursuits and failures. And I told them what I could about my new world. Honestly, there wasn't much to tell. The only bright spot was that Barbie Barlow's parents had sent her to Marian next door, but she might as well have been at the Sorbonne. Sometimes I would catch a glimpse of her in the distance across the moat, playing soccer or waiting for her ride, but I never got any closer. She was like a mirage, shimmering in the distance.

One day after school, Tommy pulled a cigarette from his pocket and ran it beneath his nostrils. It was different from other cigarettes I had seen, fat in the middle with twisted ends. "Time to smoke a doobie," he said brightly and lit up. The joint worked its way around the circle, and when it came to me I hesitated only briefly before sucking in a mouthful of smoke. I had no desire to try marijuana—it scared me—but I was more afraid of losing my friends. Somehow they had all graduated to pot without me even knowing it. I held the smoke in my mouth, acrid and musky, and consciously tried not to inhale it into my lungs. I believed what the Christian Brothers told us in health class, that a single puff of marijuana could lead in short order to ever more dangerous drugs. In no time you would be a desperate heroin junkie breaking into homes.

Tommy caught me. "Don't just hold it in your mouth," he chided. "Inhale it."

"I am," I lied.

As the leaves fell and autumn surrendered to winter, my old friends slipped away from me. There was no drama or confrontation. They merely forgot about me by degrees. They had new friends now and new social ladders to climb. Gradually they stopped calling, stopped dropping by, stopped inviting me to tag along on Friday nights. I spent most of the rest of that year alone. Alone at school. Alone at the Our Lady of Refuge rectory each evening, where I earned a dollar an hour as the office boy who answered the phones. Mostly I spent it alone in the basement with the headphones on, listening over and over to Bob Dylan sing "Sad-Eyed Lady of the Lowlands" and "Desolation Row." Mom and Dad noticed.

"How's everything at school?" they would ask at dinner. By now it was just the three of us.

"Fine," I would say. And I meant it. Things weren't bad; they weren't good. They were just . . . *flat.*

"So, anything new?" they would prod. I had always been the

chatterbox of the dinner hour, regaling my family with rapid-fire tales of every aspect of my day, even my misdeeds, at least those I thought would draw a laugh.

"Not really," I would say.

In the spring of that year, 1972, Mom and Dad sat me down. Mom did the talking, as usual, with Dad nodding silently beside her. "We've been thinking, honey," she said. "If you want to go to West Bloomfield next year, you can. We're good with that. It's your decision."

Dad chimed in: "Whatever you choose, we'll support."

I could hardly believe my ears. I knew how important a Catholic education was to them, how much they believed it was the ticket to building character and strong faith. Yet they had also watched Brother Rice turn Tim inside himself, like a turtle retracting into its shell to seal out the world. Now they saw me withdrawing, too. The joy had gone out of my life; my spirit was nearly suffocated. In the end, their fear of losing me as they had lost Tim seemed to outweigh their fervor for a religious education.

Now the decision to leave was mine. Brother Rice was not without its merits. Even as a fourteen-year-old, I recognized its academic excellence. Two teachers in particular had found a way to connect with me. There was Mr. Stark, the track coach, who taught Freshman Math for Dummies. That's not what they called it, but that's what it was. For the first time in my life, I experienced the thrill of conquering an algebraic equation.

Then there was Brother McKenna, my English composition teacher, who had all the warmth of an Arctic winter. Students loathed him. His standards were ridiculously high and inflexible. We had to write a personal essay every week, and if it had one misspelling, we would receive zero credit. A scratched-out word or sloppy handwriting would cut the grade in half. He drilled into us the seriousness of our craft and the need to edit our words, to take pride in them, to polish them like gemstones, not presenting them to the world until they were as perfect as humanly possible. Writing had always come fairly effortlessly to me, but I was sloppy and undisciplined. He returned paper after paper marked with failing or near-failing grades. Then midway through the school year, he handed back a paper marked with an A. Not a single word of encouragement, just the letter. It was all I needed. For the first time in my life, I saw there was something I could do as well or better than the other, smarter kids.

Yet the choice to leave was ridiculously easy. After thinking it over for a couple of days, I told Mom and Dad my decision. True to their word, they held their tongues and arranged my transfer.

The school year wound down, and I said good-bye to Mr. Stark and Brother McKenna, who encouraged me to keep writing with these measured words: "When you're willing to work at it, there's actually something there." The last day of school was dedicated to cleaning out lockers and turning in textbooks, and then I was free. The next day would mark the start of vacation and a lazy summer of swimming, sunbathing, and hanging out. It would also mark an event that would make my parents rethink the decision to let me transfer to public school before I even arrived.

Chapter 12

Dodge Park was located directly across Cass Lake from Harbor Hills, about a mile away as the crow flies. From The Outlot we could see its large sandy public beaches bristling with lifeguard towers, and the acres of parked cars glimmering in the sun beyond. Dodge Park covered several hundred wooded acres crisscrossed by hiking trails, but its beaches were by far the park's most popular feature. Teenagers flocked from every school district around to spend summer days there. It was more than just a place to swim and sunbathe; it was a scene. And a huge part of that scene revolved around illegal drug use. Every sunny summer day, Dodge Park took on the feel of a mini-Woodstock. The beaches and sidewalks and picnic areas were crammed with thousands of sunburned teenagers and young adults, most in cutoff blue jeans, the boys bare-chested, the girls in halters or bikini tops. Amateur musicians formed knots, strumming on guitars and banging out rhythms on congas and bongos. Marijuana smoke and the smell of patchouli oil hung in the air, and dealers openly plied their wares. Kids tripping on

LSD and hallucinogenic mushrooms, or merely stoned on pot and hashish, lay on their backs staring up at the sky. The newspapers had begun writing about the park's growing drug problem; some arrests had been made, and there were community calls to crack down more forcefully so parents could again feel comfortable bringing their children to swim.

Even though Harbor Hills had its own beach, every kid in my neighborhood considered Dodge Park the destination of choice. In stiflingly boring southeastern Michigan, it was like having our own Haight-Ashbury right across the water. I had managed to make it over there a couple of times the previous summer before Dad caught wind of the mushrooming drug culture and forbade me to enter the park. I tried to argue the point, but he was firm. "I don't care if all your friends are going," he said. "You are not. We have a perfectly good beach right down the street."

Now it was the first full day of summer vacation, and everyone who was anyone was heading to Dodge Park. I had run into Tommy the previous day after arriving home from Brother Rice for the last time, and he predicted, "It's going to be the party to end all parties." They were all getting a ride there with Doggie's older brother. "You should come with us," he said. It was the first invitation I'd gotten from him in months, and I wanted desperately to go. "Nah," I said. "My dad won't go for it."

The next morning I instead headed down to The Lagoon. Four years earlier, when I was ten, Dad had surprised us with a sailboat. Although he was a landlubber at heart, he decided a boat would be the perfect vehicle for summer family togetherness. Besides, our house came with dock privileges. It seemed a shame not to use them.

The boat was a sleek little sloop of British design with oiled teak floorboards and varnished mahogany benches that comfortably seated five. He and Mom (who never once set foot on it) had christened it *Mary Ann* after my stillborn sister, and Dad jumped into the learning curve of sailing the same way he jumped into any other life challenge—with nose-to-grindstone determination. He read books and manuals, scoured magazine articles, and attended workshops. Dad somehow managed to turn even the leisurely pursuit of sailing into an awful lot of hard work. Marijo and Michael never really took to the sailboat, but Tim and I did with gusto and in a way my father never could—with seat-of-the-pants confidence. We did no reading or studying; we simply felt the wind and let it carry us. Soon Tim and I were taking it out on our own, often with Tommy or Rock or Sack along for the ride. Tim would skipper and we would crew, trimming the jib and hiking out over the high side to provide human ballast. By the time I was in ninth grade, I had honed my sailing skills to the point where not only could I skipper the boat, but I could skipper it singlehandedly. On that first day of vacation, knowing everyone was gathering at Dodge Park, I grabbed the sails and headed out for a solo cruise.

I didn't set out to disobey my father; this I can say truthfully. But I was only on the water a few minutes when I began rationalizing my way across the lake in the direction of the party to end all parties. *He didn't say anything about going* near *the park,* I reasoned. *What's the harm in sailing past for a closer look?* And then, once I was skimming by just outside the swim-area buoys, I took another tack: *Maybe I'll pull up on shore for a few minutes, just to stretch my legs. That's not actually* in *the park, just on the edge of it.* I spotted a muddy flat off to the side of the beach and headed for it. Once my bow hit the shore, I figured: *A quick walk up the beach and back, and I'm outta here. He'll never even know. How could he ever know?* I dropped the sails and headed off into the sea of hippie humanity. It was not even noon and already marijuana smoke hovered thick in the air.

The wide sand beach was on a man-made island separated from the rest of Dodge Park by a stagnant canal. Visitors parked on the mainland and walked across a wide pedestrian bridge to the beach. I had landed the boat on the mainland side of the canal. As I began to cross the bridge I realized I was wading into a giant, bustling drug bazaar. Dealers lined each railing, nearly shoulder to shoulder, rattling off their offerings in singsongy stage whispers: *pot, hash, Quaaludes, mescaline.* Money and packets were changing hands in plain sight. Marijuana no longer scared me, but harder drugs did, and I had no intention of buying anything, even if I had thought to bring money. But the walk was so thrilling, so forbidden, that when I reached the other side I turned around and headed back across again. Back and forth I strolled, absorbing the scene.

I made my way across the crowded beach and when I didn't see Tommy or any of the old Refuge gang, I decided to head back to the drug bridge for one last pass. I was lingering in the middle of the bridge—*chocolate acid, blotter acid, rainbow acid*—when I noticed a large covered maintenance truck rumble up to one entrance of the bridge, then a second identical truck pull to the other end. I was marveling at how tightly synchronized the trash pickups were when the canvas flaps flew back and from each truck streamed a dozen armed and helmeted riot police, wielding wooden batons. They sealed off the bridge, and suddenly dozens of plastic bags and pill bottles were flying through the air and raining down into the water. It was like the Bible story, except it wasn't manna falling from heaven but marijuana and mescaline.

The cops were pointing and shouting, and one was taking photographs. It was clear they had been watching the dealings for some time and knew who they were after. I fought my way through the pandemonium and tried to squeeze my way off the bridge. "No one on or off," a cop barked, pushing his baton into my chest. I turned and made my way to the other end where I met the same blue wall. "I was just on my way to the snack shack," I pleaded to an officer, so scared my voice quavered. "I got caught in the middle." The cop looked at me, this cloddish kid in glasses and a Catholic-school haircut. "Go on, get out of here," he said and pushed me past.

I was off the bridge, but I was on the island side, separated from my boat by the murky green canal. Besides, now that I wasn't in danger of arrest, I wanted to stick around and watch the drama unfold. A huge throng of kids began to crowd around the bridge. They were pouring off the beaches, surging forward. Soon a few started shouting, hurling insults and swear words.

"Fuck you, pig!" someone shouted. The crowd began to oink and snort. The cops pushed forward with their batons.

"Back! Back!" they shouted.

"Fuck you! Fuck you!"

"Oink! Oink! Oink! Oink!"

From behind me, a bottle flew through the sky, smashing on the pavement among the police officers. Then a second bottle. Then a fusillade of bottles. Soon everything that could fly flew: cans, cups, tubes of suntan oil, half-eaten hot dogs. Some of the officers had moved onto the bridge and were handcuffing and hauling off the drug suspects. The others turned their backs to us, and when they turned back, they were wearing gas masks. A few seconds later, the first canister came lobbing into our midst, sending up a plume of thick smoke. A boy ran forward, holding his shirt over his face, and heaved it back. More canisters arrived to replace it.

The standoff lasted for the better part of two hours before the police arrested everyone they planned to arrest and slowly extricated themselves. The crowd began to dissipate. I knew I had been on the island way too long. I needed to get back across the lake. I crossed the bridge, found the boat undisturbed, raised the sails, and set off.

The local paper was the *Oakland Press,* which my father had hand-delivered as a boy back when it was the *Pontiac Press.* Back when Pontiac was something other than a dying factory town no one wanted their business named after. It was an afternoon paper, arriving on front stoops by 4 P.M.

I was home only a half hour when the phone rang. It was Rock, and he was breathless.

"Jesus Christ! Do you know about the paper?"

"Know what about it?"

"You're on the front page! Your photo. On the front fucking page! Right next to some kid throwing a bottle."

"Hold on," I said and ran to the front porch where the paper lay. I unrolled it, and there, filling the top half of page one, was a photo of a teenager with an angry sneer on his face and his arm cocked back ready to launch a one-quart beer bottle. Several feet behind the youth was a gaggle of other kids. And off to the side of them, standing alone, was a pudgy kid in black-rimmed glasses and baggy shorts. "Holy shit," I cried. "It's me." In the photo, my eyes were on the boy with the bottle and my mouth hung open in sheer dumbfounded amazement. I looked like I had just been delivered to the drug bust by turnip truck.

"Holy shit!" I said again. It was time for evasive action.

I hung up on Rock, made sure Mom was nowhere in sight, and carried the front section of the paper under my T-shirt upstairs, where I stashed it between my mattress and box spring. I raced back downstairs and scattered the other sections of the paper around on the table in what I thought would appear a natural way. Then I summoned Tim and Michael upstairs to our bedroom.

"This better be good," Tim said impatiently. I pulled out the newspaper and handed it to him.

"Holy shit!" Tim said.

"Your ass is grass," Michael said.

"What am I going to do?" I asked.

"We can't let Dad see it," Tim said.

"Must keep it hidden at all costs," Michael said.

"You guys have to cover for me," I begged. "Dad always reads the paper when he gets home." They agreed they would do what they could.

Sure enough, right after dinner, as was his routine, Dad settled into his favorite chair in the living room with the paper. I sat upstairs, silently counting the seconds. *One thousand one, one thousand two, one thousand . . .*

"Who's got the front page?" his voice boomed out.

No answer.

"Has anyone seen the front page?" Silence. "Tim? Mike?" he shouted up the stairs.

"Haven't seen it, Dad," they called back in unison.

"John? Are you up there? Did you take the front page?"

"Not me, Dad," I said.

"Doggone it all, anyway. Who's always taking the paper before I've had a chance to read it?" It was a pet peeve of his.

"Ruth!" he yelled into the kitchen. "Did you throw out the front page already?"

"No, dear," she called back.

I lay on my bed, holding my breath, praying he'd let it go. He huffed around a little while longer, threw around some dog-gones and son-of-a-guns, and then settled for the latest issue of *National Geographic*. "Doggone it," I heard him mumble to himself. "I pay for a subscription to the paper and then it disappears before I can even see it."

I looked over at my brothers and held up both thumbs. "Close one," I mouthed silently.

The next morning I lay awake in bed, my brothers asleep beside me, thinking about the previous day's events. What was the chance, I thought, that of all those people at the park, I'd be one of a handful to end up on the front page? At least I wasn't the kid throwing the bottle, I thought. Think of the trouble he's in. I began to grin. Now that it was over, it was pretty funny. And what a great story I'd have to tell the old gang. This would show them that a year at an all-boys Catholic school hadn't whipped me. I wouldn't even have to embellish; I had photographic proof of my role, front and center in the bust and subsequent riot. It even involved *tear gas*. Did it get any better than that? No one could deny me my glory. It was a new day, and Dad would be on to the next edition of the paper when he got home. The matter, as far as I was concerned, was officially closed.

As I lay there congratulating myself, the doorbell rang. I heard my mother's voice, "Oh, Father Dan! So nice to see you. Come in, please. How about a cup of coffee?" It was Father Dan O'Sullivan, a young assistant pastor who had joined the parish several years earlier and who oversaw my duties as office boy at the rectory. He was also the priest who, shortly after arriving at the parish, had put an end to the altar-boy wine-pilfering scam once and for all.

Father Dan had become a family friend, and it wasn't unusual for him to stop in unannounced, coincidentally usually at mealtime. Mom would always offer to set another place at the table, and he would always accept. His mooching tactics were transparent, but Mom didn't mind. To have a priest at her table was a great honor, and she was proud that her meals seemed the most mooch-worthy of any in the parish. But on this day, Father Dan wasn't there to eat.

"Did you see yesterday's paper?" he asked. "Did you see John?" His voice was positively buoyant, like he had just discovered I'd made valedictorian.

"John? My John?" Mom said, sounding a bit awestruck herself. "In the paper?"

"Right on the front page!" Father Dan boasted. "Look at this!" He had brought his copy along just in case we wanted an extra. *Oh God.*

Tim looked over at me with one of those you-poor-sorry-bastard looks on his face. I began to count again. *One thousand one. One thous—*

"John Joseph Grogan, you get down here right this instant."

I climbed out of bed and pulled on a pair of shorts. "I mean *now!*" she shouted. Mom stood only five feet even, but when she wanted to, she could be pretty intimidating. Behind her back, my brothers and I had nicknamed her Little Napoleon.

Downstairs, she laid into me. What was I thinking, and who gave me the right, and didn't I know better, and hadn't they raised me to be smarter than that? Even after Father Dan excused himself, she wouldn't let it go. Why did I do these things, and wasn't it a shame, and oh, mother of mercy, and glory be to the Father and the Son and the Holy Spirit, and how does this reflect on the family, did I ever stop to consider that, and won't everyone be talking about the Grogans now? She was like a boxer with her opponent on the ropes, and she just kept pummeling. "I knew we should never have let you switch to West Bloomfield," she said. "I knew it was a mistake. Should we march you straight back to Brother Rice? Is that what you want, mister?"

I spent the whole day in my room, and when Dad got home that evening, I got it even worse. He was the angriest I had ever seen him. So angry I half expected him to strike me across the face, which is saying a lot, because my father, the man who captured houseflies in his hand like a kung-fu master and released them outdoors unhurt, never hit anyone. All the spanking was left up to Mom.

Not only had I disobeyed him, but I had willingly mingled with drug users and dealers. Worse, I had joined the crowd of rioters instead of retreating. By my very presence, I had fueled a mob and had disrespected and endangered the police officers whose job it was to uphold the laws of this country. Dad was big on respecting authority.

"But I didn't—"

"Shut up," he snapped. Dad never said "shut up." "I don't want your excuses. You listen to me. If I ever—*ever!*—catch you being disrespectful to a police officer, I will kick your ass from one end of this house to the other," he yelled. "Do you understand me?"

It was the first time I had ever heard him use the A-word, and the last time, too. I knew he meant business.

"Yes, Dad," I said and slunk off to begin a long grounding that kept me chained to our yard or my job at the rectory for a good portion of the summer.

On the bright side, I knew every kid at West Bloomfield High would learn, in advance of my arrival, all about the new kid who had ended up on the front page, caught in the middle of the infamous Dodge Park drug riot. Being grounded was no fun, and I felt bad about upsetting Mom and Dad, but it seemed a modest price to pay for such notoriety. Life, I was learning, was full of trade-offs.

Chapter 13

As the days of summer whiled by, Mom and Dad gradually calmed down. They stopped threatening to send me back to Brother Rice and stopped wondering aloud where they had gone wrong. By degrees, they loosened the grip on my grounding until I was at last fully free again to sail and swim and hang out at the beach trying, mostly in vain, to catch the attention of the golden, leggy girls stretched out on their terry-cloth towels. I stayed away from Dodge Park; after the bust, I heard it wasn't the same anyway.

Five nights a week I worked until 9:00 at the rectory. Summer nights were deathly quiet there, and some would pass without a single phone call or doorbell ring. The priests were rarely there, and I would pass my three hours reading J. R. R. Tolkien and shooting pool down in the basement. By 9:03 I would be home and back in cutoffs and a T-shirt. Often by 9:10 a knock would come at the door and there would be Tommy, usually with Rock and Sack in tow, asking if I wanted to "take a walk around the neighborhood." A walk around the neighborhood was code for coming out to smoke a joint and then head to the party store for munchies. By the summer before tenth grade, Tommy had established himself as an enthusiastic devotee of marijuana. He was the hardest worker of all of us, cutting lawns all over the neighborhood, and much of his earnings went to keep him stocked in pot. He always carried a bag, and his generosity was legendary. Tommy didn't care if the rest of us seldom reciprocated. To him, pot smoking was an inherently social act, never meant to be enjoyed alone. He was always happy to share his stash.

Tommy's love of *cannabis sativa* was obvious on first sight. His eyes seemed to have grown permanently bloodshot and his eyelids took on a perpetual droop. To better see, he would tilt his head back to peer through his slits, often with his mouth slightly open in a congenial half grin. He adopted a word that summer that he found fitting for nearly all occasions: *dubious*. In Tommy's hands, the word had multiple meanings, ranging from doubtful to excellent. Often it was simply a statement of agreement.

"Dubious, man," he would say, nodding. "Definitely dubious." Or sometimes: "Indubitably. Most indubitably." In the hierarchy of high-school cliques, Tommy was a poster boy for the one known as the Stoners.

Rock and Sack were less enthusiastic. They would never refuse the pass of a joint, but they seldom bought pot of their own. I was even more ambivalent, and I still tried to fake the deep inhales, worried about getting too high and waking up one day a desperate heroin addict. That's not to say I did not enjoy the effects of marijuana. We would pass a joint and suddenly everything about this world and our place in it seemed hilarious. Simple observations became impossibly profound. Indubitably so. One night we talked at length about the poses in *Playboy,* and Tommy made an impassioned case against rear shots. They were simply, he argued, a waste of ink. "If I want to see a butt, I'll look in the mirror," he said, and I remember thinking, *Wow, exactly, man*. It was a moment of insight like few I'd ever had.

After each one of our late-night "walks," I'd parade back into the house and promptly set about making myself a snack of immense proportions, usually involving multiple pieces of toast plastered in swaths of peanut butter and jelly. Mom and Dad often commented on my late-night cravings.

"Good Lord, John," Dad would say. "Didn't anyone feed you today?"

Mom would add, "I swear that boy has a hollow leg."

But if they ever tied my munchies to marijuana, they never let on. Slightly stoned and happily full, I'd say good night, give Dad the Grogan handshake, and stumble off to bed.

I had inherited my parents' frugality, and I was way too cheap to spend ten hard-earned dollars on a small packet of marijuana, what was known as a dime bag. At my meager pay scale, that was more than three nights of work. Besides, there was little motivation to buy my own when Tommy was constantly offering to share his. I had, however, inherited Dad's passion for plants, and the previous summer I had tended a small vegetable garden in the backyard, raising tomatoes, peppers, eggplants, and green beans. That summer after ninth grade, I added one more crop to my plot: a single bushy marijuana plant.

My fascination with cultivating cannabis had begun a few months earlier, before school let out, when Tommy complained about the large number of seeds in his latest purchase. I was serious enough about my gardening that I started my vegetable plants from seed indoors to get a jump on the growing season. At that very moment, my bedroom windowsills were lined with seedlings, which I nurtured with loving attention. Suddenly I had one of those lightbulb-over-the-head bursts of brilliance: Tommy had extra seeds; I had extra windowsill space. Eureka! Just like Jesus with the miracle of the loaves and fishes, I would transform those tiny, unwanted seeds into a bounty of homegrown marijuana. I picked out a handful of the plumpest seeds and germinated them in paper cups of peat moss. Mixed in with the tomatoes and marigolds, the baby marijuana plants were inconspicuous. Besides, my parents knew next to nothing about illicit substances, despite Dad's recent purchase of a book called something like *Knowing What Your Children Know about Drugs*. I was convinced they wouldn't recognize a marijuana plant if it knocked on the door and introduced itself.

The plants were still quite tiny when Dad came into my bedroom one day and paused to admire my sturdy seedlings. The classic notched five-leaf clusters of the cannabis family smiled up at him. I remained calm. *Dad wouldn't know a marijuana leaf if it bit him in the ass.*

"What are these here?" he asked.

"Those?" I said. "What, the marigolds?"

"No, not the marigolds," he said. "These right here."

"Oh, the eggplants."

"No, not the eggplants. These."

"Oh, *those*," I exclaimed, as if finally clearing up some lifelong misunderstanding. "Those. Um, those were from a project for science class. We, um, had to grow examples of monocotyledons and dicotyledons. Brother Fallon told us we could take them home if we wanted." Dad stared at me with a look of deep skepticism. "Those are the dicotyledons," I added.

"Dicotyledons?" he asked.

"Yep, the dicotyledons." I was pretty sure I had satisfied his curiosity, and was feeling pleased at the swift-footed agility with which I had done so.

"Dicotyledons," he said one more time.

"Dicotyledons," I repeated.

He hesitated a second, took two steps toward the door, then said, "Well, get rid of them, or we can meet with your science teacher and ask all about them."

Busted. Dad apparently knew more than I had given him

credit for. As with so many things involving his children, I could tell he knew but didn't want to know. I imagine it was like the cigarettes he had caught us with in the tent years earlier. He just wanted them to go away so he could return to a state of plausible denial.

I did get rid of the plants, all but one of them. The stockiest one I could not bear to kill. I hid it among the weeds in the vacant lot across the street, protected from the chill air beneath a cloche made from a plastic milk carton whose bottom I had sliced off. And when the weather warmed suitably to plant my garden, I nestled it among the tomato plants, where I was again convinced it would go unnoticed. My sturdy little pot plant prospered there among the Big Boys and Brandywines and indeed went unnoticed for several weeks, through my post–Dodge Park grounding, until its growth began to outpace that of the plants around it. Soon it protruded a foot above the surrounding camouflage. Why I did not realize the folly of this situation, I cannot say, other than to attribute it to the unique qualities of the fifteen-year-old mind. A bushy marijuana plant towering above the tomatoes right in front of the living-room window? Why would anyone notice that?

Then one Saturday, not long after Dad had been out cutting grass, I checked my garden and the plant was gone. A hole stood in the soil where it had been extracted, roots and all. Nearby, on the compost pile, I found its wilted remains. Just to make sure Grogan's Home Grown never found its way back into the earth, Dad had snipped the roots from the stem.

What he didn't consider was that his son just might pick the corpse off the pile and dry the leaves to smoke. When I was done, I had enough dried leaves to roll several joints. One day Rock and I were walking to the shopping plaza, and I lit one up. We both coughed and wheezed. It was the harshest thing I had ever tried inhaling, worse even than Father Joe's old, stubbed-out Lucky Strikes. And as far as any mind-altering effects, we might as well have been smoking pencil shavings. All Grogan's Home

Grown gave either of us was a headache. Despite that, I continued to carry a couple of joints with me whenever I went out. Like
any farmer, I was proud of my harvest. I knew it wasn't worth
smoking, but having my own private stash in my pocket somehow made me feel more street-worthy—and less of a mooch when
Tommy broke out his own supply. I could say things like "Or we
could smoke one of mine," knowing that no one would ever take
me up on the offer.

The last day of summer vacation arrived and with it a bittersweet
edge. Every kid in the neighborhood was at the beach, soaking up
every possible ray of sunshine, knowing it was our last hoorah
before jumping into the new school year. I breathed in the beach's
unique fragrance of Coppertone, algae, and cigarette smoke, and
captured mental photographs of the girls with their oiled stomachs and legs, fixing them in my mind for another season.

That night, Tommy and Sack showed up at the door. Rock
had passed; he was the most academically inclined of us, and
his parents didn't want him out the night before the first day of
school. "I'm going out for a walk," I called to Dad and headed out
the door.

"Don't stay out too late," he called after me. "School tomorrow."

All three of us were in high spirits. The next morning I would
be tasting public education for the first time, and Tommy and Sack
were talking up the experience, telling me how great it would be.
They made West Bloomfield sound a lot like an indoor version
of Dodge Park, filled with slinky girls, wild boys, and barely dis-
guised drug abuse. As they portrayed it, no one actually attended
classes. Everyone just hung out all day in the parking lot and
designated smoking areas, chatting, flirting, and smoking. Our
laughter filled the night as we walked down Erie Drive toward
The Outlot, steering playfully into each other like bumper cars.

We were right in front of Old Man Pemberton's place when from behind us, out of nowhere, appeared a car that had crept up, lights off. First I heard the squawk of a radio transmission, then the low rumble of an idling engine. I was just turning to see the words TO SERVE AND PROTECT on the door when a spotlight blinded us. Tommy instinctively veered off and began walking across the Pembertons' lawn, his back to the light.

"Right there!" one officer shouted. "The blond kid just dropped something." They were out of the car, rushing toward him, yelling for him to stop, which he did. "Don't move!" they yelled back at Sack and me.

As they descended on Tommy, I reached into my shirt pocket, pulled out the two joints of Grogan's Home Grown, and let them fall in the grass. Then I sauntered toward them.

"All right, up against the car, Cullen." The cops knew Tommy by name. One searched him, finding rolling papers and a small pipe, as the other retrieved the plastic bag Tommy had dropped. They placed him in the backseat and closed the door, then turned to Sack and me. I recognized the older cop as Sergeant Glover, a fixture around town, and the younger one as Officer Reisler, who had lived next door to us when he was a teenager.

"Do you two have anything on you?" Glover asked. "Don't lie to me. What are you carrying?"

"Nothing," we insisted in chorus.

"We were just out for a walk," I said.

The cops stared at us. They looked almost ready to buy it. Tommy was the one who had been on their radar for months.

"Honest, we don't have anything," Sack said, those giant brown eyes of his growing as big and liquid as puddles.

To help make the case, I added: "You can search us if you want." The words were not even out of my mouth before I knew I had made a horrible mistake. I could see it on Sack's face, which went instantly gray.

"Let's just do that," Sergeant Glover said, and they pushed

both of us up against the squad car and began patting us down. Sack looked over at me the way I imagine Jesus looked at Judas at the moment of betrayal. "Nothing, huh?" Sergeant Glover said as he pulled a brass hash pipe from Sack's front pants pocket. I had forgotten about his pipe. "You just earned yourself a free ride to the station," he said and put Sack in the backseat with Tommy.

I came up clean, as I knew I would, and they never spotted the two joints in the grass. Officer Reisler led me around to the back of the car and got close to my face.

"Do you remember me? Do you remember me from next door when you were a little kid?" I told him I did. "Do you know what this would do to your father? Do you have any idea how this would crush him?" I shrugged. "Your father is a great man. Do you realize that? Do you know how outstanding your father is? He doesn't deserve this. This would kill him. You want to put your father in the grave?"

I thought he was being a little dramatic, but I just nodded and looked at my feet.

"All right, what else are you into?" he asked. "Acid? Speed? Downers? Don't bullshit me. What else?" I swore I hadn't tried any of those things, and I hadn't. "Just pot once in a while," I said, and he seemed to take me at my word.

"You want me to take you down to the station with your pals and have your dad come pick you up? Is that what you want? You want your dad to see you in the lockup?" I said I didn't. Then he started back in on what it would do to my great father, the sudden death by broken heart. "If it wasn't for how much I respect your father, I'd haul your ass in. I don't give a shit about you. But your father I care about." I nodded that I understood.

"This is what I'm going to do," Officer Reisler said. "I'm going to let you turn around and walk home. You're going to go straight home, and you're going to keep your nose clean, understand? I'm going to be watching you. I am going to be watching every step you take. Got it?"

"Yes, sir," I said. He walked around the car and got in front with Sergeant Glover. The car pulled away, and as it did, Tommy and Sack both turned and looked out the rear window at me. They didn't look angry, not even betrayed. Just scared. Scared and small and fragile. Part of me wanted to be in there with them.

I waited until the car disappeared around the curve, then I turned and ran. Ran as fast as I could. But I didn't run straight home as Officer Reisler had ordered. I cut through a neighbor's side yard and jumped a fence, then another and another, weaving through the backyards until I was at Rock's door. He answered and instantly knew something was wrong.

"What happened?" he whispered.

"Just get out here," I said.

He pulled the door shut and followed me into the dark and behind a row of shrubs where we could lie in the grass unseen. I was convinced the squad car was going to make another pass at any second to make sure I had not disobeyed. My breath came out in jagged gasps, and I could feel my hands shaking. Rock listened intently as I recounted the entire event. When I was done, he thought for a moment and I waited for him to say something reassuring. "You mean you *told* them to search you?" he asked. It was, I would learn, the main takeaway point of the whole tangled story. I had not simply stood by and *allowed* the police to pat down my best friend. I had *invited* them to. Offered it up like a party favor. *You can search us if you want.*

Rock and I lay out in the wet grass, watching the Cullen and Sacorelli houses from behind the bushes. Fifteen minutes passed before we saw Mr. Cullen start his pickup truck and drive off, his headlights sweeping briefly over us as he pulled out of his driveway. A few minutes later, Mr. Sacorelli followed. We waited out there until both vehicles returned and both fathers marched their sons silently inside.

Two of my three best friends had been arrested, and I had not. The third was trying to understand why I would have suggested a police search. In the morning, I would land for the first time in that unknown, intimidating world known as public high school. I had a bad feeling about the welcome I would receive. A very bad feeling.

After the lights went off in the Cullen and Sacorelli homes, I said good-bye to Rock and cut through the backyards to my house, where I found Dad in his chair, reading and eating peanuts with chopsticks.

"No snack tonight?" he asked.

"Not very hungry," I said. "I'm just going to bed." We shook hands, and I headed upstairs.

In the weeks and months that followed, Officer Reisler stayed true to his word, pulling his squad car to the curb in front of our house whenever he passed by. If I was outside, he would stare at me through his windshield. Sometimes he would sit there for an hour, doing his paperwork. If Dad was in the yard with me, cutting grass or raking leaves, Reisler would look me in the eyes, then look across the yard at my oblivious father trotting along behind the Gravely. He'd look back at me, and I could almost hear his words: *Do you have any idea what this would do to him?*

For the life of him, Dad couldn't figure out why the police kept pulling up directly in front of our house to idle their cars and fill out their reports. He didn't notice it was always the same officer. "There they are again," he would say, marveling as if he were witnessing a great mystery of nature. "That's the darnedest thing. They have the entire town to patrol, and every doggone Saturday they pull up here and just sit. It's almost like clockwork."

"No idea, Dad," I would say.

"Huh. Me, either." And he'd scratch his head and return to his work.

I lived in dread that one day his curiosity would get the better of him and he'd walk up to the squad car, knock on the glass, and inquire. But he never did, and Officer Reisler never divulged my secret.

It was Tommy's dad who nearly exposed me. A couple of weeks after retrieving their son from the police station, Mr. and Mrs. Cullen were passing by on their evening walk. I watched helplessly from the next room as Mom spotted them and opened the front door. "Hello there, Bevan! Hi, Claire!" she called out. *No, Mom, don't do this.* Mr. Cullen was the last person I wanted to face. *Please, Mom. Please don't . . .* "How about a nice cup of tea?" *Oh, Mom.* They turned up the driveway, and I raced to the top of the stairs, just out of sight. Mr. Cullen ran hot in the best of circumstances and was never one to mince words. Once, when a teenage driver flipped Mr. Cullen the middle finger over some traffic dispute, Mr. Cullen chased him for miles in the family van with his wife and all six children aboard, finally catching the kid at a traffic light, jumping out, and pounding on his windshield. My chest tightened and I felt my stomach twist.

At first the conversation was filled with pleasant small talk. Mom poured tea for Mrs. Cullen and herself; Dad brought out two beers. That's when the conversation turned to children.

"Don't get me started about the children in this neighborhood," Mr. Cullen said. "They're all angels, aren't they? All perfect, bloody little angels. All of them except my sons."

I heard my mother clear her throat nervously.

"If there's marijuana, it's gotta be the Cullen boys. If there's drinkin' goin' on, well, certainly it must be the Cullen boys. If anything happens in the neighborhood, haul in the Cullen boys. They're never alone when it happens, but they always are when the blame comes down." Then he changed his voice to mimic a spoiled schoolboy. "'Oh, it wasn't me, Mum; it wasn't me, Pop. It was all the Cullen boys. I told 'em not to, Mum. I ran the other way, Pop.' It's always the Cullen boys, and let me tell you"—and he paused for emphasis—"I'm bloody goddamn sick of it." I knew how he looked when he got worked up, the way the veins popped out on his temples and his forehead went crimson. I knew that's how he looked right now. "What the bloody hell, mon? I'm not making excuses for my boys. I know they're not perfect. Boys are gonna do what boys will do. I did it, too. But the parents around here need to get their bloody heads out of the sand and open their eyes."

From my parents' polite, awkward responses I could tell they were trying to figure out exactly what he was telling them—and at the same time not wanting to know. It was a comfortable pattern in our family: the less known and the less said, the better. Mom and Dad never asked Mr. Cullen to elaborate, and they never asked me to, either. For that, I was grateful.

Chapter 14

If life at Brother Rice had been isolated and hollow, at West Bloomfield High it was something altogether lonelier. At least at Brother Rice I was physically removed from those I cared about and could pretend they still cared about me. At the new school my old friends swirled around me, already comfortably ensconced in their social circles, and I hung awkwardly on the edge like a man clinging to a cliff, waiting in vain for a hand up. The bad feeling in my gut the night of Tommy's and Sack's arrest turned out to be well founded. I was the Catholic schoolkid no one wanted to be seen with, the one who had gotten his best friend busted. Some of my old Refuge pals openly shunned me. Doggie, so concerned about currying favor with the cool crowd, would walk right past me in the hallway without so much as a nod.

Tommy and Sack were more gracious. They both managed to forgive me for that night and held no grudges, but they had their own friends now. Tommy was surrounded by stoners and dopers who went through each day in a mind-altered stupor. Sack was constantly trailed by a harem of boy-crazy girls in hip-hugger bell-bottoms about whom he was too shy to do anything but blush. Rock had found his own niche, too, in the music and drama cliques. Then there was me, a clique of one.

Now that I was free from the dress and grooming codes of Brother Rice, my uniform became bell-bottoms and flannel shirts, and I began to grow my hair out. But unlike Sack's hair, a satiny black mane that fell straight to his shoulders, mine was as ornery as a Brillo pad. For every inch it grew in length, it expanded two inches sideways. By the time it reached my shoulders, my exploding jungle of kinky curls gave me the look of an active volcano. Adding to my look were my new glasses, which were an oversize aviator design in tortoiseshell frames. What might have looked hip on Peter Fonda in *Easy Rider,* on me, with my thick, soda-bottle prescription, had quite a different effect. The first time she saw me in them, Mom cried out, "What were you thinking? You look like a raccoon!" She later apologized, but moms are usually right, and this time so was mine.

Mom was right about something else, too. That fall I began dropping weight at a rapid clip without trying, and I was convinced there was only one possible explanation: I had cancer. What else could it be? I was dying, it was obvious, and what a tragedy it was, given my tender years. After weeks of working myself into a panic, I went to Mom and confided my all-but-certain terminal illness. Mom didn't miss a beat. She threw her head back and had a good laugh. "Cancer? Honey, you don't have cancer," she said, wiping a tear from her eye. "You're just losing your baby fat."

Tommy and Sack and Rock tried to include me in their social groups, and we all sat together at lunch, but somehow something had changed. I stumbled through that first year at West Bloomfield in a fog, putting one foot in front of the other, marching dutifully from class to class, but not feeling fully there. My grades reflected it.

In the course of one semester, I went from As and Bs at Brother Rice to mostly Ds. Algebra II was particularly vexing for

me. Unlike at the Catholic school, there was no Math for Dummies track; the whiz kids and the struggling students were all
clumped together. It didn't take me long to become hopelessly lost.
The teacher was an attractive woman a few years out of college
with bright eyes and long blond hair. She was funny and sweet,
and I wanted to impress her. At first I raised my hand when she
asked if there were questions, but after the third or fourth explanation that only bewildered me more, I stopped raising my hand.
There were only so many times I could say, "I still don't get it."
She gave up on me, and I gave up on algebra. I simply started
taking my best wild guesses, with disastrous results.

When Mom and Dad saw my report card, I thought they
would blow double gaskets. I braced myself for the "We should
never have let you transfer to public school" speech, but they surprised me. I can only guess they somehow understood what a
rocky transition I was having. They said what they always said
when I underperformed: "All we ask is that you try your hardest.
Your best is good enough for us." I nodded along, but I knew in my
heart I wasn't even doing that.

The biggest difference between parochial and public education, I learned that year, had nothing to do with uniforms or
prayers at the start and close of each school day. The biggest difference was that teachers in Catholic schools did not allow you
to fail. If they had to ride you every day of the school year, they
would. If they had to beat the knowledge into you, they would. At
West Bloomfield, the teachers offered learning the way waiters
offer canapés at a cocktail party. You could help yourself or wave
them away. If I wanted to learn, they would teach me; if I chose
not to, they were happy to ignore me. After nine years of Catholic education, where the nuns and brothers forced performance,
often by threat of physical pain, I was free to fail.

Complicating my academic prospects was the way I chose to
commute to school each morning. Rock faithfully took the bus or
caught a ride with his father on the way to work, but Tommy de-

clared school buses the ultimate in uncool and began hitchhiking
the four-mile route. Soon Sack and I were joining him. In rain, in
sleet, through two feet of snow, and most of the year in the dark
before dawn, we would trudge the half mile to the corner across
from the party store and stick out our thumbs. Often on the way
Tommy would light a joint to pass. Depending on the difficulty we
had getting a ride—not just anyone would stop for three teenage
boys—I would arrive at school not only late but stoned as well.
My first class was French—another course in which I was tank-
ing—and one morning the teacher asked me to stand and tell the
class something about myself. All I could think to say was *"Je
m'appelle Jean. Je suis très fatigué."* Very tired and very fried.

There was only one class in which I excelled, and that was
American literature. The teacher, Christine Shotwell, was just
out of college and, unlike my algebra teacher, not the stuff of
teenage crushes. She sported sensible eyeglasses and a no-fuss
haircut. For some reason, she took an interest in me, and I read
everything she threw at me: *The Crucible, The Scarlet Letter,
Of Mice and Men, The Old Man and the Sea.* I fell in love with
Steinbeck and Hemingway and the worlds they portrayed, so far
removed from my own. Then I discovered J. D. Salinger and *The
Catcher in the Rye.* In Holden Caulfield I found a teenager every
bit as bewildered and awkward as I was. On every page I recognized a little piece of myself. In Holden, I found a soul mate.

One day after class, Mrs. Shotwell stopped me on my way
out the door. "I was wondering," she said, "have you ever thought
about keeping a journal?" I dabbled in little satires and attempts
at humor, but a diary of my own thoughts and feelings had never
occurred to me. "I think you ought to try it," she said. "Who knows
what might spill out?" I took her advice, and soon I was hooked. I
kept the journal for myself but also for her, an adult who for the
first time seemed to care what was locked inside me. The more I
shared with her, the more her feedback—wise and heartfelt and
never patronizing or judgmental—fueled my desire to write.

. . .

Shortly after school let out for the summer, Tommy called with exciting news. Saint Mary's was hosting a large casino-night fund-raiser for its most generous benefactors. It would be a men's night of eating, drinking, gambling, and smoking cigars, and the college was recruiting neighborhood kids for a variety of jobs, working for tips.

"It's gonna be easy money," Tommy promised.

"Count me in," I said. As luck would have it, Tommy and I, and several of our friends, were assigned to the bar service. Not only were the drinkers rumored to be the best tippers of all, but our jobs allowed us to easily swipe a few extra beers for ourselves.

At the end of the night, our pockets stuffed with tips and our stomachs with leftover food, we retrieved our purloined beers from the ditch where we had stashed them, and made our way across Commerce Road and through the dark neighborhood to the smoking tree, which over the years had become more of a toking-and-drinking tree.

"Beautiful!" Tommy exclaimed, cracking open a lukewarm brew. "Is this fucking beautiful or what?"

"It's fucking beautiful," I agreed, and we all toasted with a clink of bottles. "Indubitably so."

And beautiful it was. I was back with my friends, back in the fold, accepted once again. Sitting shoulder to shoulder on the beach, feet in the water, we laughed and ribbed and prodded each other just like old times. Only one thing was different. Tommy lit a joint to share, and when it came to me I passed it along without lifting it to my lips and without feeling the need to. I had survived tenth grade without self-destructing and picked up some valuable pointers along the way. One of them was that if you had to impress your friends to keep them, they weren't really friends in the first place. I was figuring out that life was too short and brilliant to spend it suspended in a marijuana cloud. However my life was meant to turn out, it was mine alone to seize or squander. No one else was going to do it for me.

Tommy let out a whoop, and so did I. We had made it to another endless summer. I took a swig of beer and let my body sink into the cool damp sand. Indubitably beautiful, indeed.

Chapter 15

Not long into junior year, I found my niche at West Bloomfield—in the grungy, cramped office of the student newspaper.

The *Spectrum* drew a motley assemblage of students, most of whom did not fit in anywhere else. Tommy was solidly off on the tech-ed track by now, but Sack, Rock, and I, sensing an easy elective, signed on as staff writers. The paper was appallingly bad, even by high-school standards; so bad, in fact, that nearly everyone around school, students and teachers alike, referred to it as the *Rectum*. The paper offered the obligatory news on sports and extracurricular activities, uncritical reviews of school musicals, and predictable editorials (cafeteria food bad; student rights good). But mostly it contained rambling diatribes about whatever topic tickled an individual staffer's fancy: women's rights, Elton John's latest tour, the environment, acupuncture. After buying a pair of Earth Shoes, the negative-heel Danish footwear that was all the rage then, Sack was inspired to write a two-page celebration of their many virtues. Rock gushed at length about Bob

Dylan's newly released *Blood on the Tracks*. For reasons I'm still not sure of, I weighed in on Transcendental Meditation, which I had never tried and knew almost nothing about.

Our student adviser, an easygoing teacher named Ms. Pappas, provided abundant freedom but little structure or guidance and almost no quality standards. She let us get away with sloppy, lazy work, and our copy went into print riddled with spelling and grammatical errors. Where was the exacting Brother McKenna when we needed him? I did my part to help the *Rectum* maintain its reputation for mediocrity, cranking out whatever drivel required the least amount of time and energy.

There were a few students attempting serious journalism, and one of them penned a piece titled "Fact and Fiction about Gay Life." It was a thoughtful, intelligent essay that was well researched. Ms. Pappas cleared it for publication and sent the issue off to the printer. But when the *Spectrum* came off the presses and we opened it to page 24, a prominent chunk of the text was missing, replaced by an empty white rectangle. There was only one possible culprit: Mr. Cavin. Our principal insisted on reviewing every galley before releasing it to the printer.

He had held up publication in the past to demand we remove or rewrite stories he found too controversial or provocative, but this was the first time he had censored an article without informing our adviser in advance. He had simply papered over the section he did not like. It was an act that would galvanize us as young journalists. My fellow *Spectrum* staffers and I were outraged. Where were our constitutional rights? Where was our freedom of expression? Did the First Amendment not apply to us? The *Spectrum* received no money from the school district, surviving entirely on its own meager revenues from advertisements and the 25-cent cover price. Didn't that make us quasi-independent? Ms. Pappas tried to calm us, but we could tell she was upset, too, and felt just as violated.

I reacted by marching to the public library and checking out a book I had browsed through before—a book on the radical underground press. It was a topic that had fascinated me for several years, ever since visiting Marijo at the University of Michigan at the height of the antiwar movement. In my bedroom, I read through the case studies of various underground newspapers, many of which sprang to life during the counterculture movement of the late 1960s. They were to mainstream papers what espresso was to instant coffee; I found them impossibly romantic and edgy. I was especially smitten by the *Fifth Estate,* an underground paper started in Detroit several years earlier by a seventeen-year-old in his parents' basement. It had grown into one of the country's most prominent and longest-running alternative voices, providing a platform for the likes of Michigan's homegrown radical John Sinclair, head of the White Panther Party. If that kid could do it, why couldn't I?

I began to dream in earnest. What if I launched my very own underground paper at West Bloomfield High? What if we wrote whatever we wanted in it, and distributed it without anyone's permission? What if we used words as weapons to challenge the school administration? My mind raced, and I pulled out a notebook and began capturing ideas. For several days, I could barely sleep. By the end of the week I had a mission statement, several possible names, and a list of potential story topics. I laid out my plan to Rock and Sack, and they immediately signed on as my coeditors. Together, we recruited a small army of students eager to participate. Others sought us out and asked to join. Everyone, it seemed, wanted to stick it to The Man.

Most of the volunteers were boys, but among them were three girls in my grade whom I had seen around school but did not know well. They had impressed me the previous year, however, by smiling sympathetically at me in the hallway at a time when it seemed every other student had ostracized me. In the stratified world of West Bloomfield cliques, Lori, Sue, and Anna were solidly in the one known as the Hippie Chicks. They eschewed makeup and favored muslin peasant smocks and beads. Sue was tiny with a freckled face surrounded by a crown of ringlets that reminded me of Little Orphan Annie. Lori was tall and lanky with long sand-colored hair into which she was always braiding whatever she had at hand: flowers, beads, yarn, ribbon. Anna was the most exotic of the three with a deep mocha complexion and a jungle of dark, frizzy hair even wilder than mine. In the summer, when her skin was especially dark, strangers occasionally mistook her for black. The three of them were constantly together, so much so that it had become a joke around school. People called out to them as if to a single entity: *Lorisueanna.* I sensed I was just enough of an outcast at school to make me vaguely interesting to them. I found them interesting, too, if a little earnest, and though I wouldn't dare admit it even to my best friends, cute. Girls were alien goddesses I admired from afar but could seldom summon the courage to approach. Now I would be working side by side with these three, a prospect I found exhilarating.

We named our nascent publication *Innervisions,* inspired by (some would charge ripped off from) the Stevie Wonder album of the same name that had come out the previous summer. Beneath it we added the tagline "West Bloomfield's Independent Student Press." The newly assembled staff began gathering after school to write, edit, and lay out pages. Our only publishing tools were a pair of electric typewriters, which meant that the only way to typeset our copy was to hand-type our stories into narrow columns, starting over every time we made a mistake. It was tedious, infuriating work, but we stuck with it, day after day. When the copy was finally all in columns, we cut them out with scissors and pasted them onto page dummies, where we added rub-on headlines, photographs, and simple line drawings. Sack's piece, titled "What the Hell's Profanity?" made a spirited defense of foul language by using as much of it as he could work in. Rock delivered a screed about the school's ban on students leaving the campus for lunch. I busted on my drafting teacher for giving students extra credit for buying tickets to the basketball games he coached. I also penned the front-page essay explaining the mission of *Innervisions*. "This paper does not kiss ass to the parents and other adults of the community by printing only what they want to hear in order to feel more secure," I wrote in grand fashion.

Yet for all my bluster, I toiled for hours on this labor of love without daring to breathe a word about it to my own parents. *Innervisions* was filled with foul language, drug humor, and disrespectful portrayals of authority figures. One cartoon showed the vice principal with a tag on his ankle labeling him "Grade A Bullshit." Another was a drug-addled spoof of the Peanuts comic strip showing "Loosie" and a goateed Charlie Brown smoking catnip in Snoopy's doghouse. Before Dad found and ripped out my marijuana plant growing among the tomatoes, I proudly photographed it, and that picture made its way onto page 3 to illustrate an irreverent—some would say sacrilegious—biblical parody titled "The Parable of the Lids and the Busches." In it, a rock star named Messiah, surrounded by his twelve faithful roadies, multiplied two bags of pot and four beers into enough mind-altering substances to inebriate a stadium filled with five thousand concertgoers. I knew Mom and Dad would definitely not see the humor in any of it.

I was pouring my soul into something I believed in, something I was proud of, something that for the first time in my life gave me the thrill of accomplishment. Yet I could not bring myself to share it with them. I knew they would disapprove. I could see the hurt on their faces and hear the dismay in their voices. In truth, much of the content that I knew would offend them also bothered me. Nearly all the drug humor came from a single student, a senior by the name of Justin Jorgenson, who had signed on as the fourth coeditor and who funneled his considerable creative talent into juvenile humor. He and I argued bitterly over creative control. I pushed for hard-hitting social commentary; he for off-color parody with shock value. I wanted the *Fifth Estate* meets the *Vil-*

lage Voice; Justin wanted *Mad* magazine meets *High Times.* In the end, I kept the worst of it out, but only the worst.

On the morning of April 7, 1974, my cohorts and I arrived on campus with 900 copies of the eight-page debut issue of *Inner-visions,* printed on mint-green paper, under our arms. We fanned out through the hallways, bathrooms, and courtyard, quietly peddling them for a dime each. Curiosity ran high, and sales were brisk. Teachers were our best customers of all, often buying multiple copies. Several of them slipped us five- and ten-dollar bills to help defray our printing costs. The whole school was buzzing about "the new underground paper," and by third hour, we had sold 750 copies, covering our seventy-five-dollar printing tab in full. With the donations from teachers, we were already in the black with 150 copies still to sell. Life as an underground newspaper editor seemed every bit as romantic as I had imagined it would be.

The next period, all four editors—we had brashly listed our names on the masthead—were summoned out of class to Principal Cavin's office. He invited us to have seats and opened on a congenial note, telling us how surprised he was to see our "little newsletter" and complimenting us on our initiative. "Quite frankly," he observed, "I didn't think you four had it in you."

As principal, he said, he always liked to encourage students to pursue their passions, even if ours were misguided and immature. "I hardly know where to begin," he said and slid a copy of the paper in front of us. He went right to the catnip cartoon, then flipped the page and tapped his finger ominously on the photo of my marijuana plant. "Pro-drug messages," he said with a heavy voice. "And this," he said, slapping his palm down on the Messiah parable. "You find this amusing? Not only does it glorify drug abuse, it offends religious belief." He went through the issue page by page, pointing out the many transgressions that made *Inner-visions* totally inappropriate for distribution on campus.

"And this," he said, pointing to the cartoon of the vice principal labeled as "Grade A Bullshit." "This defames Mr. Coe's character."

"That's impossible," Justin, the lippiest among us, shot back. "Mr. Coe has no character to defame."

"Zip it," Cavin ordered.

What seemed to rankle him most was the letter we printed in full from our beloved and highly respected humanities teacher. Linda Miller Atkinson had turned me on to Greek architecture and Roman sculpture. She helped me see the beauty in the dribbles of a Pollock abstract and the blurry watercolors of a Monet. She began each class by turning off the lights and playing Stravinsky's *Rite of Spring*. Now she was leaving in frustration and disgust—and she had slipped us a copy of her scathing resignation letter. *Innervisions* had an exclusive.

"You had no right to print this," Cavin said, his voice tensing in a way that let me know our goal of wounding the enemy with well-aimed words had worked. "This is privileged workplace correspondence." He then began rattling off a long list of school district policies we had violated: unsanctioned activities on campus, soliciting funds without authorization, use of profanity, promotion of illegal activities, defamation of character, and the catchall "portraying students and faculty in ways not in the best interest of the school district." He ordered us to cease and desist immediately and to turn over all unsold copies.

If we wanted to produce future issues of our publication, that was fine with him, Cavin said, but with two stipulations. We would have to give it away for free. And every word would have to be preapproved by the administration.

"So more censorship," I said.

"You know, boys, freedom of speech is a big, big responsibility," he said. "Bigger than you understand. You've shown you're not capable of grasping that responsibility."

He warned us that if we didn't comply we would face serious disciplinary action. "I won't have this crap in my school, do you understand?" he said. Then, pausing to look each of us in the eye: "And I will be calling your parents."

The heady experience of a free press had lasted exactly four hours. We handed over the remaining copies we had on us and filed out. We quickly found out, however, that being hauled to the principal's office for a stern upbraiding was not without its rewards. Throngs of kids—including girls who had never before deigned to acknowledge our existence—gathered around us, asking for every detail. We gladly obliged, embellishing with abandon our martyrdom on the altar of an unfettered press. For the first time since arriving at West Bloomfield, I was at the center of attention. I had rattled the establishment; I had made waves. I had gotten people talking and thinking. Right then and there, I decided my future calling. I was going to be a journalist.

When Dad arrived home that evening, I greeted him at the door with our customary handshake, then handed him a copy of *Innervisions*. I handed one to Mom, too. Cavin had not called yet; I figured I was better off breaking the news to them myself. Besides, the community weekly newspaper had interviewed us for a story it was running on the new unauthorized student publication, and I knew from experience that there was no hiding the paper from Dad.

"What's this?" he asked.

"Just something I've been working on the last couple months," I said. "I'd like you to read it."

He and Mom sat at the kitchen table and began reading in silence, and I stood in the next room, waiting for what seemed forever. When they called me in, they didn't yell or threaten to send me back to Brother Rice. They asked a lot of questions, and I told them the whole story, starting with the principal censoring our student paper.

"You came up with this all on your own?" Dad asked.

"Yeah," I said.

"And no one helped you put this together?"

"Just us."

He paged through it once more. "I don't agree with everything you say in here," he said. "Not by a long shot. But I respect what you've done. You stood up for what you believe. That's important."

That's when I saw it on his face, a look I had seen before but not often. A look that told me what he couldn't bring himself to say, not without undermining the principal's authority, yet his expression was as clear to me as the written word: a parent's pride. My conservative, buttoned-down, play-by-the-rules father was proud of his son for breaking rules and speaking out against a perceived injustice. He was proud of me, I imagined, for finally finding the gumption to undertake something, anything, that required focus and discipline. Probably more than anything, he was proud of me for believing strongly enough in a cause to fight for it, even if it was not the cause he had hoped for.

"If you ask me, that principal got what he had coming," Mom said. "Covering over that girl's story without even telling anyone. Why, the nerve of him!"

"Can we eat dinner now?" I asked.

"Heavens, yes," Mom said. "Go wash your hands."

If *Innervisions* was all the buzz at West Bloomfield that week, Pete Grunwald's big party was the only topic on anyone's tongue when classes resumed after the weekend. Pete was a charter member of the Stoners and Potheads and never passed up an opportunity to party. When his parents decided to head off to a heating-and-cooling convention and leave Pete alone for the weekend, he went into high gear.

By the time Tommy, Sack, Rock, and I arrived, cars lined both sides of the street for blocks in either direction. The yard was filled with teens, many of whom I did not recognize, smoking and drinking beer from plastic cups. Inside, the place was a sardine can of sweating, shoulder-to-shoulder humanity. Marijuana and cigarette smoke choked the air, and Led Zeppelin blasted from the stereo. The legal drinking age in Michigan was eighteen then, and Pete had enlisted a group of seniors to buy kegs of beer, which sat on ice in the laundry room.

The house was trashed. How he was going to hide this from his parents when they returned, I couldn't imagine. But when I finally bumped into him in the crowd, he looked up from taking a long hit off a joint and smiled beatifically like he had not a care in the world.

I made it to the keg and poured a beer, and when I turned around I saw I had lost Tommy, Rock, and Sack. I also noticed couples peeling off and heading upstairs. Despite a nonstop series of crushes and infatuations, I still had not so much as kissed a girl. Until recently, I had been able to find consolation in the knowledge that no one else in my inner circle had, either, but over spring vacation, Sack had finally overcome his shyness enough to have his first make-out session—and the girl was a year older, which made his good fortune all the more enviable. I watched the couplings at the party with a combination of envy and heartache.

"Hey, Mr. Editor Man," I heard in my ear, and when I turned around, there stood Lori, Sue, and Anna, as always clustered so tightly together as to appear singular. They had worked hard on *Innervisions,* uncomplainingly taking on many of the most tedious tasks. I was grateful to them, and had grown close to all three of them.

"Lorisueanna! Hi," I said. We tried talking over the blaring music, but it was nearly impossible.

"Let's get out of here," Anna shouted, and we squeezed our way toward the door. Pete's house overlooked a large pond lined with cattails, and we walked down to the water's edge where a couple of dozen others had gathered. A kid who had taken it upon himself to play host wandered through the yard, filling beer glasses from a pitcher. We stood and drank and talked. Then, as if by some mysterious, preordained signal, Anna and Sue disappeared. One instant they were there, the next they had simply vanished. It was the first time I could remember the three of them not being together, and I half expected Lori to fly into a panic, but when I looked at her, she didn't seem concerned at all.

A canoe lay overturned at the water's edge, and we sat on it and looked up at the stars. In the moonlight, I had to admit she looked lovely. As we made small talk, I studied her upturned nose, delicate neck, and round cheeks. The magnitude of the moment was not lost on me. Here was a girl sitting right beside me in the dark—with her coterie dismissed. And she was acting like there was no place on earth she would rather be. I reached up and touched her hair spilling like a waterfall down her back. She leaned slightly into me and let out a purr. I moved my arm behind her until I had it around her waist. *Holy Christ,* I thought, *this is it!* In slow motion, our faces inched closer until our cheeks brushed; then we turned our heads and let our lips touch. I kissed her once gently, like you might kiss your grandmother. Twice. On the third peck, Lori wedged my head in her hands and shoved her tongue into my mouth. I had spent the last five years imagining what French kissing would be like, but I never imagined it could come on so abruptly. I always thought it was something you worked up to, over weeks and months. Lori's tongue was a fearsome thing, lashing and licking and darting about. Her teeth were more fearsome yet. They gnashed and clacked and nipped at my lips and tongue. This wouldn't have been an issue except that Lori was an orthodontist's early retirement dream; she had enough metal in her mouth to clad Old Ironsides with plenty left over for the *Monitor* and the *Merrimack.* French kissing with Lori was a little like French kissing with a power tool. I spent half the time marveling at my amazing luck and the other half trying to prevent serious injury.

Lori was a lioness. We smashed our mouths together, clacked

our teeth, and banged noses. Our hands roamed freely over each other. But as the night stretched on, I found myself feeling increasingly . . . restless. Restless and trapped. I found myself opening one eye to peer over her shoulder, looking for an excuse to break away.

Finally I got my break. Tommy's voice boomed down the hill. "Hey, Grogie," he yelled. "If you're coming with us, get your ass up here." I hastily excused myself from Lori, gave her a few just-for-Grandma parting lip pecks, and raced off to rejoin my friends, who grilled me for details the whole way home. I was giddy at my conquest, even if it was not exactly the earth-moving experience I had dreamed of.

The next morning I awoke late. When I walked downstairs, Mom and Dad were already home from Mass, drinking coffee and chatting at the kitchen table. The instant they saw me they went silent. They stared not into my eyes but at a spot slightly above and to the right of my upper lip.

"What?" I asked.

"Nothing," Dad replied.

Then Mom, in her don't-ask-don't-tell voice: "So how was the party last night?"

"Pretty good," I said.

"You had a nice time?"

"Okay," I said. "Nothing special."

"Did people dance?"

"No, Mom, no one danced."

"Then what did everyone do all night?"

"Just stood around and talked," I said.

They continued to gaze at the spot above my lip, their heads cocked quizzically.

I excused myself and headed to the bathroom. In the mirror, I saw what had so intrigued them. Just above my upper lip, my skin was missing. Lioness Lori had gnawed a nickel-size piece of my face off. The wound was a brilliant red and oozed a clear liquid. I was certain it was visible from outer space and could tell it would take weeks to disappear. There was no mistaking the injury. I had been mauled either by a rabid raccoon or by an overzealous make-out partner with braces. Mom and Dad knew better than to ask. My parents would spend the next three weeks dutifully pretending they did not notice the giant scab above my mouth. My real dread was returning to school the next day. The only one who would be more humiliated than I was the girl whose dangerous teeth had inflicted such injury. The one every boy in our class would henceforth know affectionately as Ole Razorblades.

Mom tapped on the door. "Honey, hurry it up or you'll miss the eleven o'clock and have to wait till the twelve-thirty."

Oh shit. Sunday. Mass.

"Be right out, Ma," I called. At least there would be no one to see me where I was heading, across Commerce Road to the shores of Orchard Lake and the Church of Tim and John.

Chapter 16

My upper lip eventually healed, and Lori and I survived the taunts of our classmates. They could tease us all they wanted; what they couldn't do was take away the notoriety we now enjoyed as one of the school's hot make-out couples. "They're just jealous," Lori said to me one day in the cafeteria, and I was quick to believe it. Still, she didn't seem any more impressed with my kissing prowess than I was with hers. Neither of us initiated a repeat engagement. But I wore my lip scab with pride until the day it finally fell off—proof positive that the awkward kid with the big hair and big glasses had finally been kissed.

As the school year wound down, my cohorts and I managed to put out a second issue of *Innervisions,* but it wasn't the same. The excitement and passion of the first issue were gone, replaced by a sort of dull, dutiful tedium. We toiled away with all the joy of taxpayers preparing for an audit. Our main motivation was pride. We didn't want Cavin and the school board to think they had bullied us into submission. More important, we didn't want the teachers and our fellow students to think it.

Work on the second and, as it would turn out, final issue was marked by apathy and bitter infighting. Many of our contributors drifted away, and those who remained turned in lazy ramblings not much edgier than the dross running in the *Spectrum*. The only one still cranking out copy at a furious pace was Justin, and it was more juvenile and offensive than ever. I hated all of it, but with the dearth of copy from anyone else, nearly all of it made it in. Mom and Dad were vaguely aware we were working on a second issue, but I knew they weren't expecting this.

We couldn't buckle to Cavin's demands, not if we were to retain a shred of credibility, but we also knew we couldn't openly defy him. He was watching now, and he would swoop in and seize all our copies within minutes of us carrying them onto school property. In the end, we decided to produce and sell the paper completely off school grounds, safely beyond his reach. The big gamble was whether the students and teachers would leave campus to buy a copy at one of several locations nearby where we would have hawkers waiting. In a front-page editorial describing Cavin's demands and our decision to move off campus, I wrote, "Please don't allow this inconvenience to prevent you from going out and buying a copy. It's a small hassle for a large amount of information and entertainment." But very few made the effort.

By midmorning, we had sold barely 200 of the 1,000 copies printed, and most of those were in the half hour before school started. Once classes were in session, sales dropped to a trickle. If we didn't come up with a new strategy soon, we faced a humiliating defeat and a big financial loss. We huddled and debated, and by late morning we abandoned the off-site selling locations and sneaked the unsold copies onto campus, where we quietly began peddling them in lavatories and locker wells. Sales by this method were slow, painstaking, and risky. Hundreds of unsold copies remained.

Over lunch, Justin came up with an idea even I had to admit was brilliant. The *Spectrum* was also on sale that day, and each of us on staff was expected to walk the halls hawking it. "We're out there selling the *Spectrum* in plain sight, right?" Justin said over lunch. "Is anyone thinking what I'm thinking?" A few minutes later we were back in the *Spectrum* office surrounded by piles of the approved paper and piles of *Innervisions*. "Start stuffing," Justin said.

We spread out across school peddling the *Spectrum* with new-found zeal. "Get your *Spectrum*! Come on, people, support your student newspaper! *Spectrum*! Get your *Spectrum*! Only a quarter!" At one point Mr. Cavin passed me and, sounding sincerely impressed, said, "Now that's the spirit, Mr. Grogan." What he did not know was that each time one of us snagged a customer, we would quietly ask, "Interested in a copy of *Innervisions* with that?" If the buyer was, he would add a dime to the purchase price and receive a copy off the bottom of the stack—with *Innervisions* tucked inside.

We felt like drug dealers pushing our dope under the noses of administrators, but the plan was working. At least until the president of the school board, a humorless man named Robert Carter, arrived on campus and stopped to buy a copy of the *Spectrum* on his way in. I watched from across the courtyard as he approached one of our double agents, an underclassman who had no idea our school district even had a president, let alone what he looked like. *No, please God, no,* I whispered. Carter reached into his pocket for a quarter. I held my breath as the unsuspecting volunteer accepted the change. *Off the top of the stack,* I prayed. *Take it off the top.* I could see the kid's lips moving and knew what he must be saying. Then I watched as the board president reached in his pocket and produced another coin. *Oh no, oh no, oh no.* From the bottom of the stack, the student handed him a paper.

Fifteen minutes later all four editors were back in Mr. Cavin's office, and this time Cavin sat quietly while Mr. Carter did the talking. He could barely contain his anger. Little flecks of saliva hit my face as he spat out a string of threats. But they were mostly hollow. We had only a few days left of school. Suspending us for the rest of the year was meaningless. They knew it and we knew it. The president tore up his copy of *Innervisions* and threw it at us, green paper fluttering down like confetti. "You're done. This is over now. Do I make myself clear?" he asked.

"Yes, sir," we mumbled and filed out of the office past Cavin, who gave us a look that said, *See what you've done? Now I'm in trouble, too.* Quite honestly, we *were* done. We did not have any more fight in us. We were tired; we were worn down; we just wanted to join everyone else out in the courtyard soaking up the sun and signing yearbooks. A free press, I was learning, involved nine-tenths thankless tedium and one-tenth glory, and then only on a good day. As ordered, we delivered the 500 unsold copies of *Innervisions* to the principal's office to be destroyed.

On the way out of school at the end of the day, I bumped into Mrs. Atkinson, our rebellious heroine, who was within days of leaving to become a lawyer. She asked me how sales had gone. When I told her what had happened, she asked how much money we had lost.

"We had a little surplus left over from the first issue," I said. "I guess about twenty-five dollars."

She opened her purse and pressed a twenty- and a five-dollar bill into my hand. "Now you're even," she said.

I wanted to throw my arms around her. I wanted to tell her how great she was, what an amazing teacher; what an inspiration and role model. I wanted to say I would never forget her and what she had taught me, not only about Greek columns and pre-

historic pottery but about questioning the status quo and challenging authority. What I said was "Gee, Mrs. A., thanks."

"Keep 'em sweating," she said with a smile. "And don't ever
think you haven't made a difference."

Perhaps Mrs. Atkinson was onto something. The next fall when I
returned to West Bloomfield as a senior, *Innervisions* was just a
distant memory. But in the offices of the *Spectrum* something was
distinctly different. The staff seemed to have more confidence,
our adviser more interest in challenging us, and the stories more
heft. We pushed the envelope more often and more aggressively.
Despite that, Mr. Cavin backed off. He deferred to our adviser's
judgment and no longer took it upon himself to impose his will
on our content. Staff members published articles on birth control,
teacher contract negotiations, and other hot-button topics without so much as a peep from the administration. I may have been
flattering myself, but it seemed Cavin and the school board didn't
want to inflame any more passions among the student journalists. Why risk waking that sleeping bear again?

That fall marked another change at West Bloomfield, one involving the inseparable trinity known as *Lorisueanna*. When the first
day of school arrived, the threesome was a twosome. Just *Lorisue*.
During the summer, Anna's family had moved out of state. In the
halls, Lori and Sue now walked in tandem, a hole between them
where Anna had once stood. They seemed somehow not quite
complete without their friend. I had grown closer to all three of
them, and I, too, was sad to see her gone. Anna had a quiet intelligence and independence I admired, and I liked her crazy hair
and shy smile.

One day after the leaves had fallen, Lori found me in the hall.
She was beaming. "Guess what," she said, grabbing my arm.

"Anna's coming back to visit! She'll be here for three days over Thanksgiving." Anna had been so miserable in her new town and school that her parents had sprung for an airline ticket back to Michigan, where she would spend the holiday weekend at Lori's house. Sue would be sleeping over, too. The threesome, however briefly, would be reunited.

"It's going to be so great!" Lori gushed. "And it gets better. My parents are going to be out of town on the last night. We'll have the house to ourselves. You *must* come over." Her braces had come off over the summer and she flashed me her newly perfect smile.

"I must, huh?" I said coyly.

"You must." More dazzling smile.

"Well, then, I'll be there," I said.

And I was. Unlike Pete Grunwald's bash, Lori's was small and discreet—a party of four. Months earlier, I had discovered a store where I could buy beer without being asked to show identification, and I arrived with a couple of six-packs. Lori made omelets. The four of us sat around, talking and listening to Arlo Guthrie records. Sue was the first to drift off, waking just long enough to head upstairs to bed sometime after midnight. Lori was next, growing quiet and finally falling into a heavy sleep on the couch a few feet from where Anna and I sat side by side on the floor, talking and looking at album covers. She smiled at me. "Guess we're the last two standing," she said.

And then her hand was on my knee, and my hand was in her incorrigible hair, brushing it back from her face. She closed her eyes. I took a moment to study her face and realized how pretty she was—prettier than I had allowed myself to notice. I kissed her cheek, then her nose. Our lips found each other, tentatively at first and then without reservation. Almost instantly I knew I was experiencing something very different from that night the previous spring on the overturned canoe. As her mouth opened to mine, I paused momentarily to marvel, *So this is how a kiss is supposed to feel.* My heart raced and breath came in short, anx-

ious jags. I forgot about everything but Anna. About the lights
that were far too bright, about my already blown curfew, even
about Lori softly snoring an arm's length away.

"You're shivering," Anna whispered.

"I know," I said and folded her onto her back on the floor and
rolled on top of her. She slid a hand inside my T-shirt. As I kissed
her, I began to fumble with the buttons of her blouse and eventually her jeans.

By the time we heard the yawn, we were in a fully compromised position. Anna's shirt was wide open; her jeans were un-
zipped, panties peeking out. My shirt was up around my shoulder
blades. From behind us, Lori yawned again, this time louder and
with a dramatic effect that reminded me of how the Cowardly
Lion yawned in *The Wizard of Oz*. Anna and I froze, our mouths
still sealed together, our hands locked in place where they had
been roaming. It was as though we had been playing musical
make-out chairs and the music had just stopped. Anna's eyes
were wide open now, and I knew she was wondering the same
thing I was: how long had Lori been awake, trying to figure out
how to extricate herself? I pictured her lying on the couch for the
past hour debating her options. Should she attempt to sneak out
silently and hope we didn't notice? Feign sleep until we eventually left for a bedroom? Let out a big, casual yawn as if, ho-hum,
she woke to these types of surprises every night? I heard Lori
rustle on the couch and then her footsteps as she stepped over us
and walked out of the room and up the stairs, pausing on her way
to switch off the lights.

"Oh, God," I whispered.

"Oh well," Anna whispered back and playfully nipped at my
lower lip.

We continued where we had left off. In the vernacular of teenage boys everywhere, I was rounding third base and making the
final sprint toward home plate when Anna pulled back almost
imperceptibly and kissed me on the bridge of my nose.

"John," she whispered, "I'm not ready to go all the way."

We were both virgins, both feeling our way for the first time. Even as I explored her breasts and tugged at her underwear, I had been worrying, too. Maybe it was everything the nuns and brothers had preached about mortal sins and our bodies as temples of Christ. Or Mom and Dad's constant ranting about the sanctity of what they called "marital relations." Or the fears they all planted of unwanted pregnancies, dashed dreams, and ruined lives. I would never admit it, but I wasn't ready, either.

"It's just . . . ," Anna began. "We're just going so fast. Can we slow down a little?"

"I can respect that," I said, feigning a worldliness I could only dream of, as if I bedded girls on a nightly basis and this once was willing to make a special exception. Secretly I was relieved beyond words.

We lay together on the floor, half naked, kissing and touching and giggling, until I thought to check my watch and was shocked to see it was 3 A.M. "I've got to go," I said. "I was supposed to be home hours ago." I didn't mention it, but it was also now officially Sunday morning, and Mom would be waking me in a few hours to get ready for Mass. We pulled our clothes together and Anna walked me to the door.

"Come over in the morning for a late breakfast?" she asked.

"That sounds good," I said.

On the drive home, I plotted my strategy for sneaking upstairs and into bed without waking Mom or Dad. The trick was to make sure Shaun didn't bark. He was a smart dog and could usually tell my approach from a stranger's.

I pulled Dad's big Monte Carlo into the garage and before opening the door to the laundry room let out a soft whistle, the whistle I had used with Shaun since he was a puppy. Then I silently turned the knob and stepped inside. Shaun was right there to greet me, stretching and shaking, his tags clinking. I knelt down and scratched his ears. "Hey, boy," I whispered. "You miss me?" I slipped out of my shoes and tiptoed through the kitchen in the dark. As I silently passed the living room, feeling for the handrail to the stairs, Little Napoleon's voice came out of the blackness.

"Where have you been?"

"Oh—hi, Mom."

"Don't 'hi, Mom' me. Do you know what time it is? Do you know how long I've been sitting up? Do you have any idea how worried I've been?" In the dark, I could hear her rosary beads clinking.

I spun a tale about watching a late-night movie with my friends and all four of us dozing off and next thing we knew, gee, look at the time, and wow, can you believe how late it is, and oh man, where did the night go? In her nightgown and slippers, she stepped closer and peered up at me. I could tell she was trying to sniff my breath for booze or other illicit substances, and on that front I was safe. My last beer had been hours earlier. "Really, Ma, it was just the four of us hanging out all night."

"For all I knew, you were lying dead on the side of the road," she scolded. Then, as if a whole new sordid scenario had just dawned on her: "Were her parents home?"

"Mr. and Mrs. Sheldon? The Sheldons? Oh, sure. Of course. Where else would they be? Mrs. Sheldon made really great popcorn. For the movie. Really buttery. Delicious."

Mom stared at me, trying to divine where the truth lay. At least there were no visible gnaw marks on me this time. "I just don't know what these parents are thinking letting boys and girls sit up half the night together," she said. "It's a recipe for trouble."

"They were right there the whole time, Mom," I said. "That Mr. S., what a night owl. Loves the Civil War. Sits up all night reading about the Civil War."

"I was worried half to death," she scolded. "Not even a phone number to call. Not even a last name."

"I should have called, Ma," I said. "But you know, we all fell asleep." I could tell from the way her voice was softening that she once again would choose to believe me, or at least pretend to.

"Now up to bed," she said, "before I blister you. You're still not too big to turn over my knee, you know."

I gave her a quick peck on the cheek and headed upstairs, my head swimming with the events of the night. *Anna, Anna, my God, Anna.* I repeated her name in my head like a mantra as I drifted off into a deep, happy sleep.

The next morning—or rather, several hours later that same morning—I dragged myself to the 9 A.M. with my parents, then headed back to Lori's house for what I pictured would be a bois-terous group breakfast around the kitchen table, all four of us jabbering away like the good friends we were. But when I ar-rived, Anna answered the door alone. Lori and Sue were nowhere in sight. It was obvious they had cleared out to give us time alone. Anna beamed at me, all swoony like, and I knew something had changed, something major. Somehow, over the course of a few hours, everything was different. We were no longer four pals, and Anna and I, without anyone asking my thoughts on the matter, had become a couple. I resisted a creeping sense of panic.

Anna made eggs and toast, and then I took her to one of my favorite places, a rambling, decrepit greenhouse on a remote country road where Dad used to take us when we were younger. Walking in from the cold was like walking into a tropical rain forest. The air was so heavy with moisture it condensed on the glass and dripped onto our heads.

We walked through the rows of greenery, hand in hand, paus-ing occasionally to kiss or merely hug. At one point we caught our reflection in a steamy pane of glass and both burst out laughing. Our hair had ballooned with the humidity, doubling in volume.

"Lotta freaks," Anna said, mimicking Arlo Guthrie from his

performance at Woodstock, and she reached up and smoothed my hair into a bulky ponytail, which she held in her hands briefly before releasing it to spring back over my shoulders. She was flying home later that afternoon, and we both knew we would not see each other, at best, for many months. Out in the parking lot, I leaned against Dad's Monte Carlo, and she slipped her arms around me and rested her head on my shoulder. Neither of us wanted to say good-bye. I was not sure what real love was supposed to feel like, but I knew what I felt in my chest at that moment had to be close. I pressed my face into her hair and breathed her in. *Anna, Anna, my God, Anna.*

"I'll write," she said.

"I'll write, too," I promised.

Chapter 17

As senior year progressed, Anna and I wrote less and less often. At first our letters were twice a week, then weekly, then monthly, and finally, as we both prepared to graduate from our respective schools, not at all. I had a new circle of friends in addition to the old regulars; she had forged bonds at her new school.

Then, a week before commencement, a new distraction came into my life. She was a sophomore whom I had met late in the year through Rock, who was in the school play with her. Becky had inherited her father's olive complexion and her mother's almond eyes. She was a talented stage performer with a beautiful singing voice, a high soprano, polished by years of professional training her blue-collar parents really could not afford. But she wasn't known for her acting prowess or her ability to hit high C on command. She was universally known, around school and town, and everywhere she went, for just one thing. Two, actually.

Becky had the largest, fullest, most magnificent breasts of any girl ever to walk the halls of West Bloomfield High School.

They began just south of her collarbone and protruded more or less straight outward in open defiance of Sir Isaac Newton for what seemed, at least to the adolescent male eye, miles before curving gently earthward again. This normally would be considered a desirable characteristic, the type of chest some women spend thousands of dollars to achieve surgically. And it would have been for Becky, too, if only she had the body to accommodate it. If only she were a little taller. But Becky was just five feet one. The effect those expansive, gravity-defying breasts had on that compact frame was overwhelming. It was like cramming the Grand Tetons into Rhode Island. No matter what Becky did or said, how well she acted or sang or competed in softball, she was recognized only as "the girl with the big knockers."

No matter what she wore—the baggiest sweaters, the most demure blouses, her father's oversize blazers—she stood out in any crowd. Men of all ages would literally gasp aloud from fifty feet away as if they had just glimpsed Haley's comet at close range. Women always noticed, too, and a surprising number of them were quick to deliver commentary beneath their breath.

Three days before classes let out for summer, Becky arrived at school with an armful of carnations, which she distributed to friends and favorite teachers. As I walked between classes she stopped me in the hall and held out a stem. "This is for you, John Grogan."

I was surprised. I had met her only a few weeks earlier and then just to chat in the hall. I was one of the few boys in school who hadn't thought to stare at her chest, at least not in an obvious way, or make lewd comments, and perhaps that helped me make her short list of flower recipients. I accepted the carnation and thanked her. Becky stood there in the crowded hall, beaming up at me as if waiting for a receipt. I had no gift to give her, not even a yearbook to ask her to sign. Until that moment, she had barely registered as a blip on my radar. It seemed only gracious to make a gesture of appreciation. I leaned over to give her a thank-you peck. But as my lips touched her cheek she turned her head so our mouths banged together. The next thing I knew, Becky's lips were locked over mine. I always despised those exhibitionist types who made out in the hallway at school. Couldn't they wait till they were alone? But I would be lying if I said I didn't kiss back. By the time we finally broke apart, I was late for class, and my carnation looked like it had been run over by a steamroller.

"Call me?" she said, holding an invisible phone to her ear.

"Absolutely," I answered and rushed off.

I graduated with a C-plus grade point average, exactly in the middle of my class. I had joined no clubs, played no sports, performed no community service. Undistinguished with a capital *U*. With that kind of academic record, I was not getting into the University of Michigan, where my father and sister went, or even into sprawling Michigan State University, which Rock was off to in the fall along with scores of other classmates. But I did get accepted into Central Michigan University, located three hours north of my home, in the middle of the Chippewa Indian reservation. Central was the kind of college willing to take a chance on a student with mediocre grades, so-so SAT scores, and scant evidence of ambition. The admissions officer seemed to like me, especially my gumption in starting *Innervisions*. And he seemed to understand and sympathize with the difficulty I had transitioning from nine years of regimented Catholic education into a laissez-faire public school.

At commencement, I did have bragging rights to one claim: I had the longest hair of any boy in the West Bloomfield class of 1975, with three or four inches to spare. My parents had learned something from their bitter and ultimately futile battles with Tim over the length of his hair. By the time I was in high school they had mellowed considerably, and on more than one occasion

I overheard Mom on the phone to another parent say, "As long as he stays out of trouble and keeps his grades up, what does that big mop of hair really matter?" They sat in the bleachers as I filed up for my diploma, big colorful bow tie around my neck, frizzy curls streaming out from under my mortarboard and over my gown. They couldn't have looked prouder.

I invited Becky to attend the school-sponsored graduation party with me, where we ended up making out so furiously next to the punch bowl that parent chaperones twice pulled us apart to tell us to cool it. Finally we abandoned the party and continued our mutual exploration outside in Dad's Monte Carlo. By night's end, it was official: without even meaning to, I had a steady girl-friend. Becky was playful, flirty, curious, eager to please. Becky was on fire. Becky was exactly the kind of girl Mom wanted to keep as far away from her sons as possible. She was convinced Becky was like girls she had known growing up; they were the ones who seduced boys, got pregnant, and forced them into dead-end marriages. Besides, Becky was a Protestant, another mark against her in my mother's mind.

Never mind that Becky was two years behind me in school and, because of a late birthday, nearly three years younger. In Mom's eyes, she was the calculating predator and I the innocent prey.

Like everyone else, Mom couldn't help noticing Becky's impressive breasts and the intoxicating effect they had on males. In one famous family encounter, my long-divorced uncle Artie was at our house for a Sunday cookout and hit it off so well with Becky that I asked them to pose for a photo. Uncle Artie gladly obliged, slinging his arm around Becky's shoulder and pulling her close to him. He pressed his face to hers and they both beamed into the lens. "Okay, big smiles," I coached. Through the lens, it looked like the perfect shot, and when the prints came back, the shot indeed was almost perfect. There they were, looking like best pals, my sixty-year-old uncle and fifteen-year-old girlfriend.

Only one small thing was amiss, and that was Uncle Artie's eyes. Specifically, where they were aiming. The photo showed Becky and Uncle Artie smiling directly into the camera, but with my uncle's eyes rolled sideways and down, nearly popping from their sockets—eyebrows forced upward into a salacious arch—staring directly into Becky's cleavage.

My brothers and I found the photo hilarious, and even Becky had to laugh. She was used to such odd male behavior and didn't seem to mind the attention. Mom, on the other hand, was not amused. The snapshot only reinforced her perception of Becky as a seductress who could use her physical attributes to short-circuit the brains of otherwise levelheaded males, forcing them to forget every last lesson their mothers had taught them. Whenever I brought Becky around the house, Mom was careful to be pleasant, but I could tell what she was thinking. To Mom, Becky's breasts were powerful man-seeking missiles in the arms race to conquer her youngest son's moral character. She had nothing in her arsenal of rosary beads and holy water that could begin to compete. Mom's singular mission in life became to keep the two of us from having any unsupervised time together. This, too, proved a losing battle.

Dad, on the other hand, was completely unfazed by Becky's breasts. He seemed oblivious to their existence. He was kind and fatherly to her, and if he in any way disapproved of her, he never gave a hint. Becky loved him for it.

That summer we saw each other nearly every night and often during the day, too. We would go to movies, go to the beach, shoot pool. I'd tag along with her on babysitting jobs. Wherever we ended up, whatever the activity, it always concluded the same way, with us mashing and groping and working each other into nervous powerhouses of barely contained, unconsummated sexual energy.

One day we took the sailboat out and made it only a quarter mile offshore before I succumbed to Becky in her bikini. I dropped the tiller, pulled her into my arms, and slid down onto the floorboards with her as the sails flapped and the boat turned in lazy circles. When we got back to the dock, Dad was standing there, looking puzzled. He often walked to the beach to watch me sail, studying my form on the water and then critiquing it after I returned to shore. Usually he had nothing but praise. Today, though, he was perplexed.

"What the heck happened out there?" he asked, genuinely baffled. "It looked like you were clipping along just fine and all of a sudden everything went haywire. I could see the sails luffing and the boat turning."

Becky and I sneaked grins at each other. "That? Oh, *that*. We were just goofing around," I said. "I let go of the tiller for kicks, just to see what would happen."

Dad appeared to buy my story. If Mom detected a potential pregnancy-inducing liaison in every unchaperoned moment, Dad seemed blissfully unaware that sex before marriage was even possible. The fact that Becky and I would choose to interrupt a perfectly good sailing tack for no reason other than "kicks" simply reinforced his conviction that teens were strange and inexplicable life-forms best given a wide berth.

Mom, meanwhile, was praying fervently each night to the Virgin Mother to keep me chaste. Much to my chagrin, her prayers seemed to be working. For all our hot and heavy foreplay, Becky and I still had not had sex. More times than I cared to count, we came tantalizingly close, but never all the way. My hot-blooded girlfriend had mastered the art of seduction but was less sure about surrendering the goods. And how could I blame her? She was still a virgin, and even more confused than I was. Night after night she would accompany me to the brink of intimacy before backing off. Summer was winding down, I would soon be off to college, and I remained a virgin. A crazed and highly frustrated virgin.

Still, I wanted to be prepared just in case. One morning when I knew it would be quiet, I headed to Dandy Drugs and—after lurking in the aisles for what seemed hours, pretending to read the labels on Pepto-Bismol and Old Spice bottles—summoned the nerve to buy a three-pack of condoms. After eighteen years without the need for a single prophylactic, I could not fathom ever requiring more than three. Three condoms seemed wildly optimistic. Three condoms, I was convinced, would last the rest of my life. I slid one into my wallet and hid the other two above a basement ceiling panel where I knew Mom and Dad wouldn't find them. I was ready when Becky was.

Then the unexpected happened. One week before I was to leave for college, the doorbell rang, and on the front porch stood Anna. Her skin was the color of cocoa from a summer of sun, her hair a shimmer of tight, frizzy curls. She wore shorts and flip-flops and a loose muslin smock, a small silver Star of David around her neck. The instant I saw her, all the feelings from the previous autumn came rushing back. *Anna, Anna, my God, Anna.*

"Hi," she said with a smile that told me the feelings had not left her, either.

"Hi," I answered.

Then we were walking through the dark, hand in hand. We walked down Erie Drive, across The Outlot to the beach, stopping along the way to fetch a blanket from the boat. Neither of us needed to say a word; we both knew where the night would take us. I led her to a grassy place beneath one of the giant oak trees, and together we spread the blanket and sank down on it.

"I missed you," I whispered. It had been eight months since our last kiss, but the transition was seamless. Here we were again, our lips and torsos and limbs pressed together as if no time at all had passed. The humid night air surrounded us and distant lightning flashed silently in the sky. I pulled my face back far enough to look into her eyes.

"You're sure?" I asked.

"I'm sure," Anna said and pulled my face back to hers.

That's when I felt a wet, cold jab on the back of my neck. I jolted upright and turned. Shaun lunged forward and began licking my face. He was wildly happy to have found us, and was panting and prancing about. "Aww, puppy," Anna cooed and reached up to pet him.

"No! No, wait," I said. "Quick! Button your shirt! Sit up!" If Shaun was here, that could mean just one thing.

I stood up, pulled my shirt down, and looked around. From the direction we had just come danced a flashlight beam, growing brighter and bigger as it drew closer. I waited until it was nearly upon us.

"Hi, Dad," I said. "Over here."

The beam fell on us briefly and then went dark.

"You remember Anna," I continued. "My friend from New Jersey? She's back visiting."

Dad said hello to her, then turned back to me. "Your mother's concerned," he said. "She sent me down to check on you." I paused to marvel at my mother's ability to sniff out possible hanky-panky from hundreds of yards away. As far as I knew, she hadn't even seen Anna come to the door. From the pained tone of Dad's voice, I could tell this was the last thing he wanted to be doing on his Saturday night. He had been ordered here against his will, Little Napoleon's foot soldier. I could tell he was embarrassed to be caught in the middle.

"We're just talking, Dad. Catching up."

"Why don't you catch up at the house. That would probably be better."

"Sure, good idea," I said. "We'll be right up."

"How right up?"

"Twenty minutes?"

He hesitated in the dark. I could picture his face, and I imagined it grimacing. I could see him weighing what he would tell his wife when he returned alone. "Twenty minutes," he said.

"Twenty minutes. Promise."

"Okay then," he said and flicked on his flashlight and walked away.

We both sat frozen until the flashlight beam disappeared on the other side of The Lagoon. Then I was on my feet, pulling her up onto hers.

"Come on, quick," I said. "We don't have much time."

"John," she said. "We can't. What if he comes back?"

"I have a place," I said. "A secret place we used to go as kids."

I threw the blanket over my shoulder and led her down into the water. "Watch the rocks," I warned as we waded knee-deep along the shoreline. Ahead of us, a small peninsula jutted out into the lake, thick with underbrush. I led Anna around the little spit of land, which separated the neighborhood beach from a private home. On the other side, a steep stairway led up the embankment to the house, but first, on the edge of the water, was a tiny secluded beach. Just big enough for two people on a blanket. Tommy and I had discovered it years earlier.

"What do you think?" I asked.

"I think it's perfect," she said.

Within seconds we were out of our clothes. She lay down on the blanket and pulled me on top of her. The sensation of our bare flesh pressed together was like nothing I had ever imagined. I was delirious with desire.

"My condom!" I nearly shouted. "I have a condom."

I fumbled for my wallet, and she helped me put it on. I sank back on top of her, felt our skin make contact again, her breasts against my chest, her stomach flat against mine. It was as if our bodies had always been meant to fit together. I was so excited. So incredibly excited.

Too excited. My orgasm came in a matter of seconds. It came with no warning. It came before I was even fully inside her.

"It was still wonderful," she said.

But I knew it wasn't. I lay motionless on top of her. She traced her fingertips along my spine and whispered in my ear. I don't remember what she said, but whatever it was, it gave me all the encouragement I needed. Seconds later I was ready for her again and she for me.

"Grab another condom," she whispered.

I froze. "Another condom?"

"Yeah. Hurry."

"Um. I don't have another one."

"You only brought one?" The disappointment in her voice bordered on annoyance.

"I didn't know."

From the way Anna recoiled on the blanket, I knew what she wanted to say: What kind of an idiot would carry only one lousy condom? What she said was: "Just hold me, okay?"

I racked my brain. "We could try to use it over again," I offered.

"No," she said, clearly appalled at the idea. "That won't work."

In the end, we did what high school kids for eons have done, and that was to err on the side of recklessness. We made love with no protection at all. Afterward, we lay together and I cradled her face in my hands. "You are so beautiful," I said.

We were late. It was time to go before Mom sent Dad in search of us again. At the house, I called inside, "Back!" I saw Dad in the living room check his watch. Anna and I sat on the porch and talked, then I walked her to her car.

"I'm glad you came back," I said.

"I am, too."

She unclasped the Star of David from her neck and put it around mine. For my birthday that year, Marijo had given me a silver cross with the word *Alleluia* stamped on it, and I removed it from my neck. Anna held her hair up for me, and I fumbled to clasp it around hers. We both started laughing.

"This will drive the parents insane," Anna said.

"Yours and mine both," I said.

We stood in the dark, rocking gently in each other's arms, our foreheads pressed together. The first hint of autumn drifted on the breeze, and with it an awareness that my life had reached a juncture. Everything was soon about to change—or perhaps was already changing. I was leaving home in a week, leaving my parents' nest and the childhood they had given me. I was leaving without my virginity and with no concept of the irrevocability of life's chapters.

I kissed Anna on the lips. Once, twice, three times. And then she was gone. Back to New Jersey, to college in Boston, to a life that, as it turned out, would remain fully separate and apart from my own.

PART TWO

Breaking Away

Chapter 18

B y 1982 I was three years out of Central Michigan University, where I had finally gotten serious about academics and graduated cum laude with twin majors in journalism and English. I was working as a reporter at a small newspaper in the far southwest corner of the state, covering murders, robberies, rapes, and lesser crimes. I lived alone in an apartment carved out of the second story of a turn-of-the-century house perched on a bluff above Lake Michigan. And I was still dating Becky. Or perhaps more accurately, Becky was still dating me.

Just as she had instigated that first kiss in the hallway of West Bloomfield High seven years earlier, Becky continued to be the driving force that kept us hanging on as a couple. I followed the course of least resistance, going along for the ride—and for the sex, which finally came to pass in my dorm room at Central Michigan after Becky went on the Pill and persuaded her mother to drive her the two hours to campus to spend the weekend.

That visit marked a watershed in my struggle for candor with my parents. I had never grown comfortable with the lies and deceit, and once in college I was determined to be more forthcoming. But my parents seldom rewarded my attempts at honesty. I learned that over and over, but never as much as I did during that Homecoming weekend when Mom called while Becky was in the room with me, waiting for her mother to arrive to take her home.

"So what's new?" Mom asked.

"Oh, not much," I said.

"Nothing at all?"

"Not really."

"Surely you must have something to report," she said, not accusatorily but with enough zeal to make me think, *Oh God, she knows.*

"Well," I said, "Becky's here for the weekend."

Long pause.

"Becky? There with you?" Mom asked.

"Yes. Her mom brought her up for Homecoming."

"For the day?"

"No, for the weekend." I glanced over at Becky and could tell from her expression that I was making a grave mistake. But my pride was on the line. I wasn't going to lie to my mother in front of my girlfriend and roommates. Besides, I was an adult now, old enough to vote, and figured it was time to be my own man. "She's actually here right now."

"She is? Where did she stay last night?" Mom asked.

"Here at the dorm."

"Where at the dorm?"

"Here in my room."

"Your room? Then where did you stay?"

Now it was my turn to pause. It was the moment of truth. I could easily lie and tell her I bunked across the hall, or I could be a man and tell it straight. "Here in my room, Mom."

A drawn breath, and then: "John, what are you trying to tell me?"

Before I could answer, she started in about the sanctity of

marriage, and the need for God's blessing of sexual relations, and the repercussions of one irresponsible act. It was time to abandon ship. The SS *Honesty* was going down.

"Mom," I interrupted. "Nothing happened. Nothing at all, okay? She slept in my bed and I slept in the beanbag. We just slept, that's all."

"Do you expect me to—?"

"Not a thing, Mom. Not a thing happened."

I quickly got off the line before the grilling could resume, but the fallout from that moment of candor continued for weeks, with Mom lamenting the decision to send me to public schools and Dad threatening to make me live at home while attending a local Catholic college.

On my next visit home, I sat with them in the living room, looked into their eyes, and repeated my lie with straight-faced sincerity: "Honest, nothing happened." I repeated the words over and over, like a hypnotist.

They finally seemed to buy it. "We believe you, dear," Mom said as Dad nodded silently in agreement, "but it was very foolish of you to put yourself in such a situation of temptation. Your guardian angel can only do so much. You were just asking for trouble."

"I can see that now," I said and promised them I would not make the same mistake again. Silently I told myself that, at least when it came to my parents, the truth was not always the best course. From that day forward, I simply told them what I knew they wanted to hear—or at least refrained from telling them what they did not. The decision was a simple one that allowed me to continue down the path of least resistance with them. The only trade-off was with my pride and integrity. It was a swap I was willing to make.

I became one of those underclassmen with a girlfriend back home, and I would see Becky whenever I returned for holidays or long weekends, during which we slinked around behind the backs of my parents, who were still hoping against all circumstantial evidence that their youngest son's virginity was intact and would remain so until marriage. Fortunately, we had allies in Becky's permissive parents, who understood our need to have alone time in Becky's bedroom with the door locked.

After graduating from high school, Becky followed me to Central, even though I had not encouraged her. It was the only college she applied to. By then I was living off campus in a coed house, and she was in a dormitory. My journalism classes were on the other side of campus from her music courses. We saw each other when we could, and I enjoyed having her there, but I continued to treat her like a part-time girlfriend. Becky, always the accommodating one, allowed me to.

Then I got out of college and moved halfway across the state, and our relationship returned to long-distance status, with weekend visits a couple of times a month. By 1982 she was out of college, too—and looking to begin a life together. She pushed to move in with me, and I resisted. I liked Becky and cared about her; we had natural chemistry and many good times together. But I could not imagine spending my life with her. The joke among my male friends was that my idea of commitment would be to invite Becky to move to Grand Rapids, sixty miles to the north, so she'd be only an hour's drive away, not three. That wasn't far from the mark. The truth was, the status quo suited me fine. I got to have a fun-loving girlfriend and lover without all the baggage of a full-time relationship. Our twice-monthly visits together, most of which were spent in bed, were just about the right amount of Becky for me. She hung on, hoping for more, even as my lackluster commitment became increasingly impossible to ignore. The relationship lapsed into a tired stasis, becoming more and more strained.

Every Sunday afternoon like clockwork my parents called to catch up, and every Sunday I perpetuated a freewheeling fiction about the life I was leading. Actually, just two aspects of it: church and Becky. In our weekly chat, one of the first questions always out of their mouths was "How was Mass this morning?" I had grown adept at hiding from them the fact that, except during visits home, I had not gone to church since the day I left for college six years earlier. "Oh, pretty good," I would say, and I'm sure it had been for those in attendance. Mom and Dad knew better than to ask too many questions, and I knew better than to offer too many details. Over the years I had perfected the art of obfuscating without exactly lying outright. I would drop little nuggets of hope into our weekly phone conversations like a sailor might drop life preservers to men overboard. I wanted to give them something to cling to. I would say things like "Saint Bart's just put a beautiful addition onto the back of the church." I was careful not to say I had actually set foot inside Saint Bart's, but that's the impression I hoped to leave.

Sometimes my efforts returned to haunt me. I prepared for my parents' first weekend visit to my new apartment by looking up the nearest Catholic church in the phone book. I found the intersection on a map and memorized the route. I called ahead and got the Mass times so I could breezily let drop, as if I did this every Sunday, "Should we shoot for the nine-fifteen, the eleven o'clock, or the twelve-thirty?" I thought I had covered all my bases. But when we arrived at the intersection where the church was located, there wasn't one church but three. I had no idea which one was for Catholics and knew I had only a few seconds to figure it out. My eyes searched for any sign of Catholicism: a statue of the Virgin Mary, a crucifix, anything. Finally I spotted a plain cross, swallowed hard, and pulled into the parking lot—of a Lutheran church. "I think we want to be over there," Dad said, pointing across the street. Then from the backseat, more playful than scolding, Mom chimed in: "Oh, Johnny boy."

When it came to Becky, my duplicity was even more creative. Each phone call they would inquire, "So, have you seen Becky lately?" They would ask it in a breezy, chatty way, just like they asked about Mass. But as with Mass, I knew they were probing for information. I was careful to give away no usable intelligence. As far as my parents knew, Becky had never once stayed at my apartment. When I visited her at the university, my tale went, I stayed with male friends, and when she visited me in Saint Joseph, I arranged to have her stay with a married couple I knew from work, who were gracious enough to open their spare bedroom to her. I gave my parents the same things my siblings had learned to give them: plausible deniability and enough leeway to allow them to believe they were succeeding in their lifelong mission to raise their children as devout and chaste practicing Catholics. None of us wanted to disappoint them.

My paper was called the *Herald-Palladium* and it served the racially divided cities of Saint Joseph and Benton Harbor, though not equally, with daily doses of crime news, ribbon cuttings, and small-town gossip. Crimes committed by blacks against whites received especially sensational play. A favorite feature was the weekly photo gallery of deadbeat dads who had not paid their child support. It was truly an awful newspaper and an awful place to work, run by a former World War II submarine commander who barked orders and threats like he was still operating under martial law. With the exception of four grandmotherly ladies who ran the women's page, the staff consisted entirely of white men, nearly all of whom smoked. An inky cloud of cigarette, cigar, and pipe smoke clung to the ceiling of the newsroom at all hours of the day.

Into this morass one snowy winter's day marched a young woman. I noticed her right away. How could I not? She arrived fresh out of Michigan State University to begin her journalism career as the *Herald-Palladium*'s first-ever woman news reporter. The whole staff had anticipated the arrival of "the girl reporter" for weeks. And now here she was, standing in the newsroom, tall and slender, with a refined bearing and sandy blond hair that fell to her shoulders. Instantly, I was smitten. When I finally got a chance to introduce myself, she cut me off and insisted she had already met me during an earlier whirlwind of introductions.

"Um, no, you didn't," I corrected her.

"Yes I did."

"Nope. You're confusing me with someone else," I said and wanted to add, *You're the first woman under fifty to set foot in this newsroom and easily the most beautiful. Believe me, if I'd met you, I'd remember.*

"I'm sure I met you."

"Not me. Wrong guy."

We continued back and forth like this until it became so awkward that the only course left was to walk away. I never did get the chance to properly introduce myself. Was I really that forgettable? To me and every other man on staff, she was the biggest event to hit the paper in years: a young, pretty, single woman breaking the gender barrier. To her, I was just one of the many faceless males, married and unmarried, who hovered around her, fawning and jockeying for her attention. Before walking off, she cheerfully dropped into the conversation what she had told all the rest, that she had taken the job primarily to be near her steady boyfriend, who was a graduate student at Notre Dame University, a half hour down the road.

"That's great," I said. "Makes perfect sense."

I had just met this woman and already I was experiencing a piercing pang of heartsickness the likes of which I had seldom felt during seven years of dating Becky. Maybe it was because Becky tried so hard and this new woman, Jenny, showed no interest in trying at all. She was already taken and, even if she had not been, could not have cared less about me. She couldn't even tell me apart from the next guy in line. Her indifference made me want her all the more.

As winter stretched into spring, Jenny and I gradually became pals. We shot messages back and forth on our computers and gossiped in the lunchroom. We began going out after work for pizza and beer and took weekend hikes in the wooded dunes along Lake Michigan. She told me all about her boyfriend; I told her about my girlfriend, making the relationship sound stronger than it was. I didn't want to sound too eager.

That spring I bought an aging but seaworthy twenty-eight-foot sailboat with a cabin that slept four, and she volunteered to meet me down at the marina to help work on it. Together, we scrubbed and painted the bottom, sanded and oiled the teak trim, waxed the decks, monkeyed with the engine. We often worked until dusk and then found ourselves in the cockpit as the sun set over the water, drinking wine or splitting carryouts. Jenny had become my closest friend, and although I steadfastly pretended otherwise, so much more. At long last I had a view of what love really was, and I was falling headfirst into it at a dizzying speed. I felt like a spider cascading over Niagara Falls, powerless to do anything but be swept away. I didn't realize it at the time, but Jenny felt that way, too. Over Memorial Day weekend we had dinner together, at which we both confessed how hollow our respective relationships had grown. At the end of the evening, back at her apartment, I leaned over and kissed her. It was a kiss that would forever change our lives. The next weekend Jenny summoned the Notre Dame boyfriend to a restaurant and broke up with him. Shortly after that, I did the same with Becky. She acted almost relieved to at last get a clear decision from me.

The relationship advanced at a breathless pace, a pace I had never dreamed possible. Every day Jenny and I seemed to fall more in love. I found everything about her intriguing, including her sharp tongue and stinging wit. Even when we had fights I swooned over her. She called me Yogi Grogie, and I called her Jen-Jen. She was always doing things to steal my heart. After buying her first microwave oven, she invited me over for an all-microwave dinner, and the pork chops came out so thoroughly overdone they had turned translucent, as hard and brittle as petrified wood. "I'm so humiliated!" she wailed, but I found her disastrous cooking skills, so unlike my mother's, irresistibly endearing. One autumn night she slept over at my apartment. The next morning when we walked outside, I saw she had camouflaged her bright orange Chevy Vega with a thick layer of fallen leaves to disguise its presence in front of my place. She was concerned for her reputation, and I found it adorable beyond words.

In phone calls home, I gushed to Mom and Dad about this new girl in my life. They sounded elated, truly thrilled. I suspect the real reason was that Becky was finally out of the picture.

"Is she a Catholic?" Mom and Dad asked in chorus.

"Um, no," I said. "She's Presbyterian." From the silence on the line, I could hear their disappointment. I knew just how Mom would break the news to the church ladies when she announced John's new girlfriend: "Well, she's not a Catholic, but if they're really in love, I suppose that's what matters most."

"Yep, Presbyterian," I repeated. But even that was a stretch. Jenny was raised marginally Presbyterian, but no one in her family was religious, least of all her. "We're a bunch of heathens," she liked to quip, and I prayed silently she would never use the line in front of my parents. It was bad enough for them to know that Jenny was not Catholic; to know she was nothing at all would be heresy.

"Presbyterians are actually quite a bit like Catholics," I offered. "Lots of similarities."

"Some major differences, too," Dad shot back. "The Protestants won't even acknowledge our Blessed Virgin Mother or the Immaculate Conception. They deny the core tenets of Catholicism." Then he recited, as he had so many times before, why Catholicism was the one true faith. I didn't even try to argue.

"She can convert!" Mom exclaimed with a eureka-moment brightness in her voice. "Lots of people convert before marrying a Catholic."

"Ma, stop it!" I said. "Let's not get carried away. We just

started dating." What I could have said, though, with absolute certainty, was that Jenny would never, ever convert. Not for me, not for any man. Not for all the love or money in the world. If I wanted her, I would have to take her just the way she was, and that was fine with me.

"It's just something to think about as you two get more serious," Mom said.

When they finally met her, during a weekend visit to my apartment, Mom and Dad seemed nearly as smitten by Jenny as I was. She was elegant and charming and clearly crazy about their son. She impressed Dad with her homemade apple pie and Mom with her spotless apartment. Mostly, she impressed them by not being Becky. In fact, she was nearly the antithesis of Becky. She had no mountainous missiles to scramble men's minds. She radiated girl-next-door wholesomeness and clearly looked forward to marriage and motherhood. Jenny seemed to like my parents a lot, too. Their budding relationship, I noted, was off to a very promising start.

Chapter 19

A small-town newspaper like the *Herald-Palladium* was a career destination for only two kinds of journalists: those with ties to the area who were willing to make professional sacrifices to put down roots, and those without the talent or ambition to move on. For everyone else it was a humble first career rung until something better came along. My break came about a year after meeting Jenny when I was hired by the *Kalamazoo Gazette* to write about politics. Kalamazoo was a college town an hour's drive due east of Saint Joseph, and Jenny helped me move into my new apartment. Several months later Jenny got her break, too, moving to the *Muskegon Chronicle* to cover education. With her move, we were now more than two hours apart, driving to see each other every weekend and occasionally midweek, as well. The long-distance commute was far from ideal, but it was bearable, and our shared hope was that the next career jump would bring us into the same city again.

Then I received a letter that was like winning the lottery, only better. I had been accepted into a midcareer fellowship pro-

gram at Ohio State University. The opportunity was amazing, a
full ride covering tuition and living expenses for a year of study,
culminating in a master's degree in journalism. The program
accepted only ten journalists a year from dozens of applications
nationwide. I knew it could be my ticket out of small-town newspaper jobs. I couldn't pass it up. But Columbus was nine hours
from Muskegon, and I knew Jenny would be crushed. This was
a part of the dream she had not counted on, a part that did not
include her. I thought about it overnight, then accepted without
telling her.

It was cowardly of me and in bad form. When I finally broke
the news to her, what made her angriest of all was that I had not
included her in the decision. We were a couple planning a future
together, and I had thrust a unilateral edict upon her. I think she
just wanted to be asked, even if she knew the only answer she
could give was "Yes, go."

We survived the year but not without some calluses to our
souls. Even though we spoke every night on the phone, it was
impossible not to grow apart with the distance. Jenny was working undercover in the local high school, posing as a student for a
series of investigative articles. I was deep into my graduate studies. We were on separate planets whose orbits no longer quite
aligned. Then it got worse.

From Ohio State, I was accepted into a second journalism fellowship program, this one in Saint Petersburg, Florida. Jenny
and I were now twenty-six hours apart. And when the three-
month program ended, I was hired as a reporter at the South
Florida *Sun-Sentinel,* across the state in Fort Lauderdale. My
dream of landing at a metropolitan paper had been realized, but
at the expense of reuniting with Jenny. Our future looked bleak.
How long could a couple go on like this, barely seeing each other,
getting by with phone calls and letters? We were both ready to
give up.

Always the good girlfriend, Jenny offered to help me move

my belongings to Florida and set up my new apartment—a fact I kept hidden from my parents because I could think of no plausible way to explain where she might sleep other than with me. While in town, she walked unannounced into the newsroom of the *Palm Beach Post* and handed her résumé and writing samples to the editors. They were especially impressed with her undercover high-school work. Two weeks later she had the job, and a month after that I helped her move into an apartment just a fifteen-minute drive from my own. Our dream had taken a few major detours but ultimately landed us where we had always hoped. Mom and Dad congratulated us heartily—especially after I made clear we had separate apartments.

Six months into Jenny's one-year lease, I said, "This is crazy. I love you. You love me. We spend all our time together anyway. Why don't we just move in together?"

Jenny blinked hard, and I thought she was going to cry. Then she threw her arms around my neck and said, "I accept."

We found a funky neighborhood we liked in West Palm Beach, just a couple of blocks from the Intracoastal Waterway, and soon stumbled upon a squat white bungalow with a front yard consisting entirely of weeds. It was the first house in the block off the main drag, Dixie Highway, and the most modest, too. In front of it was a sign that read FOR RENT.

As moving day neared, we discussed how we would break the news to our parents. Jenny was concerned that her mother and father would react badly. I, on the other hand, insisted to Jenny that my parents would have no problems at all. After all, they adored Jenny and knew how much we loved each other. They just wanted us to be happy, right? And this move was making us more than happy; we were giddy with excitement. So much so that we talked the landlord into giving us the key early so we could strip and polish the hardwood floors.

"I don't know, John," Jenny said. "Your parents are pretty conservative."

"They'll be fine," I assured her. "You just worry about your folks."

But secretly, deep inside, I was a nervous puddle. I was thirty years old and embarrassed to admit it but terrified to tell them something so simple as "Jenny and I have decided to live together." Part of me knew I was being ridiculous. I was an adult living on my own. What could they do? Encumber my allowance? Part of me struggled with wave after wave of dread. All my years of filtering the truth, of little deceits and outright lies, made it all the worse. With my help, they had allowed themselves to be deluded.

The previous Sunday, Mom and Dad had called for their weekly chat, only earlier than normal. Jenny had slept over, and we were just making coffee. As she always did, Mom asked me if I had gone to Mass yet that morning. No, I said, not yet. She then asked if I planned to see Jenny later in the day.

"Actually, I'm heading over to her place right after Mass," I said, managing to work two lies into one sentence. Jenny pretended not to overhear, and I knew she was embarrassed for me, a thirty-year-old still lying to his mother. I considered myself moral, ethical, even a little boring, with nothing to be ashamed of. Yet I dreaded the news I had to break to them, and my biggest fear was that when I did, Mom and Dad would blame Jenny. "He was such a good Catholic boy until he met . . . *that woman!*"

On the morning of our move, I pulled the rental truck up to Jenny's apartment, but before we began loading she called her parents. When she hung up a few minutes later, she said, "Wow, that was easier than I thought it would be. They really sounded pleased for us. My dad said his only regret was that he couldn't be here to help us move."

"He said that?"

"Yep. 'I just wish I could be there to help you move.'"

"Great," I said. "One down, one to go. My parents will be a breeze."

I put off calling them until all our possessions were in the moving van ready to be delivered to our new house. I wanted the move to be past the point of no return before breaking it to them.

I dialed their number and Mom picked up.

"Hi, Mom," I said. "Can you get Dad on the other line? I have some news to share with you both."

A few seconds later she was back with Dad. We made small talk for a minute and then Dad asked, "So what's this big news Mother tells me you have?"

"Well," I said. "Are you sitting down?" A nervous laugh escaped my lips. I knew they would have reservations, but I hoped they could, if not embrace, at least respect our decision. I wanted to believe they'd react as I knew they would if I announced we were engaged to be married. In my mind, this day was tantamount to that, the first step in our shared life together.

"Jenny and I have decided to move in together," I said.

Long pause, then Dad's voice: "I'm sorry? You what?"

"Decided to move in together."

Silence.

"We found a cute little house, and it seemed crazy paying two rents, and it's really convenient to both our offices. Right down by the water. And . . . we're moving in together."

Several seconds passed. I asked: "Are you still there?"

"We're here," Dad said.

"Today, actually. We're moving today. I have the truck loaded and ready to go."

Mom spoke next, and once she started there was no stopping her. "This is a big mistake—John, don't do this—do you hear me? Don't do it. Do you know how big a mistake this is? You'll be tarnishing your relationship forever. You don't want to do this—you can never take it back—you'll always regret it." Her words sprayed out like machine-gun fire.

Then Dad brought out the howitzers: "Sure, it's fine for you.

It's fine for the man. But what about Jenny? What about the woman? What's that tell the world about her and your respect for her? Have you thought about her reputation? What happens to her when you get tired of this?" His message was clear: from this point forward she would be a marked woman—stained, used, unsuitable for marriage.

"Dad," I said, an edge of pleading in my voice, "that's so old-fashioned. Things have changed. People don't think that way anymore."

"Morals don't go in and out of style," he snapped. "That's what's wrong with this age, the moral relativism. 'If it feels good, do it.' Well, you know what? Right and wrong are right and wrong. They don't change. And living together out of wedlock is wrong. It's plain wrong."

Then he got to his main point. "You'll be living in a state of sin. Is that what you want? To live with the pall of sin over you?"

Mom broke in: "This will ruin the marriage. The Lord won't bless this union. You're dooming your future." She begged me to reconsider.

"Mom, c'mon," I pleaded.

"Your marriage will be damned before it ever starts," she said.

"Ma . . ."

"Have you thought about pregnancy? About birth control? What if Jenny gets pregnant? What then? Do you want a baby born out of wedlock? That child will carry this shame for his entire life. Is that what you want?"

My God, I thought. *They really still believe I'm a virgin. I'm thirty years old and they're afraid I'll accidentally get Jenny knocked up. They think Jenny and I have never had sex. Unbeliev-able. How were they able to delude themselves for so long?* Until that moment, I never quite believed they had bought into all my deceit. Mom's voice rattled on like a Gatling gun, laying down a withering cross fire of recrimination. She worked every angle to dissuade me. I was barely hearing her words. Finally I shouted over her.

"Stop! Look, the moving truck is in the driveway. Our apartments are both empty. Everything's in the truck. We're not reconsidering. It's too late. This is happening."

A long, long silence. Then Dad's voice: "You understand our position and I think we understand yours. We should let you go now." In the background, I could tell Mom was crying.

"Okay, then," I said.

"John?" Dad said. A long silence filled the phone line. "John, you will always be our son."

"I know, Dad," I said and hung up.

"Well, that went well," I said, and Jenny slipped her arms around me from behind and said, "I could tell."

"Let's not let it ruin the day," I said. "We're moving in together!" I kissed her on the lips, then gave her a slap on the backside and said, "We've got work to do."

As we carried our combined furnishings and possessions into our new rental house, I tried hard to seal away the phone call. But the more I tried, the more it filled my head. The whole thing was really my fault, I told myself. Had I been more honest and up-front with them all along, starting years earlier, my announcement would not have hit them so hard. Part of me felt pain for disappointing them; part of me, self-loathing for lacking the character to stand tall and be myself around them; part of me, anger at them for being so rigid. I continued to worry about Jenny and what this incident would do to her relationship with my parents. How could she not harbor resentment toward them now? They made it clear what they thought of our arrangement, and by extension what they thought of us. If I was the sinner, what did that make her?

We were crazy about our two-bedroom house with the weedy

yard and drippy faucets. There were orange and avocado trees out back loaded with fruit and a little patio where we could sit beneath the palms with our coffee and newspapers in the morning. There was a washer with a clothesline instead of a dryer, which we found impossibly romantic. Off the laundry was a one-car garage Jenny would spend an entire weekend repainting to convert into a studio for me. There was even a fireplace to take the chill off winter nights. We were like kids with a new toy, and we raced from one room to the next, then made the circuit all over again.

And yet, a quiet pall hung over the day. As we carried in the last boxes, mingling our two lives at last into one, an image flashed before my eyes. An image of my parents. They were sitting together in the living room, holding their rosaries, having just prayed for my soul. They were big on praying for lost souls. Mom was weeping and red-eyed, Dad shaking his head, deep worry on his face. Both of them were wondering aloud where they had gone wrong.

Chapter 20

One week into our new life together, a letter arrived. I recognized the handwriting right away as belonging to Mom. I had not spoken with her or Dad since moving day. Now that she'd had time to calm down, maybe she was seeing things more clearly. Maybe she was writing to apologize. I tore open the envelope.

"Dear John," her letter opened, "I write this with a heavy heart." It was not the opening I had hoped for, and I could feel my chest tighten. "I have been numb since our telephone conversation. Strange that so few words could affect one so much. I just realized that this is the very first time I have had to shed tears over you. For thirty years you have given us nothing but joy and pride. I don't need to say how disappointed both Dad and I are at your decision. Somehow we thought we had instilled higher ethics and morals in you. We didn't think we had to preach; we thought we were teaching you by example." And then the razor-edged saber to the heart: "I'm sorry I have failed you."

Just like in the phone conversation with me, her words poured

192 · JOHN GROGAN

out in bursts: "Honestly, I can't understand what your problem is . . . If you love someone enough to sleep with them, it just seems to me that you would want to have your relationship blessed . . . Without doubt, this is the biggest decision you have had to make; I hope you are prepared to meet the responsibilities that go with it . . . Have you thought of the children that could result? Are you ready to cope with birth control and abortion?"

The problem, she noted, was that we had tried to make this important life decision on our own without spiritual guidance. "This is the time for both of you to turn to prayer. God is the only one who knows what the future holds. It is He, and He alone, who can guide you during this most important time of your lives. Don't be so proud as to think you can make your own decisions without His help . . . We were made to love and serve God. He is our Creator. We can't say we believe this and yet go about doing what He has asked us not to do. I am asking you to please take the time to converse with God. Tell Him how you feel, what your doubts are, your fears. Then listen! Think about making a retreat. Talk to a priest. Explore every avenue. It is your life—your future happiness."

She concluded this way: "We have loved you for the past thirty years and we are not about to stop now. No matter what your decision. Parents don't stop loving just because they are disappointed in their children. Of course, it would be much nicer loving with joy in our hearts rather than being laden with this heavy burden. But you are a man; only you can make the final decision. I think we know you well enough that you will do what you feel is right in your heart. But sometimes we are deceived by our own desires, so try to think straight . . . We will keep both of you in our prayers. We want you to find complete happiness—not just for a few months but for a lifetime."

The letter, three pages single-spaced, was classic Mom, a combination of heartfelt concern and overwrought emotions with a few well-aimed jabs of Catholic guilt skillfully slipped in. *Of course, it would be much nicer loving with joy in our hearts rather than being laden with this heavy burden . . .* When she felt strongly about something, she was incapable of self-censoring. When it came to influencing her children's lives, she had no on-off switch. It all came pouring out. What outsiders might see as meddling, I saw in a more positive light: a well-intentioned, if misguided and somewhat heavy-handed, effort to steer her brood down the right path.

I assumed Jenny would see it in the same light, which prompted me to make what in retrospect was one of the bigger mistakes of my life: I showed her the letter.

I did so without thinking. I did so assuming she would find it an amusing window into my mother's personality: the tenacious Little Napoleon in prime fighting form, grasping at every weapon in her arsenal to win this battle for her son's soul. I knew the letter was fueled by the best of intentions, but that did not soften my mother's judgmental tone. Before Jenny even said a word, I knew what a mistake I had made. I could see it in her face, at once wounded and angry.

"It's just my mom being my mom," I said, wishing I could push back the clock three minutes and bury the letter forever.

"What we share is beautiful, but to her it's just dirty. Dirty and wrong," Jenny said.

"Oh, c'mon," I pleaded. "She's just upset. It's a Catholic mother thing. They all do it. Don't take it personally."

A few days later, another letter arrived, this one bearing the crisp draftsman's lettering of my father.

"Dear John," it began. "By this time you have received Mother's letter. I want to add a few of my personal thoughts while the iron is hot. Mother did enough 'preaching' for both of us so all I want to say is that I agree with and support all she said. One of our big worries is that this may be the first step in your drifting away from the Church and losing your faith—so keep praying and don't stop going to Mass on Sunday. Your faith is precious. Please understand that we are concerned so much because we want only the best of everything for you. Now that we have said all this, we will not bring it up again. You are a grown man and it is your life."

He closed the letter: "One last thought, John. Don't do, or not do, anything because you think it is what *we* want. That would be a mistake. Do what you know is best for *you*. Whatever your decision, Mother and I will always stand by you and be your loving and caring parents. Give our love to Jenny. None of this has changed our feelings of affection toward her."

He signed it, "Sincerely, Dad."

I returned the letter to its envelope and slipped it into the bottom of my sock drawer, beside Mom's. Even though his words were more conciliatory than Mom's, they still carried the unmistakable mark of disapproval. I decided it would be best not to show his letter to Jenny. My life of filtering and parsing the truth was entering a new chapter. No longer did I need only to protect my parents from my own reality; now I had to shelter my girlfriend from theirs, as well.

That evening at dinner, I said, "I heard from my dad today."

"Oh, yeah?" Jenny said.

"He sent their love to you, and said none of this has changed how they feel about you."

"Oh, I'm sure it hasn't," she said.

"Sarcasm duly noted," I replied.

It was several weeks before I responded to either letter. I kept it breezy, telling them about work and our neighborhood and the routine we had fallen into. But I did want them to know that their doom-and-gloom predictions were not coming true. "After two months Jenny and I are very happy in our new home," I wrote. "We both agree we are the most content we've ever been. The strain of constantly commuting was proving to be a real test of our relationship. It was not a healthy way to live, and it was not a smart way to try to maintain a vital relationship. I know you disapprove of our decision, and maybe in a perfect world where we weren't thrown into a strange, sometimes hostile, culture hundreds of miles from our family and friends, things would have been different. But so far we have no regrets."

We had no regrets at all. We bought bikes and took long rides around Palm Beach. We strolled along the Intracoastal Waterway most evenings and spent weekends in Key West and Sanibel. We sipped café cubanos in Little Havana and began every morning by squeezing fresh orange juice from our tree. We planted tomatoes on our patio and coaxed grass to grow in the weedy front yard.

The night before Jenny's birthday, I stayed up late making a homemade card, which I put on the bedstand for her to find when she awoke. Inside it read:

> *He was an unreformed rock-and-roll animal*
> *In love with a lanky gorgeous blonde*
> *Who had wit, style and grace.*
> *She even laughed at his bad jokes*
> *And made him feel more handsome than he really was.*
> *He never much said it, being the (not so) strong, silent type,*
> *but he knew he was the luckiest guy around.*
> *They lived happily ever after.*
> *The End.*

Our lives felt full, complete, contented, despite my parents' disapproval and the strain it had caused. Eleven months after moving in together, I took Jenny to pick out a new stereo to replace the assemblage of college-vintage components we had each brought into the relationship. It sounded magnificent and was by far our biggest joint purchase. After we got it home and hooked up, I popped in an Anita Baker CD and danced Jenny around the living room.

When the song ended, I said, "Okay, sit down, right here on the couch. I have something for you." I pulled a tiny box from my pocket and handed it to her. Inside was a diamond engagement ring.

Chapter 21

Jenny began planning in earnest for our wedding, and I began lobbying just as earnestly to make it a Catholic ceremony. I did it for the exact reason my father had warned against—to make him and Mom happy. To fix the damage and heal the wounds. I thought a Catholic wedding would make everything right again. And not just a Catholic exchange of vows, but the whole shebang: a full Catholic wedding Mass complete with the consecration of the bread and wine followed by Holy Communion. Just like they had had.

Jenny knew how important it was to me and agreed, even though it would involve weeks of instruction from a Catholic priest. For her, it was just another of the many chores that went into preparing for a wedding—find a caterer, pick a menu, buy a dress, submit to weeks of rigorous Catholic indoctrination. We agreed to get married back at Our Lady of Refuge, and I asked my two uncles, Father Vin and Father Joe, now both in retirement, to officiate. All they needed, they told us, was the official document showing we had successfully completed our religious training back in our home parish in Florida. I had no idea what or where my home parish was, having never bothered to look up a church near our rental house, but I wasn't going to tell my elderly uncles that. I found our parish, and together we signed up for instruction. We were assigned to an assistant pastor named Father David.

When he showed up at our house one evening for the first meeting, we were both surprised to see a young man dressed in shorts, T-shirt, and sandals. He had a bushy mop of hair and a day's growth of beard; he looked more like he had arrived to teach surfing than religious instruction. Father David did not seem at all perturbed that we were living together. If he was judging us, he did not show it. Jenny instantly liked him, and by the end of the evening we were joking and laughing over wine like old friends.

The Catholic orthodoxy requires both parents, even one who is not a Catholic, to solemnly vow to raise the children in the Catholic faith, promising that they will attend Mass regularly and receive the sacraments. To Jenny, this was akin to forcing a Frenchman to pledge allegiance to Great Britain. Why, she asked, should she be required to raise her children in a religion she neither practiced nor believed in? The conciliatory Father David seemed to understand that he could not push too hard without risking losing us entirely to a justice of the peace. He proposed a compromise: that she agree only to *consider* raising our children Catholic when the time came. Sure, she would agree to consider it, she said, adding, "John's the Catholic. If he wants the kids raised in his faith, then he's going to have to be the one to do it." She agreed that she wouldn't block my efforts, and Father David seemed satisfied. We signed the pledge.

"What a nice guy!" Jenny said after he left. "He's really great. Very reasonable. He's nothing like those holier-than-thou stuffed shirts at your parents' parish." I smiled at our good fortune in finding a young, moderate priest flexible enough to bend his way around some of the Church's more rigid rules. If there was a God, then Father David was God's gift to us, the perfect priest to help me navigate the treacherous waters between my fiancée's and my parents' sensibilities.

But before our next weekly meeting, a distraught Father David called with bad news. His superiors had abruptly re-assigned him to a job that would allow him no contact with parishioners. "They seem to think I'm a bit too much of a maver-ick," he said.

"Can't you finish up with us?" I asked.

"No," he said. "I'd like to but I can't. I'm sorry."

The parish reassigned us to another priest, a rotund little man with oily skin and close-set eyes that had a slightly leer-ing quality about them. Unlike Father David, he issued edicts in absolute terms, telling us not only how we would be married but how we would live our married life. He seemed to especially enjoy talking to the young couples in our group about sex. The priest dedicated the entire final session to the joys of human sexuality. The more he talked, the more animated he became.

Father Beady Eyes wanted us to know that once we were married we could forget everything we had been told about sex being bad and sinful. "Ignore all that," he said. "Starting on your wedding night, none of that applies." Sex between a married man and woman was a natural thing, a beautiful thing, even a holy and sacred thing. We were to pursue it without hesitation or guilt, with gusto even. "Enjoy it, embrace it, celebrate it!" he said, voice rising in both pitch and volume. His eyes darted from one couple to the next, as though picturing each of us on our wedding night locked in blissful, naked, steamy coitus.

I leaned over and whispered into Jenny's ear: "I think he's enjoying this topic just a little too much."

"Way too much," she whispered back. "He's creeping me out."

The irony of the afternoon was not lost on either of us. Here was this single, celibate man who in all likelihood had never even held hands with a member of the opposite sex standing before a room full of couples offering sage sex advice. It was like hiring a blind man to teach sharpshooting.

But his lack of credibility did not slow Father down. He was even more animated as he gave his blessing to various forms of sexual foreplay. "There's nothing at all wrong with keeping things fun and interesting," he counseled. "Feel free to spice things up." There was only one restriction on our free, unfettered Catholic lovemaking, Father warned, and that was that the penis always, always, always must end up in the vagina. "You must do nothing to keep the sperm from the egg. You must do nothing to subvert God's plan."

This led Father into a detailed description of the only form of birth control we were allowed to practice: the rhythm method. The beauty of this form of birth control was that couples simply stopped having sex during those periods of the month deemed most fertile. The rhythm method was not a sin in the eyes of God, Father explained, because it simply entailed the absence of sex, not the enjoyment of it for some reason other than pro- creation. And Father insisted it could be highly effective. I knew this to be the case, as evidenced by all those families I'd grown up with back at Our Lady of Refuge with ten, twelve, even fourteen children. My own mother was one of nine, and she swore by the rhythm method. One thing we could all agree on: it worked with 100 percent effectiveness as long as you weren't having sex.

I could sense Jenny nearing her boiling point. At any second she might leap to her feet and tell Father Beady Eyes what she really thought of him and his advice. And I knew she would want to throw in something about his salacious leer as well. "We're almost through," I whispered, as I might if she were undergoing a root canal. "Just sit tight. Nearly over." I offered her my hand to squeeze.

Father left us with one final thought: "When you and your spouse are engaged in sexual union, remember you are not making love with each other. You are making love with our Lord Jesus Christ." We then all bowed our heads as Father led us in prayer that Jesus would bless our wedding-night union with his presence.

Father Beady Eyes handed us the official document showing we had successfully completed religious marriage instruction, and we bolted through the doors and into the sunshine. When we reached the car, I pushed Jenny against the door and kissed her. "Making love with Jesus!" I exclaimed. "A threesome! Now *that* I did not expect to hear."

She burst into laughter, and I could feel her relax in my arms. I knew I definitely owed her big-time for this one.

We set our wedding date for Labor Day weekend, but first came Rock's wedding. Of all my old friends from the neighborhood, Rock was the one with whom I had stayed closest. Even as college and careers took us in opposite directions, we remained best friends, traveling together, camping, and double-dating. I had largely lost track of Tommy and Sack and the others, but not Rock. Now he was getting married in Chicago, just three months before our planned date, and I wouldn't think of missing it. Only after booking our flights did I learn that the guest list included my parents, to whom Rock was almost like a fourth son after years as a regular presence in our home. Other parents from the neighborhood would be attending as well, and we were all staying in the same hotel. It would be my first time seeing them since Jenny and I had moved in together, and I feared that the sight of their son and future daughter-in-law sharing a room before marriage would be painful for them—not only on moral grounds, but social, as well. They no doubt had kept our cohabitation a secret; now it would be obvious to all their friends and neighbors attending the wedding. More salt in their already raw wounds.

And yet I kept telling myself, "You have nothing to hide. You have nothing to be ashamed of. This is their problem, not yours." In preparation for marriage, and feeling our Catholic instruction had fallen somewhat short, Jenny and I had signed up for premarriage counseling with a therapist. The sessions were designed to help couples understand and address the challenges of marriage in advance and to teach relationship skills, including how to resolve conflicts without leaving lasting scars. In the first session, I immediately launched into a lengthy description of the tension with my parents over our cohabitation. I fully expected the therapist, an affable and warm man named John Adams, to take my side and chastise Jenny for not being more sympathetic to my dilemma. I wanted him to tell her she really needed to be more accommodating of my parents' sensibilities.

But Dr. Adams seemed bewildered by my concerns. "You're how old again?" he asked. I told him, and he continued, "Do you live at home with your parents?"

"No."

"Do you rely on them to support you?"

"No."

"Do you owe them money?"

"No."

"College loans?"

"No."

"Do they pay your car insurance? Your grocery bill? Your utilities?"

By now I was getting the point. He raised his hands in the air. "So why do you let them control your life? What will they do to you?"

"Well, you see, it's just that . . ."

"You don't want to disappoint them," he said, finishing my sentence. "I understand that. But there's a way to be respectful of your parents and their mores without letting them run your life."

Dr. Adams dedicated a lot of our premarriage counseling to

helping me find a way to break free of their gravitational pull. I was overdue to live my own life without worrying how they would judge it. I needed to be myself without apology, he counseled, and then it would be up to them to accept me or not. With his advice in mind, I arrived in Chicago, determined to enjoy the weekend with my live-in girlfriend just as I would if they weren't there. I braced for the fallout.

But when we met my parents in the hotel lobby, all was breezily pleasant. They treated us to lunch, and we had an easy, comfortable conversation. Not a heavy word was uttered. We exchanged small gifts, and Jenny briefed my mother on the wedding preparations. Mom, for the umpteenth time, regaled us with the funny story of her own wedding day, how nervous Dad was and how Father Joe overslept and almost missed the ceremony. Dad sat and smiled, nodding his head as he always did when his wife held court.

That evening we sat with them at the wedding Mass, and Mom and Dad smiled up at me as I read a scripture passage from the altar, at Rock's request. They seemed to enjoy the reception. Only the next morning, as we prepared to check out of the hotel, did I finally see what simmered just below the surface. I left Jenny in our hotel room while I went two doors down to visit my parents. I was barely inside the door when they let loose. They had their son to themselves for a moment; this was their chance to speak candidly.

"John, we have something important we want to talk to you about," Dad said.

And then, immediately, Mom: "We don't think you should have a Mass at your wedding."

At first I misunderstood their intent. I thought they were trying to spare Jenny and me the longer ceremony if it wasn't what we really wanted. I figured they knew we were acting more for their sake than our own. "No, really, we don't mind," I said. "The full Mass is fine with both of us."

"You don't understand," Dad said. "We don't think it's a good idea."

"You don't?"

"We don't think it's right given how you're living."

"How I'm living?"

"Living in sin," Mom said. "John, you are living in a state of sin. And you're flaunting it. Look at you, staying together in this hotel in front of everyone."

"You'd be making a mockery of the Mass," Dad continued.

"Oh," I said.

"Jenny's not a Catholic. From what we can tell, you aren't a practicing Catholic anymore," he said. "It would be hypocritical. The Mass should not be window dressing."

The message was slowly sinking in, and I reeled from their words. I was no longer worthy. No longer fit to participate in that singularly most important, transforming experience of their lives, the Eucharist.

"Okay," I said. "We don't have to have a Mass."

"It seems to us you've lost all your faith," Dad said. Just two weeks earlier they had returned from a pilgrimage to the tiny village of Medjugorje in Bosnia-Herzegovina where believers claim the Virgin Mary had repeatedly appeared. Their breathless, unquestioning description of the alleged miracles had made me wince. Dad said he could tell from my muted response that I no longer shared their beliefs.

"Dad," I said. "Faith is a gift. You can't force it on someone. It's always come so effortlessly to you."

"Tell us the truth," Mom interjected. "Do you still go to church?"

I looked at her for a long moment. Studied her face, the face I had lied to so many times over so many years. "No," I said. "Not for a long, long time."

My mother acted as if she had taken a hit to the chest, knocking the wind out of her. She rested one hand on the chair back and stared out the window as if studying something far off on the interstate. "Oh," she said. "I didn't know that."

"It's not Jenny," I quickly added. "Don't think it's Jenny. I stopped going long before I ever met her. Long before."

We stood in a circle, saying nothing. "Look, I need to get going," I said. I was opening the door when Dad's voice boomed after me.

"John!"

I froze, then turned back. As I did he threw himself against me and buried his face in my shoulder, locking me in a grip so tight it was as if he would never let go. I felt him shaking, his chest lurching against me. Then I felt a warm wetness on my neck and heard his sobs, his jagged gasps. The man I had never seen shed a tear, my Rock of Gibraltar, was crying in my arms.

Soon Mom joined us, wrapping her arms around both Dad and me and crying uncontrollably. I imagine the sight of her husband weeping was too much to bear. I looked down at her face and it was filled with so much anguish I thought of Michelangelo's *Pietà,* showing the sorrowful Virgin Mary holding Jesus' body. I stood dry-eyed, sandwiched between them, rocking gently, awkwardly. "I'm sorry," I murmured, unsure if it was loud enough for them to hear. I was sorry, not for my actions, not for loving Jenny and wanting to be with her, not for failing to embrace those beliefs my parents embraced. But sorry for how much pain I had caused them. Sorry for the years of deception and now for the sucker punch of revelations that so quickly shredded, like shrapnel to the heart, all they had allowed themselves to believe for so long. Sorry for the gaping rift our religious differences had torn in the fabric of an otherwise loving family.

"I'm sorry," I said again, louder.

Finally Dad raised his head and wiped his face. His composure fully back, he said in a voice as strong as ever, "You're going to be late."

Back in my room, I found Jenny packing. "How'd it go with your parents?" she asked.

"Fine," I said. "We just chatted."

"Good. No more heavy stuff?"

"Nope. Not at all."

The next weekend, the phone rang and it was Dad. He sounded sheepish.

"Listen," he said. "I want you to try to forget everything we said in the hotel room in Chicago. We were out of place. It's your wedding, John. If you want a Mass, you should have a Mass."

"Thanks, Dad," I said. "I appreciate that. Jenny and I talked it over. We won't be having the Mass."

Chapter 22

M om nearly succeeded in sabotaging the wedding. Not that she was consciously trying to. I would never accuse her of that. But how else to explain the sandwich she made for me a mere ninety minutes before I was to walk down the aisle to meet my bride?

On September 2, 1989, I awoke before dawn on the foldout couch in my parents' basement. Jenny was staying with friends across town, and as tradition dictated, we were not to see or speak to each other until we met at the altar later that day. My stomach churned away like a washing machine, and my bowels rumbled. My nerves were on high alert. The previous night at the rehearsal dinner it all still seemed pretend. But now in the gray light before sunrise there was no more denying reality. My gut, quite literally, was telling me so. This was really happening. At the age of thirty-two, I was at last kissing my bachelorhood good-bye. In seven hours I would be a married man, and I was not too proud to admit the prospect terrified me. I pulled myself out of bed, slipped into my running shoes, and took a jog around Harbor Hills and Saint Mary's College. Then I picked up my tuxedo, stopped for a haircut and beard trim, and set up tables in the backyard for a champagne toast and receiving line that would take place between the wedding and reception.

It was just about time to shower and dress when Mom said, "You really should eat something. If there's any day you need to keep up your strength, it's today. Let me make you a sandwich." I had no appetite, but I knew she was right. I wouldn't make it through the long day ahead without nourishment.

A few minutes later, she brought out a sandwich on toast and I took a bite. "What is this?" I asked.

"Liverwurst and onions," she said.

It occurred to me that eating liverwurst and onions just before kissing my bride for the first time as man and wife might not be the wisest move.

"Do you think this is a good idea, Mom?" I asked.

"Why wouldn't it be? You love liverwurst and onions."

I pulled back the bread and studied the interior. Fat, thick rings of white onion, raw and pungent, towered above the liver spread. They were so strong, my eyes watered just looking at them. The sandwich might as well have had the words DEATH BREATH branded across it. Why I didn't push it aside or at least remove the onions, I can't say. Instead I took bite after bite, washing it down with a glass of milk.

Only after my plate was empty did the slow, odorous burn begin to pulsate through my mouth. As I showered, it radiated off my tongue and lips like a radioactive experiment gone wrong. I brushed my teeth, once, twice, three times, then gargled with mouthwash. None of it made a dent. I ran to the kitchen and made a poultice of white bread soaked in milk, plastering it between my tongue and the roof of my mouth. I brushed some more, swished another swig of Listerine, then puffed into my cupped hands. My eyes blinked hard. I didn't just reek. I was toxic.

By the time I was huddled in the back of the church with my brothers, who were serving as co–best men, it was obvious that moms are not always right, and that two hundred guests were all too soon going to realize that as well. Tim and Mike, standing about four feet from me, sniffed in unison. It was Tim who spoke. "Don't tell me you let Mom feed you one of those liverwurst sandwiches," he said.

"What makes you say that?" I asked and popped another breath mint.

Jenny later told me my liver-and-onion breath hit her when she was still several feet down the aisle. Her father, on whose arm she walked, confirmed that she was not exaggerating. I wouldn't have blamed her had she turned and run for the parking lot.

Despite the vapors rising off me, Jenny answered "I do" to all the salient questions. When it was my turn, I did my best to repeat my vows without once exhaling. It was really quite a feat, even if it did make me sound remarkably like Darth Vader. *Jenny . . . I . . . am . . . your . . . husband.*

And then it was over. A full wedding Mass would have stretched an hour or more, but we were in and out in fifteen minutes. I silently thanked Mom and Dad for that. Before we exchanged vows, Father Vin gave a short homily in which he reminded us that we weren't really marrying each other; we were both marrying our Lord Jesus Christ. He left out the part about the wedding night.

Late that night after the band had packed up and all the guests had gone home, Jenny and I checked into a Holiday Inn a few miles from Harbor Hills. With the exception of my onion breath, which, with the help of a barrage of gum and mints, had dissipated about halfway through the receiving line, the entire day had gone off without a hitch. I could laugh now at Little Napoleon's sandwich choice and the idea that, whether consciously or not, she was making one final attempt to derail a marriage she was convinced was doomed by virtue of its sinful prelude.

Both she and my father had been perfect hosts, graciously greeting guests, welcoming Jenny's family, and opening their home for both the rehearsal dinner the previous night and the champagne reception. They gave no hint to anyone of the pain that preceded the day.

The hotel room was unspectacular, but it was ours and ours alone. Just us and Jesus.

"We did it," Jenny said as she let her wedding dress fall to the floor.

"You're stuck with me now," I said, and we collapsed on the bed together, at once exhausted and exhilarated, and made love for the first time as husband and wife.

The next morning, Jenny and I boarded an express train to Toronto, where we spent a blissful week honeymooning. Our plan was to return to my parents' house, spend the night, then leave early the next morning for the long drive back to South Florida. This would be our first time staying at the house as a married couple and, now that we sported wedding bands, the first time Mom and Dad would no longer insist we sleep in separate rooms. I assumed we would commandeer the foldout couch in the basement, but when we arrived home at the end of the week, Mom had other plans.

"I'm putting you in our room," she announced.

"Oh, we couldn't do that, Ruth," Jenny said. "The couch will be just great."

"Nonsense," she replied. "You'll be much more comfortable."

"That's so nice, Ruth," Jenny said. "But the couch is great."

"I won't hear of it," Mom said. "This way you'll have your privacy." And from the way my mother said it—a slight, barely noticeable rise of the eyebrows—I could tell what she was thinking—and it was grandchildren. I glanced at Jenny and knew her skin had begun to crawl.

"Thank you, Ruth, it's very kind, but really," Jenny said in her firmest, no-nonsense voice, "I'd prefer the basement."

"Absolutely not," Mom shot back. "The room's all set for you."

"No, really, I insist," Jenny said.

"No," Mom said in a way that made clear she had no intention of backing down, "*I* insist."

Dad and I locked eyes, and I could tell we were both thinking the same thing: this was between the two women, and only a fool would get between them. It would be their first battle of wills as mother-in-law and daughter-in-law. The first of many to come.

"Ruth," Jenny said, her voice tensing as she carefully enunciated each word, "I do not want to sleep in your room."

"I have it all set up for you," Mom retorted. "Let me show it to you."

And then we were upstairs standing in their bedroom, and I understood why my mother had been so adamant. She had been busy converting it into a romantic honeymoon suite. Fresh flowers stood in a vase on the bedstand. Two sets of her best towels waited on the bed. The covers were turned down, exposing floral sheets she had taken the time to iron. And on the pillow sat two foil-wrapped chocolates. It was just like what Father Beady Eyes had said. Now that we were married, my mother had abandoned her crusade against sexual relations and was now anxious to help facilitate a pregnancy. I could see the color running out of Jenny's face. Her fight-or-flight instinct was kicking in and I sensed she was looking for the nearest door to bolt through.

"This bed has always been," Mom began, and I contemplated leaping across the room, knocking her to the floor, and cupping my hand over her mouth—*No, Mom, don't say it. Please, Mom, don't*—"very lucky for your father and me."

Oh no, she said it. Jenny was now beyond gray. She looked like she'd entered a catatonic state. I imagined she was repeating in her head, *This is not happening to me. This cannot be happening.* She stood perfectly still, not saying a word.

"Great, Mom, thanks," I said. "Fantastic. This will be terrific. We'll get unpacked now." I nudged her out of the room and closed the door. Then I looked around. In Mom's effort to create a romantic boudoir, she had failed to consider the many religious artifacts in the room and the effect they might have on the libidos of others less devout. On one wall was a framed portrait of the Pope staring benevolently at the bed. On another was a wooden crucifix showing Christ in the agony of death, blood trickling down his face and side. I counted three statues of the Virgin Mary, one of them nearly life-size, and another of Saint Francis. A bottle of mail-order holy water was on the windowsill. My mother's Bible sat on one bedstand, my father's prayer book on the other. And hanging from the headboard was the pièce de résistance— an oversize rosary that looked like it had been special ordered for Paul Bunyan. It was a good four feet long, and each wooden bead was the size of a walnut, strung together on a heavy chain. I plopped down on the bed, and the giant beads clanked loudly against the frame.

"It's not so bad," I said to Jenny. She just stood in silence. "It's only for one night. C'mon, honey, it's fine. Isn't it fine?" And then: "She means well. She's trying." I didn't have the heart to tell her that Father Vin would also be spending the night, and would be in my old room, immediately on the other side of the wall, his headboard inches from our own. Nor that Mom and Dad would be on the sleeper sofa immediately below us.

"We'll just have to be quiet," I offered helpfully.

Jenny at last spoke: "Don't touch me tonight."

"Oh, come on. Relax. It's just a room." And for me, it was. I had grown up with these Catholic adornments and barely noticed them.

"I mean it," she said. "You will not touch me."

That night after dinner when we retired for the night, Jenny still had not relaxed. Sex had become such a powder-keg issue between her and my parents, I guess I couldn't blame her. Before marriage, sex had been our downfall, our dirty little secret that had brought shame to the family name. Now we were supposed to embrace it with vigor in their bed with the saints and angels and Pope watching—and my uncle the priest inches away on the other side of the wall. She slid into the king-size bed and hugged the edge of the mattress as though she were expecting six or seven others to join us. I crawled in from the other side and slid up against her, draping one leg over hers. "Do not touch me," she repeated in a way that told me not to push my luck.

Despite that, I thought a little levity could only help ease the tension. I sat up on my side of the bed and began to rock. Slowly at first, then with increasing vigor. Pretty soon the bed frame was creaking, the springs squeaking. Then the giant rosary beads began to knock against the headboard. *Clank, clank, clank.* Even Jenny would have to admit this was funny. Here we were, freshly minted newlyweds in my parents' very Catholic bed, not having sex but making noises that would make it sound like we were. Hilarious! At any moment I fully expected Jenny to burst out laughing.

Suffice it to say, Jenny did not burst out laughing. She did not grin or smile or even nod. What she did was leap out of bed so quickly I thought for a moment that my mother might have left hot coals in the sheets. I then spent the next hour trying to convince my bride that walking back to Florida in the middle of the night was not practical. I eventually coaxed her back into my parents' bed, where we slept with four feet of empty mattress between us and nary a squeak or creak heard all night.

The next morning, after hurried good-byes, we began our trip south, the backseat and trunk filled with wedding gifts. We were nearly to Georgia before Jenny found it in her heart to forgive me, not only for the simulated sex sounds but, more important, for failing to take her side against my mother. I promised her then and there that she would never again have to sleep in my parents' bed.

Chapter 23

———

We were barely back in Florida as husband and wife when we began shopping for a house to call our own. Our rental place had its charm, but something felt different now, and we ached to put down roots. With marriage came a sense of security and permanence we both found reassuring. Jenny and I had insisted we did not need a marriage certificate to be fully committed to each other, that the wedding was just a formality, but we were both surprised at how much marriage changed our dynamic. For the first time since meeting, we each knew the other wasn't going anywhere. No one would be running off alone for the next job opportunity or fellowship. This was our life now, a life together. The prospect of cosigning away thirty years of it to a bank mortgage no longer felt terrifying.

Just one block away on a much prettier street, we found a small bungalow for sale. Unlike our rental house, it was meticulously kept, with a lush lawn surrounded by exotic tropical plantings. Jenny gasped aloud when we spotted it on our evening walk. "It's perfect," she said before even getting a peek inside.

"The green paint has to go, but otherwise it's just right."

Several weeks later, we walked out of a bank office with the deed and the keys to the front door—and headed straight to our new address: 345 Churchill Road. As soon as we were in the driveway, Jenny jumped out of the car and bolted for the door, key in hand.

"No, no! Wait! Don't go in! Wait for me!" I shouted after her. I wanted to do this right. I caught up with her on the porch, took the key from her, turned it in the lock, and swung the door open. Then, without a word of warning, I scooped Jenny into my arms and lifted her off her feet. She let out a surprised, joyful whoop.

"You goof!" she said, throwing her arms around my neck. "What are you doing?"

"Here we go," I announced. "Our first step into our very own home. Our new life." And with that I carried her across the threshold. We paused there for a moment just inside the entrance, silently reveling.

"Now put me down," Jenny said, "before you hurt yourself."

As the months passed, we turned the little bungalow into our own, repainting the walls, hanging Haitian artwork, and lifting the shag carpeting to discover burnished oak floors beneath. We planted a garden and brought home a behaviorally challenged Labrador retriever puppy we named Marley, who quickly wiggled his way into our hearts despite causing all sorts of havoc on a daily basis. Outside our bedroom window were a gardenia bush and a giant Brazilian pepper tree where wild parrots roosted, and each morning we awoke to the flowers' scent and the birds' chatter. Life seemed about as good as life could get.

Yet the strain with my parents remained. I had assumed all the bad blood that had preceded the marriage would wash away with the Catholic ceremony, but the wounds ran deep. Jenny had not gotten over how judgmental they had been, especially my mother's emotional prediction that our marriage was doomed to failure. In their moral certitude, she saw smugness and superiority and an implicit belief that she was somehow inferior, not quite the good Catholic wife they had prayed for their son to find. She was convinced they blamed her for pulling me away from the faith. "In their eyes, I'm your downfall," she said more than once.

My parents were hurt, too. Hurt by my belated honesty. Hurt by our rejection of their values. Hurt by Jenny's barely concealed contempt for everything they believed and by my acquiescence in that contempt. My parents' medieval interpretation of Catholicism, with its literal belief in guardian angels hovering over our shoulders to protect us from the dark agents of Satan, struck both of us as almost comically superstitious. The difference was that I had grown up with it and took it all in stride. Jenny, on the other hand, was unable to hide how bizarre she found it all. To her it was all hocus-pocus, no different from tossing salt over one's shoulder for good luck. She met their various expressions of faith with a sort of bemused bewilderment, usually accompanied by a grimacing cringe, which I knew my parents interpreted as mocking. In their eyes, her discomfort was disrespect.

On one of Jenny's first visits to my parents' house, shortly after we began dating, Mom cornered her in the kitchen and pulled from her apron pocket a small glass bottle with a hand-printed label. *Oh no,* I thought, *she's got the holy water.* I watched as she uncorked the bottle and moved closer to Jenny. *Put it away, Mom. Put it back in your apron. You barely know this girl yet.* Without a word of explanation, Mom wetted her thumb with the contents and made the sign of the cross on Jenny's forehead as she murmured, "In the name of the Father and of the Son and of the Holy Spirit." Dad looked on approvingly. As with most things they did, the act was well-intentioned. They wanted to bless this potential new member of our family and ensure that the Lord smiled on our new relationship. Jenny could not have looked more shocked had my mother clicked her heels and flown off on a broomstick. "It's just something old-fashioned Catholics do," I told her later, but that moment set the tone for many more to come.

Those days were far behind us now. With the help of my strong-willed wife, I had finally broken free from my parents' influence. I no longer felt the need to lie or obfuscate. I was unapologetically my own person now, officially in the category known as "non-practicing Catholic." But this freedom came at a cost. It was as though a wall of bulletproof glass had risen between my parents and me. I could still see and hear them through it, but it wasn't the same. We avoided religion, politics, and social issues such as abortion and gay rights—any hot-button topic that would expose the gaping rift in our values. They didn't ask; I didn't tell. They no longer gushed about the latest prayer hour they had organized at church, or inquired of me about Sunday Mass. Their faith and my lack of it had become our taboo topic. As it hovered over us, suffocating the relationship, we all pretended it did not exist.

More than anything, I think they realized they had met their match in Jenny and needed to clam up or risk losing me entirely. If my mother was Little Napoleon, then Jenny was her Waterloo. Mom seemed to understand she would not win this fight—not without losing her son as a casualty of war.

Soon enough there was another prize on the horizon that my parents did not want to risk losing a part of. Jenny was pregnant. The prospect of a grandchild excited them beyond words, and when the first pregnancy ended in a miscarriage, my parents grieved with us, even as they attributed the loss to God's mysterious plan. Soon enough we were expecting again, and in May 1992, we brought Patrick Joseph Grogan home from the hospital. We chose his middle name after Jenny's father, but I was happy to let my parents believe I was carrying on their Mary-and-Joseph tradition. A week later, Jenny's parents arrived to spend ten days with us, and the visit was comfortable and easy. Her mother took over the cooking and cleaning, and each day as I worked, Jenny and the baby would join her parents on an outing—to the mall, the Japanese gardens, even the beach, where Jenny could sit in the shade and nurse her newborn son.

Two days after Jenny's parents left, mine called from a camp-ground outside Atlanta where they had arrived the previous day in their motor home. They were on their way to see us and their first grandson, but the trip had another purpose: to make a pil-grimage to a farm in Conyers, Georgia, east of Atlanta, where apparitions of the Virgin Mary had been reported by the farm's owner. The Catholic Church refused to endorse the alleged sightings, but the farm woman's word was good enough for Mom and Dad.

"Our Blessed Mother says we all need to pray if we are to have any hope," Mom said. Then she put Dad on the phone, and their pilgrimage to the latest alleged miracle site made more sense to me. He had news to share. On the day Patrick was born, Dad's doctor had found a cancerous tumor on his prostate, and he was scheduled to begin radiation as soon as he returned from our place. He assured me the doctors were confident they could knock it into remission.

"Why didn't you tell me sooner?" I asked.

"You were having your first baby," he said. "I didn't want to put a damper on your joy."

"I never want to be kept in the dark, Dad," I said. "Whatever the news, and whenever you get it, I want you to share it with me, okay?"

"Fair enough," Dad said.

When they pulled up in their recreational vehicle the next evening, they both looked older and more fragile than I had remembered from just a few months earlier. For the previous dozen years, they had happily tooled all over the country and Mexico in their rolling home on a Chevrolet truck chassis, sight-seeing, visiting relatives, and making pilgrimages to various shrines and holy sites. But now I could see the strain on their faces, the weariness in their shoulders. At seventy-six, they were slowing down, and the rigors of long-distance road travel were clearly becoming too much for them. I realized with a tinge of sadness that this chapter of their lives would soon be coming to a close.

This was their first time visiting us since before we had decided to live together two years earlier, and I wanted it to go well. But they were barely in the door when I sensed Jenny's stress levels rising. As my mother cradled the baby, cooing over him, Jenny hovered nearby, clearly anxious. After dinner, she pulled me aside in the kitchen.

"Look," she whispered. "I don't want your mother trying one of her secret home baptisms on our baby." I dismissed her concerns as ridiculous, but they were not without foundation. When my mother was a schoolgirl, she would secretly baptize the non-Catholic children she babysat. Even as an adult, she saw nothing wrong with this and told the story with great affection. She had been taught that lay Catholics could perform an emergency baptism in certain circumstances. In her eyes, she was rescuing her young charges from an eternity in limbo, that perpetual waiting room between heaven and hell that the nuns taught us was the final destination for the world's millions of pagan babies. Jenny had heard the story, too, and now that she had her own child, she was unnerved by the possibility of her mother-in-law performing mysterious religious rituals over him without her knowledge.

"No one's performing any secret baptisms," I assured her, but I could see she wasn't convinced. She would not let Patrick out of her sight.

On the surface, my parents' visit was comfortable enough. Mom took over most of the cooking, and Dad puttered around the yard. We made easy small talk, sticking to our unspoken list of safe topics. We sat down to meals, and they made no attempt to pray over the food. They were in our home and clearly playing by our rules. Yet as their stay progressed, my mother increasingly picked up on Jenny's discomfort. At one point when she had me alone for a moment, she said, "Jenny acts like I've never held a baby before. What, does she think I'm going to drop him or something?"

"Chalk it up to new-mom jitters," I told her. "Don't take it personally, Mom."

From my father's glances, I knew he was offering her similar counsel when they were alone in their RV parked in the driveway. While I was at work, they wanted to free Jenny up so she could run errands or catch up on her sleep without having to worry about the baby. But Jenny deflected their offers, taking him wherever she went, whether it was to the store or into the bedroom for a nap. They couldn't help but feel snubbed.

Despite Jenny's worries, my parents had no intention of attempting an emergency baptism on their grandson, but that did not mean they had forgotten about the promise we had made when we married in the Catholic faith. One evening I returned home from work to find them alone in the living room. Jenny had taken the baby and gone shopping. "She didn't say when she'd be back," Mom said with a wounded look.

I had barely kicked my shoes off when they jumped at the opportunity to speak to me privately. "Say, we've been meaning to ask you," Dad began, and I braced for what I knew was coming. "Have you set a date for the baptism?"

"We're talking about it," I said. And we had been.

"The baptism is important," Dad said. "Without it, Patrick cannot have eternal salvation."

"It's something we're working on," I said.

"What's to work on?" Mom snapped. "He's already almost a month old. I don't know what you're waiting for."

"We plan to get to it," I said.

Her face grew grave. "You do know that if something, God forbid, were to happen to him, he couldn't go to heaven. He would be barred forever from entering our Lord's kingdom."

"I'm not too worried about that," I said.

"Well, you should be."

I felt the blood rising in my cheeks. "Do you really think God would cast aside an innocent infant just because his parents didn't get around to having him baptized?" I could not resist adding: "And do you really think a Catholic baby is somehow more sacred in God's eyes than a Jewish baby or a Muslim baby—or a baby that's nothing at all?" The Catholic belief that it was the "one true faith" had stuck in my craw for years.

"We're all born with original sin," Dad said. "By baptizing him, you'll wash that sin away and let Patrick become a child of God."

I held my tongue and stared at the floor.

"Let's all pray together," Mom suggested, and before I could protest, she grabbed my hand in one of hers and Dad's hand in the other. Dad closed the circle by gripping my free hand with his.

"Let us bow our heads and pray," he began. "In the name of the Father, and of the Son, and of the Holy Spirit."

I bowed my head as we recited the Lord's Prayer, but all I could think was that if Jenny walked in the door, her worst fears would be confirmed: secret incantations going on behind her back. I strained to listen for the sound of a car door slamming. Of the thousands of Our Fathers I had recited aloud, this one was the longest. When it finally ended, I said, "You really don't need to worry about it. Patrick will be baptized. We just need to do it at our own pace." Then I excused myself and went to the bathroom to splash water on my face.

The next morning, on the sixth day of what was to have been a ten-day visit, my parents announced they had decided to cut their visit short and leave the following day for home. The official reason was that South Florida's steamy weather was too uncomfortable for them, which I knew to be true. Mom especially wilted in even moderate heat and humidity. They were also worried about Dad's prostate cancer and the radiation regimen that awaited him. "I have to admit I'm not looking forward to what's coming," he said. "I might as well get back home and get it over with." But I knew the strain with Jenny had something to do with it as well.

Oddly, that evening was the most relaxed of the visit. Jenny and my mother were both noticeably at ease. They chatted amiably, and we all laughed as Mom told funny stories from her childhood and mine. I asked more about the cancer, and the planned bone scan that would tell him whether it had spread beyond his prostate. Dad said, "It's in God's hands. Whatever the Lord chooses for me, that's what it will be."

Mom chimed in: "We have dedicated our lives to spreading our Blessed Mother's message, and we still have a lot of work to do. I can't do it without your dad, so I know the Lord is going to give him many more healthy years with me."

"We still have too much work to do," Dad agreed. I knew they were not just putting on brave faces. This was what they believed. I marveled at their complete and unshakable faith.

The next morning Jenny packed them a picnic lunch and I helped load the motor home. Everything stayed upbeat until Dad leaned over to say good-bye to his grandson. As he stroked the back of his hand on Patrick's cheek, Mom began to weep. Her bullish confidence seemed to have vanished overnight. I imagined she was wondering if her husband would live long enough to see his grandson again.

The juxtaposition of my son's life just beginning and my father's in jeopardy was not lost on me, either. I wanted to say something profound to Dad, but the words did not come. Instead, I gave Mom a long hug and Dad the famous Grogan handshake, squeezing his hand in mine a little longer than I might have otherwise. I told them how much it meant to me that they had made the trip. As I watched them lumber off in the motor home, a pain seared my heart like an electric shock. Even though inside the house waited a wife who loved me and a beautiful son who would be my joy for the rest of my years, I could not help feeling oddly alone. Standing on the curb watching as they turned the corner, I saw it clearly: one family just beginning on life's voyage, another approaching journey's end.

In September, when Patrick was four months old, Jenny and I brought him to Michigan to be baptized in the sanctuary of Our Lady of Refuge. True to her word to Father David, Jenny said she would not stand in the way if that was what I wanted. And even though I no longer even pretended to be a practicing Catholic (when asked, my stock response was "I was *raised* Catholic"), it was what I wanted. I was hard-pressed to explain why. I was no longer a spiritual Catholic, and maybe I never had been, but I still considered myself Catholic. It was part of who I was and part of what I wanted my children to become. I knew that my parents—Dad in particular—considered this the exact wrong reason to baptize a child. The words *cultural Catholic*, with their embrace of the nostalgia of the faith without the faith itself, were anathema to him. Yet I could not deny that the term fit me.

Whatever my reasons, Mom and Dad rejoiced at the news of our decision. When I called home to tell them we would have him baptized at Refuge, they both immediately began planning the guest list.

"Um, Jenny and I were thinking we'd keep it small," I interrupted. "You know, just immediate family."

"Nonsense," Mom said. "We need to invite the neighbors. And the relatives. And the prayer group. I'll host the reception afterward."

"Mom," I said, the exasperation rising in my voice.

"What? You want to show off your baby, don't you? Besides, if you don't, people will start to wonder if there's something wrong with him."

"Wrong? Like he's the Hunchback of West Palm Beach?" I said.

"People talk," she said. "My grandson is perfect in every way, and I want to show him off."

More important, I suspected, she wanted to show off the fact that her grandson would no longer be a godless pagan baby. I diplomatically tried to temper her enthusiasm, telling her we needed to be respectful of Jenny's sensibilities as the mother. "You don't want to spook her, Mom," I said.

"Why on earth would this spook anyone?" she responded. "By the way, now that you've started a family, don't you think it's time you think about returning to Mass again?"

In the end, I won a few concessions, but Mom largely got what she wanted. Jenny repeated that this was my event, and she was going to stay out of it, which mostly she did.

Father Joe's lifelong love of Lucky Strikes had finally caught up with him, and he had died of cancer the previous year, slipping away peacefully in Marijo's former bedroom, where my parents had nursed him around the clock in his final months. But Father Vin remained healthy and vital, living in a log cabin in the Michigan woods, and he happily agreed to come out of retirement to officiate.

We asked Rock and his wife to be the godparents, and they drove in from Chicago for the big day. As they held Patrick in their arms, Father Vin launched into the rites of baptism, a surprisingly large part of which involved driving the devil from our baby's tarnished soul.

I knew it was going to be hard on Jenny when Father Vin announced to the thirty or so people gathered in the sanctuary that he was going to start off with "a prayer of exorcism."

"Almighty Father," Father Vin prayed, "you sent your holy son into the world to cast out the power of Satan, prince of evil, and to rescue man from the kingdom of darkness. We pray for this child to set him free from original sin and make him a temple for your whole spirit to dwell within him." From the side of my eye I could see Jenny's mouth tighten.

"Do you reject sin?" Father Vin asked in a clear voice, beckoning us to answer on Patrick's behalf and our own.

As a group, we responded, "I do." Jenny sat motionless, a look of quiet distress spreading across her face.

"Do you reject the glamour of evil?"

"I do."

"Do you reject Satan, father of sin, prince of darkness?" Jenny's hands, resting on the pew, tightened into ashen fists. The thought of an exorcism being held over her precious infant was too much for her. I imagined she was waiting for Patrick's head to start spinning on its neck like Linda Blair's did in *The Exorcist,* and I could tell she was fighting the urge to grab her baby and bolt for the exit.

I leaned in close until my lips rested against her ear. "Lamaze breathing," I whispered. "Quick, shallow breaths. Blow it away." I made little puffing sounds. "We're almost done."

Three times, Father Vin splashed water over Patrick's head as he chanted, "I baptize you in the name of the Father, and of the Son, and of the Holy Spirit." He used his thumb to rub sacred oils onto our son's forehead, chest, and back in the sign of a cross and placed a starched linen bib on him to signify his purification from original sin.

"Patrick Joseph, you have become a new creation," my uncle pronounced. "I claim you for Christ our savior by the sign of the cross."

Then it was over. The neighbors and relatives crowded around to coo over Patrick. Father Vin playfully hoisted his great-nephew in the air and congratulated him for uttering barely a squawk during the ceremony. "You're a Christian now," he said. "All baptized."

Off to the side, I slipped my arm around Jenny and rubbed her back.

"That Satan is so far out of here, he's halfway to Pluto by now," I said, trying to make her laugh. "Father Vin kicked Satan's ass! If Patrick takes the wrong path in life, we won't have the devil to blame."

She gave me a little smile.

"You okay?" I asked.

"I'm okay," she said. "Definitely ready for a beer."

"Me, too," I agreed. "Maybe a couple." And on the way home for Mom's punch-and-cookie reception, I made a quick detour to the party store on the corner where Tommy and I used to loiter and bought a twelve-pack.

Chapter 24

Thirteen months after Patrick's baptism, Jenny and I welcomed another member into our family. We baptized him Conor Richard, but this time we did it on our own turf, at the local parish in West Palm Beach where Father Beady Eyes had coached us on the rhythm method. It was a group ceremony, with several babies being baptized together, and the priest was more subdued than my uncle about exorcising Satan from the souls of the innocent. Because of the distance and my parents' advancing age, they did not attend, and that simplified matters, too. Jenny and I were both surprisingly relaxed, and later I sent photos to my parents so they would have proof their second grandchild, too, had been accepted into God's embrace.

Then came our daughter, Colleen Ruth, and our family was officially complete. We were five now, and it felt right. As with Conor, we had her baptized in a group ceremony at the church near our new home in Boca Raton. This time there wasn't even a priest present; a married deacon handled the duties. My aging parents could rest easy at last, knowing their grandchildren were no longer destined to spend eternity in God's waiting room. I felt I had done my duty and could relax.

The Lord apparently still had more work for Dad to do, as Mom had predicted, because he banished Dad's prostate cancer with the same vigor Father Vin had used to banish Satan. After several rounds of radiation therapy, his doctors pronounced the cancer obliterated and told him, "You'll die of something else before this ever comes back." He attributed his good fortune to the power of prayer and returned to his robust ways.

The Lord must have had more work for Mom, too. The year after Colleen's birth, Mom's cardiologist determined that her arteries were almost completely blocked. She was just one over-exertion away from a stroke or heart attack. At the hospital, doctors tried to open the passages with shunts, but ended up rushing her into emergency open-heart surgery, from which she emerged, after a lengthy recovery, feeling better than she had in years. She no longer had to stop to catch her breath or pop nitro-glycerin pills to control palpitations. There was only one adverse side effect of the quadruple bypass surgery, and it was a major one. Doctors warned us that Mom might seem forgetful and mentally adrift for several weeks because of the amount of time she spent on an external heart pump during surgery, and they were right. What they had not predicted was that Mom's mind would never quite fully return, never quite be as sharp again. The day of her surgery marked the beginning of a long, gradual descent, barely noticeable at first, into memory loss.

She also struggled with debilitating arthritis, and as my mother grew more frail, Dad took on more and more of the household responsibilities—vacuuming, grocery shopping, even expanding his cooking repertoire. He still cut his own grass, shoveled his own driveway, trimmed his own hedges, and found time to regularly weed and water the flower beds around the church.

As a couple, my parents retreated more and more into their faith. Their friends were dropping around them on what seemed

a near-weekly basis, and their own close calls had given them a
deeper sense of their mortality. I had not thought it possible, but
with each year they became even more fundamentalist. With the
exception of the evening news, they no longer watched anything
on television except for EWTN, the Eternal Word Television Net-
work, founded by a scowling, scolding nun named Mother Angelica, whom they adored for her conservative screeds against
the depravity of society. In a modern world from which they increasingly felt estranged, Mother Angelica played to their sensibilities. With her black-and-white reduction of life's complexities,
she was the comforting anchor to their past. When Pope John
Paul II came to America, my parents sat glued to EWTN for days,
videotaping his every appearance and motorcade.

As our lives moved in their separate orbits, we fell into a
rhythm. My parents and I spoke on the phone every week or
two and exchanged cards on birthdays and anniversaries. Every
winter they would fly to South Florida to spend a week with us,
and every summer Jenny and I would load the kids in the minivan and drive the thirty hours to spend a week with them. Unlike
those earlier visits, they did not push any agenda, did not even
try to pray aloud before meals in our presence. Each morning
they would arise and slip out the door for Mass, not inviting us
or even telling us where they were going. Jenny and I would be
careful not to comment on their devotion to EWTN or the growing number of Virgin Marys populating the house. Jenny and
my mother had arrived at their own separate peace, finding a
common bond in the kids; nearly all their discussions stuck to
that neutral ground. Dad and I, too, hammered out a safe zone,
talking of careers, home repairs, and our shared love of gardening. I would help Dad with yard chores and take the kids to the
playground at Our Lady of Refuge and to The Lagoon to fish for
bluegills or the Harbor Hills beach to swim where Tommy, Rock,
Sack, and I had spent so many hours.

As we sat down for dinner on the screened porch one summer

evening, Colleen in a high chair, the boys kneeling on their wrought-iron seats so their chins would clear the glass tabletop, I asked without warning or forethought, "Grandpa, are you going to lead us in a prayer?" I'm not sure what brought the words to my lips, but I knew I wanted my children to at least experience a taste of that safe, ordered world I enjoyed at their age. And I wanted to give my parents permission to be themselves around their grandchildren. My father looked up at me and blinked a couple of times. It wasn't easy to surprise the old man, but I had managed. He missed just one beat, then raised his fingertips to his forehead in preparation of making the sign of the cross, and began, "In the name of the Father, and of the Son, and of the Holy Spirit." The boys followed his lead and did their best to bless themselves. "Bless us, oh Lord, and these thy gifts . . ." At the end, he ad-libbed, "And thank you, God, for blessing us with John and Jenny and our three beautiful grandchildren, and for bringing them safely home to see us." The kids joined their grandparents with a loud "Amen."

With the kids young, it was easy to pretend the question of their religious upbringing was settled. But soon enough Patrick arrived in second grade and at the age where he should have been preparing for his first confession and First Holy Communion. My parents waited in anxious silence for an announcement, but that was not going to happen. Not for him or for his younger brother or sister. In the years since Patrick's birth, Jenny and I had settled into a life wholly our own. Something about the heady responsibility of having three tiny lives in my hands helped me put my relationship with my own parents in perspective. My priorities were with Jenny and our children now, and I embraced my new role as husband, father, and home owner. I was who I was, and as Dr. Adams the marriage therapist had counseled me several years earlier, it was now up to my parents to accept their son, or not, for the man he had become. I could tell they were trying their best to do that.

I gradually grew more comfortable in my skin as a nonpracticing Catholic, one with no particular animosity for the religion but also one who disagreed with enough of its teachings to know I did not belong. For as long as I could remember, one of Dad's favorite targets of antipathy was that certain kind of Catholic who chose Church rulings to obey or ignore as if they were options on a menu. There were few people on earth Dad held in more contempt than these cafeteria Catholics. "Doggone it all anyway," he would carp. "These people pick and choose what they want to believe like they are at the drive-thru window at McDonald's."

For all our disagreements over religion, on this we were in accord. So many of my contemporaries called themselves practicing Catholics when in actuality they were practicing only what they wanted. They embraced the feel-good aspects while conveniently disregarding whichever of the Church's hierarchical edicts they did not like. They might practice birth control, support abortion rights, roll their eyes at the Church's condemnation of homosexuality, and question why women were banned from the priesthood, and yet they still called themselves Catholics. I knew Mom and Dad were deeply disappointed in my choices, but at least they couldn't accuse me of picking and choosing off the Catholic prix fixe menu.

The clergy child sex abuse scandal that would rock the foundations of the Catholic Church was just beginning to come to light as my boys were entering grade school, and this vaporized what little was left of my crumbling faith. The actions of the pedophile priests against the most vulnerable and defenseless members of their flocks were sickening enough, but even more so were the calculated efforts of their superiors to silence the victims and bury the truth. I knew that for every predatory priest and every amoral bishop protecting him there were hundreds practicing their vocation with Christlike piety. Priests like my two uncles. Yet the blossoming scandal screamed of the highest order of hypocrisy. The molesters and their protectors perpetrated their evil while holding themselves up each Sunday in their snowy white vestments as the embodiment of Christ. They were the ultimate cafeteria Catholics, but I would never say that to my father. I could only imagine how devastated he was by the spreading scandal, though he would eventually chalk it up to "a few bad apples" corrupted by liberal elements within the Church and the depraved culture of modern society. I could only bite my tongue. As I put it in one late-night phone call to Tim, who unlike me had fallen away from the Church with a great deal of lingering anger, "It's a good time to take a break from being a Catholic."

On our own, Jenny and I set out to do our best to raise our children as moral and ethical beings, to instill in them goodness and compassion and generosity. We would not be seeking the help of any organized religion.

Mom and Dad breathed not a word. They dared not. As each child reached and missed Catholic benchmarks—first confession, first communion, confirmation—they kept their lips sealed. Jenny had made it clear that she would not tolerate any more meddling, and there had been enough flare-ups and power struggles that they knew she was not bluffing. They had gradually accepted that I shared her resolve. They weren't going to jeopardize access to their son and grandchildren by opening their mouths again.

Instead, they began to mail us things. First came a giant, heavyweight family Bible with gold-edged pages and a note encouraging us to make it a central part of our lives. Next came a wall-size crucifix and a note suggesting we display it prominently in our home. Then came a statue of the Virgin Mary and a thick treatise explaining the Catholic catechism. There were children's prayer books and Bible stories, and birthday gifts of rosaries.

Finally, a copy of *Catholic Parenting* magazine arrived with a handwritten letter from Dad saying he had bought us a one-year subscription. "Hopefully you and Jenny will find a few things in each issue that will be helpful," he wrote.

We had been silent on the subject for too long, and I knew

I owed him my thoughts. Just because my parents no longer badgered me didn't mean they had stopped worrying. In a letter thanking him for the subscription, I wrote, "I know we're not raising the kids quite the way you would like, but I want you to know that we put a lot of thought and energy into the spiritual side of their upbringing. We are working hard, and to the very best of our ability, to raise them as moral, principled people. We're doing it our own way, but our end goal, I think, is the same as yours."

A few months earlier, I had joined the *Philadelphia Inquirer* as a metropolitan columnist, giving my unvarnished opinions on a variety of topics. It was the same basic job I'd had in my last several years at the Fort Lauderdale paper, but with one big difference: the columns were now posted online. Mom and Dad were able to read each one the same day it was published, and Dad especially followed my work with zeal. I was past the point of trying to shelter him from my views, which in my column included harsh indictments of the Catholic Church over the child abuse cover-up. Still, I felt the need to explain.

"As you may have gathered from my columns, I'm a bit jaded about the institutions of men—the political, judicial, corporate, and, yes, religious," I wrote to him. "But that doesn't mean I'm jaded about what the institutions represent—democracy, justice, enterprise, faith. We humans are frail and flawed, and it goes against my grain to have one group of flawed humans trying to tell another group of flawed humans how to live. Besides, you know I'm not much of a joiner. So I'm picking my way delicately through the minefield of parenthood on my own, trying to steer the right path, making course corrections along the way. All I can promise is that I will keep an open mind."

I concluded: "I'm sorry for the pain I know I've caused you and Mom, but I know you respect that each of us must follow our own moral compass. Please, try not to worry too much, which I know is easier said than done. You have been a great father to me. I'm trying hard to be the same to my kids. Thanks for teaching by example."

Dad did not respond for two months. When he did, he apologized for the delay and explained that caring for Mom, who was becoming increasingly dependent on him for even the most basic needs, "is becoming more and more of a full-time job." He added, "I am not complaining. I thank the good Lord that I am able to take care of Ruthie, and I pray that I will always be able to do so."

Then he turned his pen to what I had written.

"I was pleased and comforted to hear that you and Jenny are working hard on giving the children day-to-day guidance in spiritual matters so that Christian principles will be the foundation of their value system as they grow up." He said he understood our desire to try to do it without the help of organized religion. "However, I sincerely hope that, when the time is right," he added, "you will introduce them to the beauty of their Catholic heritage."

"I haven't given up on the Church, but I do feel the need to proceed with caution regarding it," I responded. "I know you're praying for Jenny, the kids, and me, and I really do appreciate that. We can use all the help we can get."

And I meant it.

PART THREE

Coming Home

Chapter 25

That winter, a cherished life came to a crashing end back home in Harbor Hills. The giant maple tree that for decades had dominated the backyard of my parents' house had fallen in a blizzard. Dad called to break the news as if we had lost a family member. The tree had self-seeded there when I was a toddler and grown tall and magnificent over the years, shading many a cookout and giving us kids sturdy branches to climb.

"The end of an era," Dad said and called a tree service to come remove it, stump, roots, and all.

As spring neared, Dad looked out the living-room window, and where once he had seen loss he now saw possibility. "Say," he said in one of our weekly chats, "I'm thinking now that the maple tree is gone and the sun can get through again, that maybe that spot would be a nice place for a little flower garden. Something Mother could sit and look out on."

For all its magnificence, the maple had been a flora bully, hogging water and nutrients and blocking life-giving sunlight from reaching the soil, creating an inhospitable zone where only a few tough clumps of grass and wild mint could hang on. With its demise, the patch of earth was again available for a new generation of plant life. "I thought maybe you could give me some ideas," Dad said.

When Jenny and I moved with the children to Pennsylvania in 1999, it was so I could try my hand as a gardening editor. I spent three years as editor of *Organic Gardening* magazine before realizing daily newspapers were where my heart lay and taking the job at the *Philadelphia Inquirer*. Dad was an accomplished gardener in his own right, but he mostly stuck to marigolds, petunias, and other tried-and-true annual flowers from the garden center, and he hoped I could steer him toward more interesting varieties.

I was thrilled to be able to help. My father was so self-sufficient, even at eighty-seven, that he did not give me many opportunities. Over the next several weeks, we discussed at length the merits of different plants, the strategy of mixing perennials with annuals for season-long color, and of choosing varieties of differing heights to give the garden three-dimensional breadth. I was enjoying the process enormously, partly because I loved gardening, but more, I realized, because it gave us a shared father-son project over which to bond, just like in my childhood with science fairs and home improvements.

One evening, after the snow had melted and the ground thawed, I grabbed my spade and a bushel basket and headed into my yard. At one garden bed, I stooped over and rooted around until I found the tiny spears of a dormant hosta poking through the mulch. With my shovel, I dug the plate-size root clump out and quartered it into four equal chunks. One I replaced in the hole, and the remaining three I wrapped in newspaper and placed in the basket. I moved on to the purple coneflower and repeated the process. Then to the brown-eyed Susans and bee balm, the phlox and daisies, the fragrant anise hyssop and the lustily prolific daylilies. Soon my basket overflowed with a variety of perennials Dad could pop into the ground and watch take root. One of a gardener's greatest joys is the joy of giving. It is an easy, painless act of generosity because of the garden's endless bounty, which reminded me of the miracle of the loaves and fishes we learned about in school: the more you shared, the more there was to share. Putting together this care package from my garden to Dad's pleased me greatly. I worked with a smile on my face.

A few days later when the box showed up on my parents' porch, Dad wasted no time in calling me. "Holy smokes!" he said. "What's all this? It's like Christmas in March!" It was the most excited I had heard him in a long time. I had not sent him anything he could not have ordered from a nursery, but he acted as though I had shared exotic riches from a far distant land. "This is fantastic!"

"That'll get your garden started," I said. "You can fill it in with some annuals later."

And that is what my father did, hoeing up the circle where the maple had stood, working compost and leaf mulch into the soil, and tamping in the dormant plant divisions. My father's exercise was a vote of confidence in the future. From the lifeless brown clumps of roots would sprout new life. And Dad would eventually realize his sweet and selfless wish: that the woman to whom he was so deeply devoted could sit on the porch in the fresh air, her daydreams adrift on the breeze, and soak in the garden's soothing presence. The garden would rise and flower and stand as a modest testament to nature's exquisite exuberance and sweeping rhythms, and to its unsentimental resilience. For forty years, the old tree had graced our yard, and now in its absence a new generation was about to take root, one that would not have been possible had the towering giant remained. Seasons change, trees fall, seeds sprout. From death and decay spring new wonders. Life moves irrevocably forward.

Like garden plants, the four Grogan children had taken root in various ways and places. Marijo had become a social worker outside Ann Arbor and spent her days helping hard-luck families piece together broken lives. Tim was an economist working for a business magazine in New York City. After earning an MBA and working for a time as a financial analyst, Michael had become incapacitated with a bevy of ill-defined and energy-sapping symptoms that doctors eventually diagnosed as chronic fatigue syndrome. He quit his job in Southern California and moved back in with Mom and Dad to begin a long, slow recuperation.

I was the only one of the four to have married. Marijo, like me, had drawn our parents' disapproval when she moved in with her longtime partner and soul mate, a British psychologist named Kent, forgoing marriage and instead opting for an informal commitment ceremony in the woods behind their home. Tim, too, had lived with a woman for several years before the relationship soured. He and Michael remained unattached, and the four of us joked about the amount of prayer energy Mom and Dad burned imploring God to find them good Catholic girls to settle down with.

The chasm religion had cleaved between my parents and me brought competing emotions: the heady feeling of liberation tempered by the dull, aching sadness—sometimes palpable, sometimes barely registered, but present every day—of knowing I had caused my parents so much heartache. In their own ways, I suspected, Marijo, Tim, and Michael had each struggled with a similar conflict, but it was something none of us talked much about. Our parents' expectations were difficult to meet, and we all knew how much it meant to them that we follow in their very Catholic footsteps.

As I moved through my forties and watched my children grow from toddlers into lanky preteens, life seemed to finally find its equilibrium. Mom had survived open-heart surgery and a hip replacement. Dad had beaten prostate cancer, and appeared to have struck a truce with the leukemia discovered lurking in his bloodstream the previous year. Every four months he submitted a blood sample, and every four months the doctors returned the same report: status quo. My parents chugged on, day to day, finding comfort and joy in their faith and learning to accept that their children, to varying degrees, had not and would not. We were all thankful that Mom, with her memory and physical vigor waning, had Dad to care for her, which allowed them to stay in their home, living the independent life they so cherished. Neither of them could bear to consider a retirement community or, worse, assisted-living facility. With his abundant energy and sharp mind, Dad continued to astound all of us. Despite the sleeping leukemia within him, his only apparent concession to age was half an aspirin and a thirty-minute nap each afternoon.

In addition to all his other duties, he took on one other role that had traditionally been my mother's—the family's worrier-in-chief. As Mom's mind gradually let go, drifting like clouds across a wind-whipped sky, so did her matriarchal willpower and seemingly superhuman capacity for fretting about those she loved. That job was now Dad's alone.

Our lives, connected by blood yet now so clearly separate and distinct, marched on. Some days, the good ones, I could believe they would continue this way forever.

Chapter 26

Not long after Dad got his new garden planted, he called, but it was not to talk about plants. "Say, John," he began, "I wanted to give you a little update on my leukemia."

I could hear something in his voice, buried beneath the calm and confidence. Something that sounded like fear.

"Everything's still holding steady, right?" I asked.

"That's just it," Dad said. "The last blood test has the doctor concerned. My platelets seem to be dropping. Just a little, but he doesn't want to see that."

I had only the vaguest notion of platelets, and he explained to me what the oncologist had explained to him, that they were the blood's clotting agents, produced in vast quantities by cells in the bone marrow. Platelets coursed through the blood like microscopic masons with buckets of cement, ready to rush to the site of any injury and quickly mortar the wound. They are what save all of us from bleeding to death. In a healthy adult, 150,000 to 450,000 platelets swim in a tiny microliter of blood.

If those levels drop to 20,000 or below, the patient is at serious risk of bleeding uncontrollably from even a minor bruise or cut.

"But I'm not anywhere near that," Dad said. "I'm just a little on the low side of normal." He said the doctor wanted to see him every two months instead of every four. "He just wants to watch it more closely, that's all."

We danced around the topic a little more, both advancing the fiction that the dropping platelets were really no cause for alarm. Dad wasn't even going to tell Mom. He was fiercely protective of her, and with her mind drifting as it was, he was afraid she would have a hard time grasping anything but the word *cancer*. One thing she knew from experience—from her father, several siblings, and countless friends—was that cancer seldom carried a happy ending. He didn't want to worry her.

That's when I asked, "Dad, do you want me to come home?"

"Oh heavens no," he answered without hesitation, as if I had just proposed sending him on a transatlantic cruise or some other indulgence of mind-boggling extravagance. "You have your own family to worry about, and your job. You've got your hands full. Jenny needs you there. Besides, there's nothing to do here. I feel fine. I'm keeping up on everything. We're just going to watch this thing a little more closely."

"Okay," I said. "But you'll call me if you need me, right?"

He assured me he would.

"You'll be in all of our thoughts, Dad," I said, groping for the right words.

"John?"

A moment of silence hung on the phone line.

"And maybe your prayers, too?"

"My thoughts and prayers, Dad," I said. "My thoughts and prayers."

· · ·

For the next six months, Dad maintained his routine, even as his platelet counts trickled in the wrong direction with each new blood test. His oncologist told him about a newly approved chemotherapy regimen that had shown some early promise against Dad's form of leukemia. He asked my father to consider the treatment as a preemptive move while the leukemia was still largely inactive, but when the doctor described the debilitating side effects and told my father he would be laid up for several weeks, too weak to take care of himself or my mother, Dad recoiled. The decision to submit to the treatment was a huge one because it would mean crossing the line for the first time from independent living to a life totally reliant on others. For Dad, that would be like voluntarily stepping off a cliff.

"I think it makes more sense to just keep watching it," he said. "As long as it's still in check, I don't see the sense in trying anything that drastic."

Then on October 25, 2004, a Sunday morning, came another phone call. This time it was my brother Michael. "I'm calling from the hospital," he said. "It's Dad."

With his training as a financial analyst, Michael tended to see the world as numbers guys do—in binary code, absolutes without shadings of gray. He had been living at home for more than a decade as he slowly recovered from his maddening case of chronic fatigue syndrome, my parents nursing him for years just as they did when he was their baby. Now he was stronger, though still easily fatigued, and it was his turn to be there for them. Michael's nature was to get right to the point.

"Dad's been admitted," he said. "They're afraid if they send him home he could bleed to death."

Bleed to death? I struggled to process the words. "Start at the beginning," I said.

The night before, Michael had come home from a play to find my father in the bathroom hemorrhaging blood from his rectum. "Buckets of blood," my brother said. Dad had packed towels around himself to try to stanch the gush, but the towels just became sodden. The blood kept coming. At the emergency room, a test showed that my father's platelet count had nose-dived. I remembered the magic number of 20,000. Anything below that and you were at risk of spontaneously erupting into uncontrolled, potentially fatal bleeding. My father's count, Michael reported, was down to 1,500.

"Fifteen thousand, you mean," I corrected.

"No," Michael said. "Fifteen hundred."

The bleeding had erupted at the site of an old injury—a tissue burn caused by the radiation Dad received to treat his prostate cancer a decade earlier. "The doctors cauterized it and got the bleeding to stop," Michael said. "But they can't let him go home. If the bleeding starts again, they're afraid we couldn't get him back here in time."

"So they'll give him more platelets, right?" I asked.

"That's the plan," he said. "Until they get the platelet count up to twenty thousand, he's not coming home."

My mind bounced from one thought to the next, the consequences, immediate and distant, cascading around me. Dad's alarming drop of platelets meant he could begin hemorrhaging at any moment. But equally grave, it also meant the sleeping dragon that was his leukemia was awake now. Even if doctors pumped him up with a steady transfusion of platelets, wouldn't these new recruits, too, eventually meet the same fate? I felt a slow, sickening hollow spread through my stomach.

And then there was Mom. Mom, who could no longer care for herself. Mom with medications so complex they required an engineer's flowchart. Mom, who would forget to eat without my father gently badgering her. Mom, who was utterly helpless without him.

"So, Mike," I asked, "has Dad said anything about Mom?"

"Not yet," he said. "We haven't had a chance to talk."

Michael, as it turned out, had dropped my father at the emergency room and, at Dad's insistence, returned home to be with Mom. My father did not like to leave her alone in the house for even a half hour, worried that she could tumble down the stairs or fall in the bathroom or turn on a stove burner and walk away. My brother was now doing his best to shuttle between house and hospital, trying to take care of my mother and be there for my father. It had only been a few hours, and already it was clear how impossible it would be for him to sustain.

Thanks to my father's stamina, my parents had managed to live independently into their late eighties, still in the same house. Now, that independent lifestyle was in jeopardy. I had known for years that all it would take to bring their house of cards crashing down was one small mishap—a broken hip, a chronic illness, even a bum knee that would knock my father out of commission. It appeared that day had arrived. And yet I am an optimist by nature, and denial, in the face of a harsh reality, can be a sweet narcotic. I kept telling myself that the platelet transfusions would stick, that the dragon would return to hibernation, that in a best-case scenario, Dad could return to normal and hold things together for another year. Another year might be all he needed.

On my last visit home, I had found a card on my mother's bed table from the previous Christmas. Inside it was my father's handwriting. "Dearest Ruth," it read. "I thank the Lord every day for giving you to me, and for watching over us all these years. My prayer now is that He will bless you with peace, happiness, and healing, and that I will always be able to take care of you. I love you, Ruthie. Richard."

As a child, I thought my father was invincible, a sort of humble superhero whom nothing could hurt and no one could take from me. I grew up convinced he would live forever. That fantasy was long past, but I wanted him to have a shot at his last wish. I wanted him to be able to be there for the only true love of his life as long as she needed him. Like Dad, I didn't want her to have to experience a life without him.

. . .

Michael and I stayed in touch throughout the day, and by mid-afternoon my father had been admitted to a private room in a brand-new wing of the hospital. The switchboard patched me through, and Dad picked up.

"Hey there," I said. "What's the big idea getting sick on us?"

Dad laughed. "I guess I didn't have enough on my plate," he said. "I needed something else to keep life interesting."

"Well, you sure did that," I said.

His voice sounded as strong as ever, and he assured me he was feeling fine, no worse at all for the tremendous blood loss of the previous sixteen hours. He felt so good, in fact, he said it was like he was on vacation. "You should see the room," he gushed. "I feel like I'm at a resort! It's just like a hotel. The docs just want to keep an eye on me. This will be my excuse to get a good rest and catch up on my reading."

He didn't want me to worry. He never wanted any of us to worry. In his eyes, it was the father's job to worry, not to be worried over. "I really couldn't feel better," he repeated. "I almost feel guilty taking up this big, beautiful room when there are so many sick people who could really use it."

"Dad," I said, feeling my way carefully, "I'm thinking maybe I'll come home for a few days."

"Oh, you don't need to do that," he said. "Heck, I hope to be back home in a couple days. Mike said he'll keep an eye on Mom until I get back, and until then I'm just going to lie here and relax. We've got everything under control. You don't need to come home for me. Really."

"Okay, but you'll let me know, won't you?" I said. "You'll let me know when you need me there."

The next day on the phone, Dad told me his leukemia specialist had visited him and planned to start him on the newly approved chemotherapy course that Dad had earlier rejected. The time for procrastinating was over. The treatments would last for six weeks and would be coupled with a strong course of steroids, which he said would help his platelets rebuild. "The doctor says it'll knock me back a good bit," Dad said, "but he's hoping it will send the leukemia into remission so I can get out of here."

The chance for a preemptive attack on the sleeping monster had passed. Now it was awake and on its feet—and ready for a good fight.

Chapter 27

My father's stay in the tastefully decorated private room at Saint Joseph Mercy Hospital in Pontiac would not be quite the luxury getaway he had at first imagined. He had been in the room only a day when his specialist, an oncology hematologist named Dr. Franklin, ordered a spinal tap, a procedure Dad described in his understated way as "not the most pleasant experience of my life." The purpose of the procedure was to extract a sample of bone marrow to better learn how aggressively the leukemia was advancing. The marrow was where the leukemia's secrets lurked. The worst part was not the tap itself, but what came after: the waiting. Dr. Franklin promised he would be back in touch by midafternoon, and Dad lay in his room alone, watching the clock, summoning the emotional strength to receive whatever prognosis awaited him. I called midafternoon, and he told me, "I'm just sitting here waiting to hear back. Now they're saying it won't be till the end of the day."

Dad regrouped and braced himself for the dinner hour. But his meal arrived and with it a message that Dr. Franklin had gone home for the night. A nurse assured him the doctor would drop by on his rounds first thing in the morning, and Dad spent a mostly sleepless night waiting for the sun to rise. Dawn came, but not the doctor. Another nervous day of waiting. The string of delays for a man whose life was on the line came close to feeling like criminal torture, the kind of psychological abuse banned by civilized societies. With each phone call Dad sounded slightly more desperate. "They're not telling me anything," he said. "I'm just sitting here." He was hoping the results would show the leukemia holding steady and the steroids and transfusions working together to boost his platelet count so he could go home. "I'm ready to get out of here," he said.

When Dr. Franklin finally showed up, it was not with the report my father had hoped. First he delivered the brighter news: Dad's platelet counts were indeed creeping up, from 1,500 to 4,000, still dangerously low but moving in the right direction. No longer was the doctor setting a specific threshold before he would release my father; now he simply said he wanted to see "continued significant improvement" before he'd consider letting Dad out of the hospital. The second half of his report, we later learned, was what had caused the delays. Dr. Franklin had sought a second opinion to be certain of his findings: the leukemia was spreading aggressively, rampaging unchallenged through my father's bloodstream. That new chemotherapy regimen, the one he had broached with my father months earlier, was still Dad's best shot at bringing the disease to its knees, he said, and they would begin immediately. Later that day, as Dad described it to me on the phone, we both agreed it sounded straightforward enough. Six quick, painless treatments one week apart. And if his platelet count continued to rise, he could go home and receive them as an outpatient. Other than that, he just needed to rest and let the powerful meds do their job. The chemo, the doctor had explained, would have a cumulative effect and each week would grow more powerful in its counterattacks on the cancer cells. The side effects would also increase exponentially, the doctor warned, but that was the cost of admission. "I guess I'm not going to be feeling too great for a while," Dad said. But six weeks and it would be behind him.

"Let's talk about something else," he said.

"Well, I have some news," I said, pausing to consider how to transition from life-threatening disease to a development that was the highlight of my career. "You know that book I've been working on?" I asked.

"The one about you and Marley?" he said.

"Well, guess what? I sold it over the weekend. To a publisher in New York."

"No kidding," Dad said, his voice brightening. "Give me all the details."

Over the months, I had sketched out the basic premise for him in our weekly phone calls. *Marley & Me* was my own story, the story of starting out with Jenny as newlyweds and the incorrigible Labrador retriever that crashed into our lives and changed the family we would become.

Almost from the first day we brought him home, Marley had proved himself to be unlike any pet we had ever owned. He lived life in a big way, with verve and insouciance and a boundless joy seldom seen in this world. Quite early on, I discovered he was a good source of story fodder. At dinner parties or around the watercooler at work, and later in my newspaper column, I began recounting Marley's over-the-top antics and misdeeds, and I found they made people laugh. But Marley was more than just a punch line; he had grown to become an important member of our family, shaping us even as we tried to bend him to our will. Like most journalists, I had dreamed for years of one day writing a book, but I always searched for a topic from other people's lives—something suitably important to merit a book-length examination. Only gradually did I begin to realize that the book I was meant to write was quite literally lying at my feet. And so, in early 2004, not long after saying good-bye to Marley for the last time, I sat down and began to write.

While I was working on the book in the early morning hours before my regular job, my conviction at times faltered. Some days I honestly could not imagine anyone other than friends and family wanting to read it. Dad's confidence, however, had never waned. He was always my biggest cheerleader.

"Six publishing houses bid on it, Dad," I said.

"I'll be doggoned," he said.

How ironic, I thought, that I would receive some of the most exciting news of my life within hours of my father receiving some of the worst of his. My insides were a scramble of mixed emotions.

"That's great, John," he said before signing off. "That's really, really great."

We talked by phone every day. I filled him in on the most recent book developments and he gave me the latest medical update. The first round of chemo, he reported, had gone fine and he was feeling no side effects. "It was no big deal," he said. The steroids, on the other hand, were making him agitated, animated—and uninhibited in sharing his opinions. He spent his days in his hospital room reading the papers, watching CNN, and growing more and more worked up about the impending presidential election. As far as I knew, Dad never voted for a Democrat in his life, but he mostly kept his political views to himself. This election was different. He loathed his fellow Catholic John Kerry, seeing him as the manifestation of secular godlessness and liberalism that was ruining this country. Dad began firing off emotional letters to all four of his kids. He knew we all leaned liberal and that we considered George W. Bush's first term a disastrous mix of mind-boggling incompetence and blustery hubris. But the election, he had convinced himself, was not about ideology or competence but rather good and evil, faith and cynicism. In a letter dated October 26, he wrote, "This is a fight for the soul of America! Morality and spiritual values versus our decadent culture. If Kerry wins, our nation will be following the path of the Roman Empire to destruction."

He asked Michael to mail copies to each of us. My brother added a note of his own: "He's been sitting in his hospital bed with nothing to do but watch the news, and his blood has been boiling. I think it's quite a good sign that he has summoned the energy to write this note that expresses the passion of his convictions—all while waiting for news on his personal fate. Please take these comments in that light." I did, and so did Marijo and Tim.

As children we grew up with our parents' conservative views as a given, the uncompromising fixed prism through which we viewed the world. Abortion was murder; birth control insulted God's will; sexuality was a sacred procreative duty reserved solely for the sacrament of marriage; homosexuality was an abomination. As adults, each of us, to varying degrees, had rejected those tenets. The terrain was so emotionally fraught that we had learned years earlier to simply dance around it. If Dad needed to vent about the election, that was fine with us. It all seemed so immaterial to what really mattered in our family. Bush or Kerry, who cared? We just wanted our father to get better and get home.

When Dad was not raving about politics and the decline of Western civilization, he was working through a checklist of personal business that had suddenly taken on new importance. From his hospital bed, he talked to his lawyer, updated his will, and named Michael the executor of his estate and his medical guardian in case he became incapacitated and could no longer make his own decisions. He also filed a document with the hospital giving clear instructions about the topic none of us was prepared to discuss: end-of-life decisions. True to his Catholic faith, he wanted nothing that would unnaturally shorten his life. But he was also clear that when his time came, when all hope was gone, he did not want heroic or extraordinary measures to keep him alive. He would fight this thing with all he had, but nothing more. He was certain in his conviction of heaven and hell, and he had done his best to lead a good and moral life. When the call came to leave this life for an eternity in heaven, he was not about to say, "Sorry, Lord, not quite ready yet."

There was one last piece of unfinished business: Ruthie. Dad was figuring out that even if he were allowed to return home, he would be in no shape to care for himself, let alone his wife. After less than a week in the hospital, he could already see Michael becoming overwhelmed as Mom's full-time caregiver. It was just too much for him—the pills, the meals, the linen changes, and pull-up diapers. That was one aspect of my mother's care he just could not bring himself to do: help with her bathroom needs. In the past, she had stubbornly rejected the idea of visits from nursing aides. Her mind might be drifting, but her modesty was firmly intact, and she was not going to allow a stranger to see her naked. Marijo, who lived more than an hour away, was driving out regularly around her job as a social worker to take care of Mom's hygiene needs. It was not sustainable. Dad knew this; we all did.

From his hospital bed, Dad finally did the one thing he had fiercely resisted for so many years as Mom declined: he requested an application to Lourdes Nursing Home. It was a lovely nursing home, or as lovely as these places get, run by Catholic nuns and situated on a bluff overlooking Watkins Lake outside Pontiac, less than a mile from the original homestead where the first of our Grogans had settled after arriving from County Limerick, Ireland, in 1850. Lourdes was where his mother had spent her last few years, and Dad was so grateful for the respectful care she received that he became a generous donor of both his money and time.

The truth was my mother should have been in a nursing home,

or at least an assisted-living facility, five years earlier, as her mind and vigor and continence left her. And no doubt she would have been if not for my father's energetic outpouring of care. He feared nursing homes like a deer fears fire. They were the last stop on life's trolley line, an admission that you were ready to relinquish all you had worked to build. Now he was seeing his options running out, at least for the short term. Independent living, that thing he cherished most, had been predicated on his ability to stay healthy and vigorous, able to mind all the details. He was the knight guarding the queen's castle, and now the invaders had robbed him of his sword and shield.

While he recovered from the debilitations of chemotherapy, he would need a place with full-time nursing care, not just for himself but for Mom, too. Lourdes, he told me, had one suite designed for married couples. It consisted of two small bedrooms, a sitting room, and a bathroom. A retired priest celebrated Mass in the chapel down the hall two mornings a week. "That would be ideal," he said. He portrayed it as a short-term solution until they could move back home. "Just until I'm back on my feet again," he said, but there was something in his voice that told me he knew what I knew: that nursing homes are rarely short-term.

A nursing home might be the solution, but admission could take months. Michael, still struggling with his chronic fatigue symptoms, clearly needed help with Mom. Tim was in New York, and I in Pennsylvania, both holding down full-time jobs. Marijo was self-employed with a full roster of clients. We exchanged nervous phone calls and e-mails, all with the same underlying question: what about Mom?

Over the years, from adolescence into adulthood, Tim was always more my friend than my brother. We traveled and camped together, hung out at each other's homes, played clunker rock 'n' roll together on our electric guitars, swigged beer, confided in each other about most everything, and over the years helped each other out of various scrapes. Even when he was a teenager trying desperately to assume the mantle of cool, he let me, the chubby, bespectacled brother six years his junior, tag along with him and his friends. My very first trip away from home without my parents was with him. I was a freshman in high school, he was a college student—and our favorite band of all time, The Kinks, was coming to Toronto. It was a five-hour drive, but we didn't care. We jumped in the family's green Chevrolet Nova and set off despite Dad's protests: "Doggone it all anyway! You can't just go driving halfway around the country to see a rock concert." We bought tickets from a scalper on the street and after the concert joined the surging scene on Yonge Street. That night, Tim secured us beds at the YMCA, and when an old man with a creepy glint in his eye began hovering around me, Tim swooped in and that was the last I saw of him.

I always assumed my brother would be a lifelong bachelor. After a couple of long relationships that had not worked out, he had settled into the single life in New York City, working long hours at his magazine and living in a series of small apartments. He marched through much of his forties and into his fifties alone. But the year before Dad got sick, Tim found himself seated on a commuter train beside a young woman from the Philippines en route to her job as a nanny. They struck up a conversation, then met the next day for coffee at Penn Station. A romance bloomed, and when Dad learned that Elizabeth had somehow convinced Tim to attend Easter Sunday Mass with her at Saint Patrick's Cathedral, he knew his prayers had been answered.

In August 2004, two months before he was hospitalized, Dad walked Elizabeth down the aisle of Our Lady of Refuge and gave her hand in matrimony to his eldest son. Father Vin officiated, and Michael and I shared best-man duties. Marijo was Elizabeth's maid of honor. Mom was in the front row, beaming, alongside Jenny and our kids. It was a happy day. Our whole family was together, something that had become a rarity as the years passed. Tim, the perennial bachelor, the one the family worried most about, had found a good woman, and they were off on their new life together.

My father adored Elizabeth. Unlike his own children, she was an unquestioning Catholic who accepted the Church's teachings and edicts just as he did, without reservation or parsing. Her traditional values were in lockstep with his, and he was convinced that God had brought her into his fallen-away Catholic son's life for a purpose. "This is no coincidence," he said after the first time he met her.

Now with him hospitalized and the question of Mom's care looming larger by the hour, it was Elizabeth who stepped forward. On November 3, 2004, less than three months after her wedding day and two weeks after Dad was admitted to the hospital, Elizabeth flew to Detroit to take over Mom's care. We were all grateful, but Dad saw it as more than simply the generous act of a good-hearted person. The Lord, he was convinced, had sent a guardian angel not only into Tim's life, but into his as well.

Chapter 28

Jenny had watched my hand-wringing mostly from the sidelines. This was my father, not hers, and she didn't want to interfere, but I could tell she was growing impatient with my dithering. Dad was entering his third week in the hospital, and still I procrastinated about flying home to see him. I kept waiting for the right opportunity, the best window. Maybe late November would be good. Maybe right after Christmas; wouldn't that cheer him up? Maybe after the New Year once we had the holidays behind us. Jenny couldn't hide her frustration. It was obvious what she would do if it were her father—she would have been on a plane weeks earlier.

Finally, one morning over coffee, she spilled out, "Will you wake up? What are you waiting for? Do you want to put it off until he's gone and then spend the rest of your life with regrets? God, open your eyes, John." Her voice softened. "Look, I know you're hoping he beats this. We all are. But c'mon. What if he can't?"

She was right. I had lulled myself into believing my father

would live forever. He always managed to beat back adversity. I had convinced myself he'd pull through this crisis, too. But she raised a legitimate question: What *was* I waiting for? A bedside visit did not constitute an admission of defeat, did it?

I left for work and spent the drive into Philadelphia mulling over the question, when suddenly I remembered a moment from long ago, in the winter of 1987. I was still single then and had just arrived in Florida to begin my new job at the newspaper in Fort Lauderdale. Jenny would land her own job in the area and follow a few weeks later, but for that moment I was alone and had no idea what our future held. It was my first time living so far from home, and I knew no one. Always the loyal parents, Mom and Dad soon arrived in their recreational vehicle. They had driven hundreds of miles to help their youngest son—the one Mom reminded me had been so hopelessly homesick during his first year at sleep-away camp—get settled. For two weeks they stayed, camping at an RV park a few miles from my new apartment. Every evening after work I would drive directly there to sit in the dinette of their motor home with them, eating Mom's meatloaf and telling them every detail of my new job. I had been hired to cover the world's most boring beat: transportation. But they hung on every word as if I'd just arrived from a fascinating adventure abroad. Mom pasted each of my articles in a scrapbook, and Dad read and reread every one, peppering me with questions about the inner workings of road construction, toll structures, and traffic flow in Palm Beach County.

It would be our last great visit, the final one in which they could claim me as all their own. For those two weeks, I was still their youngest son, faithfully caught in the orbit of their gravity and happy to be their satellite. Soon enough, Jenny and I would be living together, and then married and parents, and everything would change forever. I missed the parents I had then as I knew they missed that son.

When I arrived home from work that evening, I said, "So I was thinking of flying to Detroit and spending a few days."

"I think that would be good," Jenny said.

The chemotherapy was doing a job on Dad. In our daily phone calls, he continued to keep up a good game. The hospital room was like a resort, the nurses were spoiling him, the food really wasn't too bad. But I could hear it in his voice, which had grown somehow smaller and weaker, slightly higher and reedier. The booming confidence was gone. He told me the treatments were not making him too nauseated, but they had sapped his strength. His limbs felt like deadweights, and sometimes the simple act of reading exhausted him. One day he confessed to being so enervated he couldn't pull himself out of bed to walk to the bathroom. He had to ring for a nurse to help him up. Never in his life had he felt so helpless.

When I told him I had booked my ticket, his voice brightened. "I'm glad you're coming home, John," he said.

"I'm glad, too, Dad."

A week before I was scheduled to arrive, Dad received a happy surprise. He was getting discharged. His platelet counts were still not great, but with the chemotherapy, transfusions, and steroids, they had steadily risen, and Dr. Franklin was satisfied Dad could rest just as well at home as in the hospital. Any bleeding at all and he was to return immediately. And he was to avoid public places and contact with strangers. The chemo had compromised his immune system, and Dr. Franklin did not want him exposed to germs he might not be able to fight off. Once a week for the remaining three weeks he would come to the hospital for his chemo treatment and blood work. Other than that, he was home free. Elizabeth had efficiently taken control of the household chores, meals, and Mom's care. She had let him know she would be honored to nurse him as well. He was too weak to be proud and had gratefully accepted.

"I might as well be lying in my own bed as here," he said. "Of course, I'll have to take it easy."

"Oh, you mean no heavy lifting?" I asked. "You won't be out climbing on the roof and cleaning gutters?"

"Not right away," he said.

"You better take it easy, mister," I admonished, "or when I get home, you'll have me to contend with."

I could feel his smile through the phone line.

Chapter 29

I flew into Detroit Metropolitan Airport on the morning after Thanksgiving. Michael met me in baggage claim.

"How is Dad doing?" I asked as we drove home through a steady drizzle.

"Status quo," Mike said in that infuriatingly opaque way of his.

"What's that mean?" I asked.

"Holding steady," he said. "Of course, the chemo is taking its toll."

"How?"

He hesitated as if considering where to begin, then simply said, "Well, you'll see."

As I walked in from the garage to the laundry room, I plucked from the recesses of my memory one of the corny family expressions I had grown up hearing whenever a close friend or relative arrived. "Hey, hey," I called out. "Look what the dog dragged in!"

"Ruth! He's home!" I heard my father's voice from the next

room. After a long moment, longer than I had expected, he came around the corner, and I sucked in my breath. I barely recognized him. Dressed in pajamas and a robe, he leaned heavily on a cane as he shuffled gingerly toward me, his slippered feet not lifting off the linoleum. My always ramrod-straight, speed-walking, up-with-the-sun father was stooped over as he inched forward in a manner that can only be described as doddering. What was most shocking, though, was his face. It was as round and puffy as a beach ball, his skin stretched tight as if ready to pop. He had told me the daily steroid treatments had caused him to retain fluids and swell, but I wasn't expecting this. I noticed his wrists and hands were just as swollen.

"John! You're home!" he said jovially but in a voice weaker than I had known. I took his hand in both of mine and gave it the vigorous Grogan shake.

"I'm home, Dad," I said. "It's good to see you."

"Well, I'm not much to look at right now," he said, "but I'm getting along. Come on in and say hello to your mother."

I followed behind him as he inched his way into the living room, where she sat in front of the window, her own cane across her knees. "Look who's here, Ruthie," he announced.

"Hi, Mom," I said, dropping to one knee in front of her so we could be eye to eye. "It's John."

"Who'd you think I thought it would be," she shot back, "the milkman?" I saw a little of the old glimmer in her eye and smiled. "Come here and give your old ma a kiss," she said, and I smacked my lips against her forehead and then her cheek.

"Where are Jenny and the kids?"

"Remember, Ma? I came alone this time," I said. "You've got your baby all to yourself for a change." For effect, I draped my arm over her shoulder and pretended to sit in her lap, putting no weight on her.

"Oh, what a darling baby you were," she marveled and patted my leg.

264 · JOHN GROGAN

"And it's a good thing," I said, "or you would have sent me back."

"You were my little pistol," she said.

We made small talk about my flight and the house and all the leaves that still needed raking.

"We're in crisis mode around here," Dad announced. "With this darn cancer and the hospital and everything, I've given up on all my fall chores. I'm just letting everything go."

"Don't worry about that, Dad," I said. "Reinforcements have arrived."

My mother now slept most of the day, as many as eighteen hours out of every twenty-four, and since returning from the hospital, Dad was quickly exhausted and taking extended naps, too. I planned to fill the quiet hours working around the place. Elizabeth, in addition to caring for both her new parents-in-law, had the inside of the house looking the best it had in years, but outside awaited a long backlog of jobs.

"There's a new yardman in town," I said, "and I hear he works cheap."

Mom looked up at me with clear, green, faraway eyes and asked, "Are Jenny and the kids here?"

One missed beat. My eyes met Dad's. "Not this time, Mom," I said as I would another half-dozen times throughout the day.

Dad eased himself down into the chair next to me, and I asked about his swollen face and hands. He pulled up his pajama pant legs to reveal ankles that looked like something out of a circus sideshow. They were the size of clubs, with large sores and cracks marbling the skin. "It gets stretched so tight, it splits right open," he said. Michael had been cleaning them for him and wrapping his legs in gauze. The pain was impossible to ignore, but he did his best, offering it up, as he had with all hardships over the years, for the poor souls in purgatory.

"The worst part is my mouth," Dad said. "It's so dry I can hardly swallow. Everything I try to eat tastes like sawdust." He opened his lips to expose a swollen, cracked tongue that looked like it should belong to a tortoise. The chemo, as Michael had hinted, was wreaking havoc on him.

A few days earlier he had been inching his way down the stairs when he fell backward on his butt. He wasn't hurt, but he was stuck on the step, unable to pull himself back to his feet. He had to call for help, and it took both Michael and Elizabeth to haul him up. My dad, the man who as recently as a few months earlier had started each morning with sets of jumping jacks and push-ups, had lost nearly all his strength.

"I'm weak as a kitten," he confessed.

"But just think, Dad," I said, searching for a bright spot. "You've only got three more weeks to go. You're halfway through."

"I just hope it works," he said.

"If you weren't getting better, the doctors wouldn't have let you come home," I offered, and he nodded as if that made sense.

After lunch, both Mom and Dad went upstairs to sleep, and I headed into the yard under a leaden sky to rake leaves. When all the trash cans were filled, I climbed on the roof to clean the gutters. Dad had been fretting about his clogged gutters for weeks. The older he got, the more obsessive he had become about the little details of his daily life, especially those that interfered with his routine. If he discovered a new box of cereal opened before the old one was finished, he would shout through the house, "Who opened the new cereal?" and continue to grumble until the old box was finally used up. While visiting him the previous summer, I had volunteered to cut the grass, and drove him crazy by circling the yard in a counterclockwise pattern when he had always—for forty-five years—gone clockwise. At least now he could stop worrying about the gutters. I saved the mucky, soggy leaves to show him all that had come out.

After a few hours of work, I ducked my head inside, but they were both still asleep, so I decided to take a walk—to the first of the twin attractions that had brought my family to Harbor

Hills. I followed the same path I had taken every school day for eight years, from our back door to the side door of Our Lady of Refuge. The school had a large addition now, and the new church covered the soccer field, but the original buildings looked the same. The door was locked. I walked around to the front of the school, past the football field where I had played offensive guard for the Refuge Ravens, past the convent where Tommy and I had scrubbed floors, and pulled on the door. It swung open. School was out for the holiday, and the place was silent. But that smell, the permeating aroma of floor wax, chalk, and overripe bananas, with a slight undertone of stale vomit, was just as I remembered it. I walked into the classroom where Tommy had played the Fugs song and sat in a desk approximately where mine had been. I peered through the locked door into the principal's office where we had been sent for punishment. I found my second-grade classroom, where I had embarrassed myself while fantasizing about Sister Mary Lawrence. On the teacher's desk was a wooden ruler, and I gave it a practice swing through the air. It whistled just like I remembered them whistling in the instant before contact.

"Wow," I said aloud to the empty room. "Forty years."

Back home, Dad was awake and looking more rested. When I announced that I would be cooking dinner, he volunteered to keep me company. The one positive side effect of the steroids was that they made my reserved father unusually chatty and animated. He leaned against the counter and talked my ear off as I sautéed onions and garlic. He especially enjoyed describing the cooking skills he had found late in life. When we were kids and Mom was not around to cook, Dad had only two items in his culinary repertoire: Campbell's tomato soup, into which he would melt cubes of Swiss cheese, and fried bologna sandwiches. We kids found both indescribably delicious, which always amused my mother, whose gourmet gifts her well-fed brood mostly took for granted. Since she had given up on cooking, Dad had taught himself to make stew, chili, various casseroles, and his specialty, chicken vegetable soup.

"You've become a regular Galloping Gourmet," I said, and I could tell he liked the comparison even if he knew I was teasing.

"As they say, necessity is the mother of invention."

My second day home went much like the first. We lingered at the kitchen table over breakfast, talking about everything and nothing in particular. I told Dad about my work at the newspaper and in my garden; I brought him up to date on the kids and their hobbies. He talked about projects he wanted to get to around the house and gave me updates on various neighbors I had known growing up. The Selahowskis from next door were living in Florida now and Cindy Ann, the girl who had showered me with unrequited love at the age of six, was working as a music teacher. Tommy's parents were also in Florida where they had been enjoying an active and healthy retirement until Mr. Cullen was diagnosed with stomach cancer, which he was fighting as only Mr. Cullen could. Tommy, Dad had heard, was divorced and living in Phoenix, where he managed commercial properties. There were funerals to report on and moves to nursing homes. My parents were at that stage of life. For many years now, the obituaries were the section of the paper they turned to first.

When Dad went upstairs to join Mom for a nap, Michael and I put up storm windows. Then I took another walk. This time I headed to the other pole of my Harbor Hills childhood: The Outlot. In front of the Pemberton house, which long ago had changed hands after the old man died, I paused. Right here, I thought, was where the police car had rolled up behind us. I walked a few steps onto the lawn. And here was where I dropped those two pathetic homegrown joints of mine. I looked down into the grass, half expecting to find them still hiding there.

I walked on, past where we had the Labor Day picnics and

bike parades, and down to The Lagoon where the *Mary Ann* had spent fourteen consecutive summers before being retired. As I stood on the wobbly boat dock, it came back to me, an event that even in that long-ago moment I had understood was a turning point: the final voyage on the *Mary Ann*. It was the last time Dad and I would ever sail together.

In 1981 I was two years out of college and working across the state at the *Herald-Palladium*. Even though I lived three hours away, I came home that spring, put a fresh coat of wax on the sailboat, and launched it for the season. Dad was retired by then, and I thought that if the boat were in the water he might use it. Even in retirement, he worked too hard; I wanted him to have a leisurely pursuit. But when I returned home in August for a weekend visit, I learned he had not been out once. Honestly, he had been making excuses not to sail ever since I was old enough to take the boat out alone.

"I'm going for a sail, Dad," I said. "Want to join me?"

"No, you go ahead," he said. "I've got so much to do around here."

"Aw, c'mon," I beckoned. "Come with me. For old times' sake. Just a short one." I persisted until he agreed.

The day was blustery but nothing we hadn't handled before in our sturdy day sailer. I started out at the helm, steering the boat through whitecaps and spilling wind from the sails when gusts hit. *Mary Ann* heeled up playfully and plunged forward. Across the lake, I offered the tiller and mainsheet to Dad, who accepted them reluctantly. He had not sailed much at all for many years, and I could see he was nervous. But the old magic quickly came back to him, and I caught him grinning as he peered up into the rigging, checking his sail trim.

"We've had a lot of good sails on this baby," I said, and he nodded in agreement. "Remember how you used to tell me that life was like skippering a sailboat? How you needed to pick a dot on the horizon and be careful not to veer off course?" Dad smiled at his attempt to find a life lesson in the everyday.

"Small corrections," he said. "I think that's what I used to tell you. Life is all about small, continuous corrections."

"At least if you don't want to run aground," I said.

He was opening his mouth to say something else when the big gust hit. I felt it on the back of my neck first, and then, a fraction of a second later, in the sails. All experienced sailors know what to do when a big gust hits: nose into the wind and release the sails to spill their load. Dad knew this, too, and had done it countless times. Instead, he just gripped tighter to the tiller and rope controlling the mainsail. I let the jib fly and scrambled onto the high side of the boat. Dad sat frozen, staring at the water pouring in.

Another second and he shouted: "John, take it!"

I lunged toward him.

"John! Help!" In his voice was something I had never heard before: panic.

Dad had always been the cool, collected one in our household. When I was still in preschool, Mom knocked a can of paint off a ladder in the living room, sending it splashing over the curtains, couch, and carpet. She sank to her knees and wept. But Dad instantly leaped to the rescue, barking calm orders to each of us—"Marijo, towels! Tim, a bucket of cold water! Michael, sponges!"—and got most of it up before it stained. Dad was always at his best in a crisis. He had always been the shepherd of his flock, the one we all relied on to fix any problem, right any wrong.

Not on this day. As the boat tipped beyond the point of no return, I realized our roles had finally reversed. He was the lamb now, and I the protector. Suddenly his heart attack from a few years earlier loomed large before me, as did two of the doctor's stern warnings: avoid stressful situations and avoid shocks to the body, such as a sudden plunge into cold water. An electrifying surge of adrenaline coursed through me.

I grabbed the tiller, but it was too late. *Mary Ann* was already dropping onto her side, her cockpit filling, her mast and sails settling onto the lake's surface. We both flopped into the water. Terror flashed in my father's eyes.

"It's okay, Dad," I said. "We're okay. See, everything's okay." I got him into a life jacket and helped him straddle the gunwale sticking out of the water. Then I swam around the boat, gathering up paddles and seat cushions.

"We'll have this puppy back up in no time," I called to him. In fourteen years of sailing, it was the first time either of us had capsized. "We're fine, Dad. Just a little wet."

And within a few moments, he was fine again, his calm, steady demeanor back. "Guess I'm a little rusty," he said sheepishly.

"That was one big gust," I said. "I didn't see it coming, either." And with that, I stood on the centerboard, gripped the gunwale, and rocked backward until the boat pulled upright again. Dad clung to the side as I bailed, and soon enough we had drifted onto a sandbar where we could stand and Dad could easily climb back in.

"Way to go, Pops, breaking our perfect record," I ribbed him as we tied up to the dock.

"Quite a day," Dad said.

"Quite a day," I agreed. And it was. As I pulled down the sails, I realized that my father would never again step aboard the *Mary Ann*, and I would never again share those shoulder-to-shoulder afternoons on the water with him, the closest thing to intimacy we ever had. There are moments in life that fade from memory so quickly they are gone almost before they are over. Then there are those that stick, the ones we carry with us through the years like precious parcels of clarity stitched close to our hearts, becoming part of who we are. Standing together there, soaking wet, I already understood that this was one of those moments.

I saw the paths of our lives crossing like jet contrails in an empty sky. Mine was rising toward adulthood and future's bright promise. His had begun the gradual descent toward life's inescapable conclusion.

A pair of ducks landed on the surface of The Lagoon, snapping me back to the present. Twenty-three years had passed since that last sail. Twenty-three years, and how far our opposing trajectories had carried us.

Chapter 30

———

ohn, do me a favor, will you?" Dad asked. We were sitting in Marijo's old bedroom, converted years earlier into a television room, where we had just finished watching the six o'clock news. From downstairs I could hear Elizabeth bustling about in the kitchen and smell the ginger and garlic drifting up as she prepared her specialty for dinner, an Asian noodle dish filled with chicken, shrimp, and vegetables.

"Sure, Dad," I said.

"Go into my room, next to my bed, and bring me the box you made me."

I walked across the hall and found it on the bed table, beside his flashlight and alarm clock. It was my first time seeing it since eleven months earlier when I mailed it to him for his eighty-eighth birthday. I was never quite sure what to call it. It wasn't fancy enough to be a jewelry box, and besides, Dad had no jewelry except for a couple of pairs of cuff links and his wedding band, which had not left his finger in fifty-six years. It wasn't really a keepsake box. It was just a box, handmade by me from hardwoods

I had salvaged from the forest behind my house in Pennsylvania. Squat and solid, it had a drawer in the bottom and a lid on top that swung open.

Woodworking had always been a hobby for me, though one for which I had no particular gift. Over the years, I had made picture frames and cutting boards and toy cars for the kids. In recent years I had begun scouring the woods for fallen logs of particularly beautiful varieties—red oak, black walnut, black cherry—sawing them into planks, and planing the planks into boards. Dad's box was more than a year in the planning and making. My whole life I had given him predictable gifts: aftershave and neckties and fat biographies of dead presidents. But he wasn't getting any younger, and there was no denying we had grown apart in the years since I had married. It was our lifelong cross to bear together, the burden of our religious differences. Dad was blessed with the gift of faith; I was born with the curse of skepticism. He was hardwired to believe, I to doubt. Making the box, just like planning the garden, had been my attempt to pole-vault the chasm, to let him know I still cared.

I picked up the box, which was heavier than I remembered, and stroked the satiny, hand-rubbed finish. Mom was asleep on her side in the bed, her legs tucked up in a half curl, childlike. I didn't want to wake her, not that there was much danger of that. I tiptoed out with the box and set it on Dad's knees.

"I thought you'd like to see what I'm using it for," he said and lifted the lid.

Inside was a trove of family treasures, many of which I never knew existed. He pulled them out one by one and gave me a brief rundown on each: his grandfather's silver and ebony rosary; his father's wire-framed eyeglasses; his mother's driver's license; both parents' wedding bands. From a small manila envelope, he poured out a pile of military insignias and bars he had earned in the navy. "We used to call this fruit salad," he said.

He opened the little bottom drawer and pulled out the gold

watch his father received from the Rapid Vehicle Motor Company in 1909 for being on the first expedition to reach the summit of Pikes Peak in Colorado in a motorized vehicle, and the lucky rabbit's foot my grandfather had carried with him. In a small pouch was a collection of General Motors service pins, each with a small diamond, marking various milestones in his forty-year career. Dad described each item to me. So I would know. So someday when I rummaged through the box with my children or grandchildren, or they with theirs, these objects would mean something, would be something more than faded bric-a-brac. Each had a story to tell, the story of our family. Each was a strand connecting us to our past. I could tell that Dad did not want them to slip into oblivion.

From the very bottom of the drawer he removed a folded sheet of paper that I recognized as the note I had slipped into the box before shipping it to him. Now he held it in front of us and read aloud the words I had written almost one year earlier. My note described the process of building the box, from selecting the logs to rubbing on a final coat of wax. It described how I beveled the lid and chiseled out recesses to fit the hinges. I confessed how many mistakes I had made along the way, and the resulting compromises I was forced to accept in what had begun as a quest for perfection. The box was a lot like life in that way, I suppose.

I ended the note this way:

The kids watched the box slowly take shape, and that was good. They knew it was for their grandfather, which made it all the more special for them. Colleen, in particular, took an interest and built a simple pine box of her own, with my help, beside me. It was a good opportunity for one-on-one father-daughter time and reminded me of the hours you and I spent together at the workbench in the basement. I learned a lot from you down there.

That is the story of your box, Dad, built with humble hands and an open heart. I have no idea what you possibly will use it for, and I bet you don't, either. But I hope you will place it where you will see it in the morning, or perhaps late at night. And each time you see it, I want you to know how much I appreciate all you have been—and continue to be—to me. You're all any boy could ever ask for in a father.

Dad refolded the note and returned it to the bottom of the box. "It means a lot to me, John," he said.

Then Elizabeth called from downstairs that dinner was ready, and I said, "I guess it's time to eat."

After dinner, while Michael and Elizabeth did the dishes, I gingerly broached a topic I had been rehearsing for days. In my suitcase was a video camera that I had packed with the intention of interviewing Dad on tape for posterity. Mom was the family chronicler, a natural-born storyteller. Her tales were burned into all her children's memories. But Dad rarely offered glimpses into his past, not because he was secretive but simply so modest he couldn't fathom anyone wanting to hear about his life. I wanted to capture his story in his own words before it was too late, but therein lay the awkwardness: *before it was too late.* Once the chemotherapy kicked in, I fully expected Dad to beat his leukemia, but how could I ask him for this interview as he battled a potentially fatal disease, without sounding like I had already given up? I might as well be asking him to record his last will and testament. No matter how you dressed it, the request was what it was. Children ask their parents for these things only when they know time is running out. I stammered around before finally spitting it out.

"Say, Dad, I was thinking," I said. "I'd like to interview you about your life. I brought my video camera."

"That's fine," he said, not missing a beat. "I'd be happy to."

I set up the camera on a tripod, framed him in the viewfinder, and pushed the record button.

"Where should we start?" I asked.

"You're the interviewer," Dad said.

"Okay, how about at the beginning. When and where were you born?"

"December 10, 1915. On the Franklin Road in Pontiac, Michigan. Two-forty-one Franklin."

"Were you born in a hospital or at home?"

"At home. A doctor would come to the house back in those days."

"Let's back up. Who was the first of our Grogans to come from Ireland?"

"James. My great-uncle James was the first. He came over right after the Civil War and bought a small farm on Scott Lake Road, just about ten minutes from here. A few years after he got the farm, James sent for his younger brother Patrick," Dad continued. "Patrick was my great-grandfather." Dad loved that I had named my firstborn after the family forefather.

"What's your first memory?" I asked.

"That's easy," Dad said and told me a story I had not heard since childhood. When my father was still a toddler, his mother contracted tuberculosis and was shipped off to a sanitarium in Ohio to recover. Dad was sent to live with his grandmother while his father stayed behind to work. His mother—my grandmother Edna—was gone for two years, and Dad knew her only from the letters she wrote home. Then one afternoon he awoke from his nap to find a stranger leaning over him.

"I opened my eyes and there was this kind-looking lady gazing down at me. She was smiling at me, and I knew it was Mom. I knew right away. I don't know how but I did."

His voice cracked, and he forced a small laugh to shake off the emotion. "I get choked up, even now, when I think about it," he said. "That was my first memory."

I continued to lead him chronologically through the steps of his life: his childhood as a Catholic schoolboy; the births of his sister and brother; his father's heyday as a sought-after crackerjack mechanic in the nascent days of the automobile, followed by his long, discouraging struggle to rebuild his career after the Depression hit. He described the family moves to Cleveland, New York, Philadelphia, and back to New York as his father chased short-lived jobs, and the string of apartments, neighborhoods, and schools that came with the family's itinerant lifestyle. I was amazed at the detail of his memory. He recalled the street addresses of every place he had lived, some for as little as a few months, and the names of teachers he had not seen in eighty years.

When Dad was halfway through his junior year in high school, in the Germantown section of Philadelphia, his father lost yet another job, and this time had run out of options. The family moved back to reclaim the homestead on Franklin Road in Pontiac after its new owner defaulted on a land-contract loan. They arrived to find the house of my father's birth being used as a brothel. My grandfather chased off the prostitutes, plowed up the lawn for a vegetable garden, and took a job as a field hand, fixing cars in his driveway at night for extra money.

Dad's plan was to graduate from Pontiac High School and try for a job in one of the auto factories to help support the family. "College wasn't even a dream," he said. "We didn't have any money." But as the school year drew to a close, an amazing thing happened. As Dad liked to point out, it illustrated the life-altering impact a single kind act by one individual can make.

"My French teacher, Miss Blanche Avery, bless her soul," Dad began, and then paused for several seconds before continuing. "She called me up after class one day and asked, 'What are you going to do after you graduate?' I said, 'I don't know; try to get a job, I guess.' She said, 'You really ought to go to college.' I told her, 'Well, I don't have any money or anything.' That's when she offered to—" He stopped in midsentence and I could tell he was fighting to maintain his composure. "She offered to pay my tuition out of her own pocket." His voice broke again, the magnitude of this teacher's generosity still overwhelming him all these decades later. "I said, 'No, no. No, I couldn't. My father would never allow that.' Then she started talking to me about scholarships. She said, 'Let me talk to the principal.' It turns out the principal was friends with the personnel manager over at Pontiac Motors, and the next thing I knew they were talking about me being a good fit for GMI."

"General Motors Institute in Flint," I said.

"Yes. It was a cooperative. You worked one month, went to school one month, and earned your way as you went. You had to be sponsored by a GM plant or division." Pontiac Motors sponsored my father, and he spent the next four years alternating between classes in Flint and working in various automobile jobs in Pontiac. "I made fifty-five cents an hour, and my tuition was thirty-five dollars a month, plus room and board," Dad said. "If you were careful, you could even save a little."

GMI was not accredited to offer academic degrees, but Dad was able to transfer the credits he earned there to the University of Michigan, where he graduated with honors from the College of Engineering in 1939, making him the first of our line of Grogans to receive a college degree. I asked how his father had reacted to such a point of pride.

"Dad wasn't much for showing his emotions," my father recalled. "He wasn't what you'd call gushy or demonstrative. But I think he was proud. I'm sure he was proud of me."

With his newly minted degree, my father returned to Pontiac Motors as a junior draftsman, living at home and helping to support his family. Not long after, his father succumbed to prostate cancer, dying at the age of fifty-six, a broken man. "We were all right there around his bed with him when he drew his last breath," Dad said.

My father settled in as the sole breadwinner for his mother and younger brother and sister. Then came December 7, 1941, and the Japanese attack on Pearl Harbor. My father could easily have ridden out the war in safety and without even losing face. He had ironclad double deferments. Not only was he supporting a widow and two dependents, but his plant had rapidly retooled to serve the war effort, and he was put to work designing large armaments. He was needed on the home front, by both his family and his country. He enlisted anyway.

"Why did you do that?" I asked.

Dad ran his fingers along the tablecloth and thought for a moment. "It just seemed like the right thing," he said.

"How are you doing?" I asked. "Getting tired?"

"Mouth's a little dry."

I got him a glass of water and changed videotapes, then asked, "Tell me about meeting Mom." A slight smile spread across his face, and I could see how in love with her he still was. I had heard her version of their courtship many times, but I wanted to hear it from him.

After the war, Dad returned to Pontiac, reclaimed his old job at Pontiac Motors, and moved back in with his mother and younger sister and brother. As was his habit, he resumed attending Mass each morning before work, where the associate pastor, the Reverend Joseph Howard, befriended him. Part of the reason Dad caught the young priest's eye, no doubt, was my father's generosity. Dad always believed in sharing whatever money he had with the Church. The entire time he was in the South Pacific, he kept track of the weekly offerings he was missing back home. Upon his return, he dropped a check for the accumulated lump sum in the collection basket. Not long after, Father Howard invited the newly returned navy lieutenant to the Howard family home in Ann Arbor for Sunday dinner and to meet his mother. What the priest failed to mention was that his younger sister, Ruth, would also be there. She had spent the war working at the Willow Run fighter-plane factory outside Ann Arbor and at age thirty was still single and living at home. My uncle Father Joe was playing matchmaker.

As Mom countless times told the story, she was not at all interested in the quiet, bookish man. She was pretty and confident and too proud to swoon over the first eligible bachelor her older brother dragged home on that August day in 1946. My father, on the other hand, was smitten by the petite brunette with the slightly off-kilter sense of humor. She had a natural way of filling his awkward silences with her laughter and endless banter. He felt comfortable around her. In his methodical, bashful way, Dad began courting her and eventually won her heart. (Mom's version always included a hilarious account of her shy suitor's weeks-long attempt to summon the courage to kiss her for the first time.) They married a year to the day after that first dinner, on August 16, 1947, with Father Joe and Father Vin officiating. Eleven months later they brought Marijo home from the hospital.

For two hours Dad talked as I recorded. He described the early blissful years of their marriage in a one-bedroom apartment in Detroit with a cardboard box for a dining-room table. He described their first house, on Pembroke Street in Detroit, and how he built a sandbox in the tiny backyard. He described the heartbreak of losing Mary Ann, and the promise of moving to Harbor Hills when I was one year old, where his children would enjoy the advantages he never experienced. He filled me in on everything he could think of that came before the point where my own memories began. Then he said, "I'm feeling a little tired now," and I turned off the camera and watched him, cane in hand, slowly climb the stairs to his bedroom.

Before dawn the next morning, the whole house was awake and bustling. Elizabeth fried eggs; Michael warmed up the car and scraped frost from the windshield. I would soon be leaving for the airport. It was time to return to my own family. Even Mom managed to crawl out of bed and come downstairs in her bathrobe to see me off. She sat at the kitchen table nursing a cup of instant coffee, and I kissed her on the cheek and said, "I'll try to get home in the spring, okay?"

"That would be nice, dear," she said.

Dad was in his pajamas and bathrobe, too, but he insisted on walking me out to the car. I loaded my bag in the trunk and turned back to him, standing in the garage, looking fragile. I walked over, extending my hand for the customary Grogan handshake. As I did, he hooked his cane over his wrist and extended both arms to me. I hesitated for a moment, then stepped into them. I felt them wrap around me, and mine around him.

"Aw, Dad," I said, "this has been great."

"Thanks for coming, John," he said. "I know it's not easy to get away."

As we stood there embracing, I remembered the last thing Jenny had said to me as she dropped me at the airport three days earlier. Her words rang in my head: "If there's anything you've been wanting to say to him, you probably should say it this trip." Now here I was leaving and I had not said the one thing I knew was long overdue. I drew a breath and summoned my courage.

"I love you, Dad," I said.

His words came back so quickly, so instantaneously, they seemed almost an echo of my own. They burst from him like water bursts from a broken pipe. It was as if they had been poised there for decades, hovering just inside his lips awaiting permission to be released.

"I love you, too, Johnny," he said.

Johnny. He had not called me that since I was a little boy. *Johnny.*

I clung to him for a moment longer, then got into the car with Michael. "Keep getting better!" I called out the window as we backed down the driveway. He waved one last time, and we were gone.

Chapter 31

When I returned home, Jenny asked, "Just how depressing was it?"

"A little sad," I said. "Just a little. The clock's definitely ticking. Even if Dad makes a full recovery, he's so weak now. I don't know how he can keep taking care of Mom and the house and everything. On the brighter side, Mom seems to be holding her own, and Dad was tired but in good spirits. He's still got a lot of fight left in him." I told her about the toll the chemotherapy had taken and the mementos he had pulled out of his box to share with me. I described my walks around the neighborhood and the taped interview with him on my last night home. "Whatever happens, I'm so glad I did that," I said.

"It's good that you went," Jenny said. "At their age, you just don't know."

As if to prove her point, two weeks later the phone rang. My father was back in the hospital. On December 12, a nurse came to the house to check on him. She took one look at his cracked and oozing ankles and ordered him immediately to the emergency room, fearing they were infected. But it wasn't his swollen extremities that kept him there. The doctor who saw him put a stethoscope to his chest and did not like what he heard: the faintest hint of congestion. Infection was the biggest risk of the chemotherapy regimen my father was on. Not only were the powerful drugs that coursed through his bloodstream attacking every cancer cell they encountered, they were attacking every white blood cell as well. And those white blood cells protected him from opportunistic invaders. Without them he was defenseless.

An X-ray confirmed the doctor's concern. A tiny spot of pneumonia had taken root in one lung. "You can barely see it," Dad said on the phone from his hospital bed. "But they don't want to take any chances. So I'm back in again. They've got me on an antibiotic IV to nip it in the bud."

The nurse had been wrong about my father's ankles, but had she not ordered him to the hospital, the spot of pneumonia could have gone undetected for weeks as it grew silently, filling his lungs with oxygen-robbing mucus. We both agreed her overreaction had been a blessing and saved him from a serious setback. "My guardian angel was looking out for me," Dad said.

With just one treatment remaining, the doctors suspended his chemotherapy, saying they needed to hold off on the final dose until the lung infection was under control. The chemotherapy was working better than hoped, sending his platelet count to near-normal levels. But the side effects had increased exponentially with each week, rendering him helpless. Two days before entering the hospital, on December 10, my father had celebrated his eighty-ninth birthday in bed, too enervated and nauseated to make it downstairs to eat the salmon dinner Michael had prepared for him, knowing it was a favorite. And now the drugs had compromised his immune system as well. I marveled at how a medication intended to save a life could go so far toward destroying it.

Unlike his earlier hospital stay, this time there was no private room that reminded him of a swanky resort. He was in a bare-bones cubicle with a loud, complaining roommate and inattentive nursing staff. When I called the next day, he sounded frazzled, nearly desperate. He was too weak to sit up and feed himself, but the orderlies simply left the food on a tray beside the bed. "I can't get the food to my mouth," he said. "I can't take a sip of water."

"Sit tight, Dad," I said. "We're going to fix this." And we did, browbeating the staff to give him the attention he needed and urging them to assign him the next available private room. Michael began to advocate for him more aggressively. In hospitals as elsewhere in life, we were learning, the old bromide proved true: the squeaky wheels really did get the grease. I tried to monitor him as best I could from afar by phone. Each report was more discouraging than the last. The doctors were having no success stamping out the pneumonia. They tried different antibiotics in different combinations without luck. He was now breathing with the help of an oxygen mask to compensate for his lungs' decreased capacity. During one visit, Michael overheard an attending physician in the hallway tell a colleague, "This thing is mushrooming. Nothing we throw at it is touching it."

My father's immune system was shot, allowing the pneumonia to rampage with impunity. I began to think of it as a violent predator on the loose in a small town where the populace had no sheriff, no posse, not even any pitchforks with which to defend themselves. Dr. Bober, my parents' longtime family physician, was our liaison with the hospital staff. She briefed Michael, who in turn briefed the rest of us. Dad's case was proving a medical conundrum, she said. His doctors needed to suspend the chemotherapy if they were to have any hope of reining in the potentially deadly pneumonia. But with the cancer-fighting drugs stopped, his platelet levels had resumed their perilous plummet, erasing most of the progress he had made. The leukemia was back on its feet, stronger than ever. Now there were two predators on the loose, both intent on taking him. To treat one served only to enable the other.

"Hang in there, Dad," I said on his third day of hospitalization. "They've got a new antibiotic they're going to try tomorrow. We just need it to kick in. Once the pneumonia is tackled, we can go after the leukemia again."

"I don't have any choice but to hang in there," he said.

On the fourth day, I called from my cell phone as I shopped for Christmas presents. The phone rang a dozen times before my father picked up.

"Hi, Dad," I said. "Is this an okay time?"

"No, it's not," he said, his voice distraught. "It's not good at all. I need to go now." He hung up, and a wave of dread washed over me. Only later would I learn that a priest was at his side at that moment, administering the Last Rites, the Catholic sacrament for the dying. That's why he couldn't talk. Dad was not done fighting; he hadn't given up. But he realized the growing gravity of his situation and wanted to be prepared. I was focused on his physical well-being; he was thinking of his spiritual.

As I drove home, I did something I had not done for many, many years. I prayed. I began just as I had started my prayers each night as a young boy. "Dear Jesus, dear God the Father, dear Holy Spirit, all the saints and angels in heaven," I said aloud. "Let the new antibiotic work. Please. Let the chemo work. Let Dad get better. Let him get over this hump so he can have another couple years. Or one. That's all I'm asking. One year. Mom needs him. We all still need him. Amen."

I made the sign of the cross just as the nuns had taught me to four decades earlier, touching the fingertips of my right hand to my forehead, chest, and each shoulder. Even alone in the car, I felt embarrassed. I had stopped believing in the literal power of prayer many years earlier and came to think of it as a strictly contemplative act whose value lay in self-examination and revelation. How many Jews had prayed in the concentration camps?

How many murder victims had prayed in the instant before the trigger was pulled? How many sick and dying had sought God's intervention in vain? And yet here I was. I no longer knew if I believed in the miracle of prayer. At this moment, my father's life in the balance, I knew with certainty I wanted to.

Later that day, we finally got some good news. A private room had come available. At 4 P.M. Dad was wheeled into his new quarters, and almost instantly he sounded better, more tranquil and at peace. I felt a surge of optimism. Here he could get the rest he needed, build his strength, fight back. The new antibiotic held promise, and the chemotherapy regimen had already proved its efficacy, if only he could get well enough to tolerate it again. But the new accommodations were short-lived. His doctors had been monitoring both his respiration—the number of breaths he took each minute—and the oxygen in his blood as indicators of how efficiently his lungs were working. The numbers had been gradually slipping all week even as the doctors enriched the oxygen mixture coming through his breathing mask. A healthy adult averages twelve breaths per minute, but Dad was taking as many as thirty. Even as he gasped, the oxygen levels in his blood could not keep up. The numbers had passed a threshold that triggered a hospital protocol: my father was being transferred to the intensive care unit.

"I don't want to go to the ICU," he pleaded to Michael. "The ICU is Death Row. People don't come out of there." Michael assured him that it was where he could get the best, most advanced treatment. Regardless, there was no choice. At 10 P.M. a team of orderlies wheeled Dad out of his private room and into the ICU.

The next morning I called Tim at his office in New York City. "We need to get home," I told him. Tim completely agreed. With Elizabeth still there, he had been planning to drive home to spend Christmas, anyway. Before leaving he just needed to wrap up an assignment or two at his magazine, he said, and take care of a few other work duties. Then he should be clear to head to Michigan, maybe as early as the middle of the following week, which would get him there for Christmas Eve. It was my brother's turn to deny reality.

"Next week?" I interrupted. "Tim, don't you see? We might not have until next week. We need to go now."

There was a pause on the line, then my brother said, "I'll be at your place at eight tomorrow morning. We'll drive in together. We can get there by dark."

"I'll be ready," I said.

Chapter 32

The next morning, Jenny drove me to an exit along Interstate 78 to rendezvous with Tim as he headed west from New York City. We shared the same sense of urgency now, and the half hour saved was a half hour sooner we would be at our father's side. As I slipped into the passenger seat of my brother's car, Jenny handed me a bag of sandwiches. "This way you won't have to stop to eat," she said. I kissed her good-bye and said, "I'll keep you posted."

Tim and I were only a few miles down the road when the stories began. I'm not sure which of us started them, but once we started we went on for hours. Funny stories, embarrassing stories, painful stories. The time-polished gems my mother told at the kitchen table; the tales she had no idea existed. Family stories had always been the thread that stitched together the tapestry of our lives. They amused us in good times and soothed us in bad. They filled the awkward silences when things were not right and fueled the warmth when they were. Mostly they provided the context that made us something more than six people related by blood—the context that made us that messy, imperfect, spectacularly infuriating and confounding and essential entity, a family.

"Remember the time we snuck down to the lake on the way home from church in our Sunday-best dress shoes, and you fell in?" I asked.

"You little shit," Tim said, grinning. He had sworn me to secrecy that day, knowing that a spanking with the George-and-Suzie Stick awaited him if Mom found out. Ruining his shoes was bad enough, but sneaking to the lake without permission—and dragging his baby brother along—were the graver offenses. His plan was to hide the shoes under his bed until they dried, and Mom would never be the wiser. But as we tiptoed through the kitchen, the euphoria of having my older brother's fate in my hands was too much to bear. "Mom! Mom!" I exploded. "Timmy fell in the water in his brand-new church shoes!"

"You whopped my ass pretty good for that one," I said.

"You deserved it," he answered, and I couldn't disagree.

I was a tireless troublemaker. One Easter when I was about six, I was hunting for my basket and opened the door to the clothes dryer to find Michael's basket hidden inside, his name printed in big block letters on a card stuck in the colored grass. I quietly closed the door, looked both ways, and turned on the dryer. It made a horrible racket as the eggs and chocolates and jelly beans tumbled in the steel drum. I thought it was the funniest prank I had ever pulled—until Mom led Michael to my basket, plucked out my name card, and replaced it with his. She opened the dryer, tossed in my tag among the broken eggs, linty jelly beans, and melted chocolates and said calmly, "This one's yours now, Johnny." Suddenly I was no longer laughing.

"You've got to admit," Tim said, "she had a good sense of justice."

We recounted the family camping trips to Michigan's Upper Peninsula, the frigid winds howling in off Lake Superior forcing us all to wear winter coats in July.

"Do you remember Mom's pork and beans over the camp stove?" Tim asked.

"Oh God, yes," I said. "Nothing has ever tasted so delicious."

We laughed about our elaborate schemes for skipping Sunday Mass, and the pranks we played on the nuns. One of my finest moments was the day in sixth grade when the ancient and decrepit Sister Mary Clementia screamed over our voices that she wanted to hear a pin drop. She pulled a large stickpin from her veil, held it in the air, and yelled, "Silence! I'm going to count to three, and I better hear this." As she began her countdown, I folded over the lid to my milk carton, placed it on the floor, and poised my heel above it. "One . . . two . . . three." Just as she released the pin, I stomped on the empty carton with everything I had. It exploded with a boom that nearly sent Sister through the ceiling. I had to stay after school every day for a week, writing over and over "I shall not misbehave in school," but it was worth every minute for that one instant of Hitchcock-worthy terror on her face.

Tim said he could beat that. At Brother Rice, there was the equally ancient and decrepit Brother O'Hara, who each morning like clockwork would enter the classroom and stomp his foot in the trash can to compress the litter. One day Tim and his classmates filled the can with water and sprinkled a layer of crumpled papers across the surface. In came Brother O'Hara and plunged his leg knee-deep in water.

We recounted the family vacations to miracle sites, the Thanksgiving morning family hikes through the woods as the turkey roasted in the oven, and the way Shaun loved to leap into snowdrifts. There were Mom's aniseed cookies and homemade eggnog at Christmas and Dad's dramatic manger scene beneath the giant twinkling star he suspended in the upstairs bathroom window with strings of white lights stretching down to the ground.

"Remember the Christmas Dad was in the hospital after his heart attack?" I asked. "And the two of us trying to put up the tree without him?"

"What a disaster," Tim said. We were adults by then, and the task was simple enough—we simply needed to drill a hole in the bottom of the trunk to accept the spike in the stand—but together Tim and I broke one drill bit after another, growing more and more hysterical as we did. What made it all the funnier to us at the time was the contrast between our ineptness and Dad's effortless competence. He had done the same procedure for years without once breaking a bit.

"Dad always made everything look so easy," I said.

That made me think of a story Tim had not heard: Shortly after I got my driver's license, Michael called from a party asking for a ride home. I jumped to volunteer, anxious for a chance to drive alone. Mom and Dad were cautious with teens and cars— forbidding their children to drive without a parent for a full year after becoming licensed—but they agreed to this trip. It was about twenty minutes away, and I'd have my brother with me for the drive home. Dad gave me directions. I whistled for Shaun to join me and set out into the night. Soon I was hopelessly lost, driving up and down back roads without streetlights, drifting deeper into the gritty neighborhoods surrounding Pontiac's factories. Panic rising in my chest, I pulled into the driveway of a darkened house to turn around, and as I pulled out, I cut the wheel too hard and the back tire of the family Monte Carlo dropped into the ditch. I gunned the engine again and again but the car would not budge. Outside, I dropped to my knees and could see the axle resting on the ground. Shaun must have sensed my anxiety because he began to yip. The front door of the house opened, and a woman in a bathrobe appeared in the beams of my headlights. Someone who would help, I thought.

"Turn those goddamn headlights off!" she barked. "And get off my property. We're trying to sleep."

"But—" I began.

"And shut that dog up!"

"May I use your phone?"

"Off my property or I'm calling the cops!" she yelled and slammed the door. I was now unhinged. I locked Shaun in the car, still barking wildly, and ran down the dark road until I came to a house with lights on. I knocked on the door and begged the man who answered to let me call my father. He sized me up, then told me to wait outside while he called for me. Fifteen minutes later, Dad pulled up. I had never been so happy to see one of my parents. He could see my distress. "Everything's going to be fine," he said. "These things happen." I warned him about the angry lady threatening to call the police, and he was not at all ruffled. "We'll be out of her hair in a few minutes," he said.

My can-do father pulled a jack and a large piece of lumber from the trunk of his company car, hoisted the Monte Carlo up until the axle was clear, wedged the wood under the tire, and expertly backed it out of the ditch. He could have criticized me or ridiculed my incompetence. He could have grumbled about having to come out at midnight to rescue me. Instead he put his arm around my shoulder and simply said, "Driving's like anything else; you'll get better with practice. Now let's go fetch your brother before he thinks we forgot about him."

"Dad got us out of a lot of jams over the years," Tim said as we drove through the mountains of central Pennsylvania.

I couldn't talk about Dad and cars without telling the story of the time I walked into the house during a weekend visit home from college and breathlessly described the beautiful woman I had encountered minutes earlier: "So I pull up to the red light and in the car next to me is this total fox."

"A fox?" my guileless father said in astonishment. "A fox? Right there in the car? Alive? A live fox?" Somehow he had managed to turn my moment of roadside lust into a *Wild Kingdom* episode.

Not even Mom was that clueless. "Oh, Richard," she scolded, shaking her head.

. . .

Just as the sun set, we pulled onto Erie Drive. Elizabeth and Michael greeted us at the door, and we all ate dinner with Mom, who seemed listless and detached despite our best efforts to keep the conversation upbeat. She appeared only marginally aware that her husband was hospitalized, and even less aware for what reason, but she was definitely not herself, and I wondered if she missed him on a more primal level. The man she had spent the past fifty-seven years with was suddenly not in her bed at night, not at the breakfast table in the morning. The man who had cared for her every need over the past decade had disappeared.

After dinner, Mike volunteered to do the dishes, and Elizabeth, Tim, and I headed to Saint Joseph Mercy Hospital for the 8:30 to 10 P.M. visiting hours—one of three times during the day family members were allowed in. When we arrived in the ICU, a nurse directed us to place masks over our mouths and noses. Dad was in a respiratory infectious containment room, and the masks were to protect him from our germs and us from his. Once we were masked, she opened the door to his room, and there he lay amid a warren of machines, pumps, wires, tubes, and monitors. A heavy plastic mask with a rubber gasket was clamped over his nose and mouth, connected by a hose to an external respirator that rhythmically pumped powerful bursts of oxygen into his lungs. Needles and tubes poked into his bruised, puffy arms. I swallowed hard.

"Hi, Dad," I said and squeezed his knee through the blanket.

"Hey, Dad," Tim said and touched his shoulder.

He smiled apologetically through the mask, and I could tell he was embarrassed by all the fuss being made over him. I knew what this eternally humble man was thinking: wouldn't all these fancy machines and medicines and experts be better used on someone who really needed them?

"How was the trip?" His voice came muffled through the heavy mask in between breaths, and it was difficult to hear him over the whir of the machines. "The trip," he repeated. "How was it?"

Tim and I filled the room with happy chatter, telling him about the drive, the gasoline prices, the weather, and our disdain for the Ohio Turnpike. I filled him in on the kids and work and the antics of our new dog, Gracie. We talked about anything we could think of to keep the conversation afloat. Each burst of monologue was followed by an awkward silence. We made vague, optimistic comments about Dad's prognosis and the high hopes for the latest antibiotic cocktail. "Once that kicks in, we're going to see a big difference, I bet," I volunteered.

Dad seemed distracted, like he was not quite paying attention. Then he blurted out what was on his mind. Through the mask, muffled and cottony, came the words "What do you think we should do about Mother?"

Tim and I exchanged glances. "Mom?" I asked.

Dad through the mask, each phrase separated by a deep forced breath: "If I get out of here . . . it's going to take months . . . to get back on my feet . . . Elizabeth can't stay forever . . . she needs to be home with her husband . . . Mike can't handle it alone." He waited for a breath to pass and added: "We need to talk about Mom. What's best."

"Lourdes," I said. I knew it was where he wanted her to end up if the day came when he could no longer care for her. "They'd take good care of her. And you, too, as you recover and get your strength back."

"Lourdes," Dad said, pausing to summon his most emphatic voice, "is the *best*." It was an important declaration for Tim and Elizabeth to hear. In the Philippines, where Elizabeth grew up, sending an aged parent to a nursing home was unheard of, and Elizabeth was lobbying to bring Mom back to New Jersey to stay with them, even though they lived up a steep staircase with no elevator and had only one small bedroom. Marijo, too, was trying to figure out how she could care for Mom around her job as a social worker. I even considered our house, despite knowing that the strain on our marriage would be devastating.

My father seemed intent on heading off all these well-intentioned, misguided plans. He knew firsthand the hours and level of commitment her care required. "She belongs at Lourdes," he said. "She won't like it at first. She'll be angry, but she'll get over it. She'll forget and be okay. Lourdes is the best."

Tim and I looked at each other and nodded. We promised to make an appointment to talk to the administrator about getting them both in there after Dad was released from the hospital. Dad nodded his approval, and with the topic settled he visibly relaxed. Even here in the ICU, my father was mentally running through his to-do list, taking care of business. He always was a detail man. He reminded us that the lawn mower and snowblower needed to be winterized and the hoses drained before they froze.

The conversation dwindled, and eventually we sat in silence by his side, listening to the breathing machine do its work. The nurse ducked her head in the door and gave us the five-minute warning.

"I guess it's time to go, Dad," I said.

"We'll be back in the morning, okay?" Tim added.

Dad nodded and we began to slip into our coats. That's when Elizabeth, in her broken English, offered, "Daddy, you like we say prayer?"

His eyes brightened and he nodded up and down.

We all bowed our heads and began the Lord's Prayer together. "Our Father who art in heaven . . ." But there was a problem. Tim and I no longer remembered the words that had been drilled into us thousands of times. It had been years since we had recited the prayer on our own, and whenever we were in a family gathering, we simply took our cues from Dad, mumbling along and blending in. But on this night, Dad's voice was buried inside the breathing mask, nearly impossible to understand. Elizabeth's English was too broken to help. We were adrift and couldn't even fake it: ". . . hallowed be thy name; thy *blah-blah blah,* thy *blah* be *blah-blah* . . . On *blub-blub* as it *blah-blah mumble."*

The prayer stretched on forever as we stumbled along. We might as well have been trying to recite *Beowulf* from memory. There was no hiding our rustiness. I looked at Dad and his eyes were closed as he prayed aloud. Then I made the mistake of looking at Tim. As soon as our eyes met, he let out the slightest giggle. That triggered my urge to giggle, too. I felt a laugh pushing its way up from my chest and took a gulp to try to hold it in. My shoulders began to shake. The situation was awful; beyond awkward. But something about it was unbearably funny, too. Little honks of air escaped from my nose. Tears welled in my eyes. I stared hard at my knees, trying to think unfunny thoughts. The more I tried to be serious, the worse it got—exactly like when Father Stanislaw, the old Polish priest from the seminary, would sing off-key at the solemn Good Friday service when we were kids. The more you knew you should not laugh, the more hilarious everything seemed.

From across the bed, I heard a piglike snort and glanced up to see Tim shaking, his eyes squeezed shut, as he plowed blindly ahead: ". . . give us *blah blub,* our *blah-blah blub* . . ." I joined back in: "and de-*blah-blah* us from *mumble,* for-*blah-blub* and *blub-blah.* Amen." We both said the "Amen" in loud, ringing voices. We had that part down. Tim and I wiped our eyes and tried to pretend the prayer had gone off like clockwork. Dad just looked at us with tired, resigned eyes.

In the doorway, with Tim and Elizabeth already down the hall, I turned back to look at him. He was staring up at the ceiling, each forced breath pushing his chin up and his head back into the pillow. The doctors had told him to work at inhaling deeply; the oxygen infusion into his lungs was part of the cure. Breath was life, and he concentrated on pulling each one deep inside him. "Good night, Dad," I whispered and raised two fingers to my lips, throwing him a kiss.

Chapter 33

As the days to Christmas ticked down, we settled into a routine. I took the morning visitation, Tim and Elizabeth took the afternoon slot, and Mike and I returned together for the final visit of the night. Marijo shuttled back and forth from her home and office an hour away to join us whenever she could. When we weren't with Dad, we mostly sat with Mom, telling old stories, massaging her shoulders, keeping her company.

That afternoon, as a gray, dreary dusk fell, I sat alone in the living room with Mom. Tim and Elizabeth were at the hospital; Mike was out running errands. Elizabeth had draped a few strings of holiday lights over the long-silent piano and through the houseplants on the windowsill in a valiant effort to give the place a hint of holiday cheer. But the decorations just made the house seem all the more forlorn, a vestige of its former holiday self, when the fireplace had roared and the air was filled with children's joyous shrieks and the scent of pine boughs. Sitting there, I could not resist the lure of memories from long ago when my parents were in their prime and committed to sinking endless energy into making Christmas magical.

Every other family I knew as a kid simply went to the store and bought Christmas lights for their trees. Not ours. Dad spent hours hand-wiring his own lights of a special design, guaranteed to never cause a spark because they ran in series on a single wire. What that meant was that if one bulb went out, they all went out. Part of our family ritual every year was unscrewing bulb after bulb and testing each one to find the culprit. Some years we would work late into Christmas Eve trying to get those crazy lights figured out. Then we'd all race out into the cold to make it to Our Lady of Refuge for midnight Mass, which, with its giant nativity scene, banks of red poinsettias, and curfew-busting mystique, seemed magical indeed.

The house had never seemed so silent.

"Just you and me, Ruthie," I said as we sat in the growing gloom.

"Just me and my number three son," she said.

"Are you hungry? Can I make you something?"

"Maybe a little, sure," she said. I helped her to the kitchen table, my hands under her armpits in case she stumbled, and warmed a plate of leftovers in the microwave.

"You were hungry!" I exclaimed when she finished. "You cleaned your plate." I felt the familiar swell of satisfaction as when my own kids ate everything put before them. She was more like them now than I would ever have imagined. My mother had come full circle. She had stopped worrying about her children, stopped fretting about our life choices and spiritual well-being, stopped trying to bend us to her will. All the flashpoints that had seemed so important and consumed so much of her emotional energy had washed away like flotsam on an outgoing tide. We had to hide candy from her now, pester her to eat her vegetables and drink enough water, remind her to brush her teeth, and bribe her with treats to take her medicines.

Back in the living room, I steered her to her favorite chair, and we sat in the glow of the colored lights, the house so quiet I could hear the whisper of air rising from the heating vents.

"Just five days till Christmas, Ma," I said.

"Will Dad be home for Christmas?" she asked.

"I don't know, Mom," I said. "I don't think so."

We sat for a long time, listening to the heat.

"No snow yet," she said eventually, looking out into the twilight.

"Maybe by Christmas," I said.

That's when she began to sing. Soft and reedy, her weak voice carrying a certain warble, as if coming from a tiny bird or a little girl.

"I'm dreaming of a white Christmas . . ."

I marveled at my mother's mind. From what part of her faraway memory had the song surfaced? I had not heard her sing "White Christmas" in decades.

My choices were to sit and listen to that plaintively lonely voice, or join in. Together we sang through the verse, conjuring images of snowcapped evergreens and children awaiting Santa's arrival.

Neither of us knew more than the first verse, and so we sang it over again. Over and over. When she had sung all she wanted, she stopped and sighed.

"That Bing Crosby, heavens how he could sing," she said, and then she was asleep in her chair, the silence again enveloping us.

The next morning, Tuesday, I arrived at the hospital at 10 A.M. to find Dad propped up and breathing comfortably through a light plastic mask that rested loosely over his nose and mouth. The big suction mask with the forced air pressure sat idle in the corner. "My blood oxygen has been pretty good," he said, "so they thought they'd give me a break." Through the light mask, I could hear him perfectly.

"That's great, Dad," I said. "You're making progress."

"I'm not so sure, John," he said. "I don't know anymore." He looked searchingly at me. "What do you think? Do you think I can beat this?"

On this matter of utmost significance, he had not before asked my opinion. I hesitated. My honest response was that my optimism soared and plunged on an hourly basis. One moment I saw the possibility of a full recovery and a continuation of the lifestyle for which my parents had worked so hard. The next moment I realized their days of independence were over. Even in a best-case scenario, my parents would need to live in a facility with nursing care. There would be no more driving or lawn cutting or grocery shopping. And the moment after that I was all but certain Dad's worst fear would come true, and he would never be leaving the ICU. The doctors were running out of options. The pneumonia and leukemia were in a race to the finish, and neither showed signs of slowing. I had no clue whether he could beat this thing. With each day it seemed less likely. I was trying to be realistic. I didn't want to patronize him.

"I don't know, Dad," I said. "We just need to keep fighting. We need to keep pushing."

"And praying," he added.

"And praying, Dad. You can't give up."

He nodded in agreement. "I just want to get better so I can be there for Mother," he said. "I want to take care of her for however long she has left." He remained hopelessly devoted to her. She was his everything, and it seemed his only wish was to outlive her by one day. I lifted the mask up and held the straw from his water glass to his lips so he could sip.

"One day at a time, Dad," I said.

"You know I've been fretting about Christmas."

"You mean you haven't gotten out to buy my gift yet?" I deadpanned.

"I don't want to spoil Christmas for everyone."

"Oh, Dad, you're not."

"You should be home with Jenny and the kids," he said. "We both know that."

"I'm playing it by ear," I said. "I may fly home on Christmas Eve. We'll see."

I had already spoken with Jenny about the possibility of missing the holiday, and she had told me she and the kids would be fine. "You need to be there right now," she had said.

I changed topics. "Mike and I went to Lourdes yesterday and talked to the administrator," I said. "She was great. Told us how much they all admire you and appreciate all you've done for them over the years."

Dad's eyes widened with expectation. "And?"

"And they have a long waiting list, but she said they'll do whatever it takes to find a spot for you and Mom," I said. "We got to peek at the suite near the chapel, the one for a couple. It has two bedrooms and a sitting room; it would be perfect for you and Mom. The paperwork's done."

"That's good," Dad said. "It's good you took care of that."

I didn't tell him the suite would soon be available, nor why: the current occupant, an aged priest, was days from death. Nursing homes were a lot like the ICU that way, the last station on the stagecoach ride of life.

We sat quietly for a few minutes.

"Say," he began, and I could tell from the way he was wetting his lips that he was about to say something he had been rehearsing. "This is a good time to talk to you about something." He held out his hand for me to take. I slipped my fingers through his and sat beside him on the bed.

"Sure," I said.

"What are you doing about the kids' religion?"

My heart sank. Our taboo topic was back on the table. We both knew the answer to his question, and it was *nothing*. "Dad,"

I said in almost a whisper, letting his name hang on the air. "I'm doing my best. I know it's not how you did it, or how you want me to do it, but I'm trying to raise them right."

"You are raising them right, John," he said, and he squeezed my hand. "You're a good father. I just worry about them growing up without religion and prayer in their lives. Prayer, especially, is so important."

I wanted to give him assurances, to tell him what I knew he longed to hear, that his grandchildren would receive the sacraments and attend Mass every week and be raised as good Catholics. I knew I couldn't say that and be true to myself—or honest to him. I owed him my honesty. I respected him too much to give him any less. Besides, he was an intelligent man; over the years, I had gradually come to realize that all my sugarcoated half-truths had not fooled him for a moment. Mom maybe, but not Dad.

He must have sensed my discomfort. "I know you have issues with the Church," he said.

"Yeah, I do," I said. "But I haven't given up on it just yet. I'm not done trying to figure it out." And that much was true: I hadn't, and I wasn't.

"That's all I can ask," he said.

Lunch arrived, and I pulled up his mask and fed him his soup and yogurt one spoonful at a time.

That evening Michael and I arrived for the 8:30 visit and again we found Dad breathing comfortably through the lighter mask. I was figuring out that the nurses switched masks when they knew family members were expected so he could talk and be heard more easily. After we left, they would switch back to the heavy ventilator mask. All the ICU nurses were caring, but one, a woman about my age named Michelle, was particularly kind and was Dad's favorite. She seemed sincerely fond of him and always had a cheerful word. Michelle routinely let us stay past visiting hours and sometimes slipped us sodas and snacks. It was just like her to think to switch masks so her patient could have more meaningful time with his children.

Dad had good color in his face and was relaxed and resting comfortably. Michael and I had a pleasant visit with him. We told him more about our trip to Lourdes and the suite it had on standby. We gave him the daily update on Mom, assuring him she missed him but otherwise was doing fine.

The ICU staff had begun timing meal deliveries to our visits because Dad was too weak to feed himself, and they were too busy to do it for him. Another bowl of pureed soup—one of the few things he could swallow with his swollen mouth—arrived and I again fed it to him by the spoonful, just as I did with my children before they were old enough to feed themselves.

"I'm helpless as a baby," Dad apologized between bites.

"You've been through the wringer," I said. "Now open up; here comes another bite."

On the drive home that night, I told Michael I had made a decision. I would fly home that Thursday and return three days later, the day after Christmas. "Dad's holding his own," I said. "He's eating well. He's breathing comfortably, even on the lighter mask. I can't imagine anything changing too dramatically in the next few days."

"It should be pretty much status quo through the holiday, I'd think," Michael agreed.

"I'll dash home for Christmas and be back the next day."

That was the plan.

Chapter 34

I awoke early the next morning and booked a flight home for Christmas, then called Jenny.

"Are you sure you should be leaving?" she asked.

I assured her my father was stable and in for the long haul. "Last night he actually looked the best he has all week," I said. "Whichever way this goes, it's going to be a long, slow process."

I showered, ate a bowl of cereal, and headed to the hospital for my regular ten-to-noon shift. When I arrived, I knew right away something was wrong. The door to Dad's room was wide open, a crash cart in the doorway. Michelle intercepted me in the hallway, her face drawn and white. "I'm so glad you're here. Your dad's had a very rough morning," she said. "Twice his blood oxygen crashed. We had the respiratory team in here. They really had to work on him to get him out of danger. It was touch and go." The goal was to keep his blood oxygen saturation as close to 100 percent as possible. All week it had been hovering in the 90s, which was good. At an oxygen saturation level of 86 percent, alarms are triggered. On this morning, the alarms rang at

8 A.M. and again ninety minutes later, and both times the levels plunged, bottoming out below 70 percent even as he gasped 40 breaths per minute. Blood oxygen levels that low for more than a few minutes could result in stroke or damage to his brain and other vital organs, Michelle said.

"He's resting now," she said, "but this is a threshold day for your family." I remember thinking how odd a word choice that was, *threshold*. It was as if she knew our family would soon be stepping through a doorway, crossing from one chapter of life into another, never to return again. "We need clear direction on what you want us to do," she said. "If it happens again—and it will, it's just a matter of when—we'll need to intubate him and put him on a ventilator." She hesitated. "If that's what the family wants." She didn't have to tell me the ramifications of being ventilated, or what the alternative meant. I looked through the doorway at Dad. The big suction mask was again clamped over his face, pushing his head back into the pillow with each forced breath. His mouth was agape, struggling to accept each gust. His eyes were shut, his body still. There was now even more equipment surrounding him.

The respiratory therapist who had worked on him joined us. "If we intubate him, he likely will never come off," she said. "At this stage, it's nearly impossible to wean them off the vent again. You need to know that. I've been doing this for sixteen years, and I haven't seen anyone in your father's condition come off it yet."

"I see," I said. But I didn't see at all. The words were pinging off the inside of my skull like pinballs. I felt blindsided by the surprise attack of information. I had arrived planning to tell him about the flight I had just booked; he was going to assure me he'd be fine until I returned. That was how our visit was supposed to go. Now all I could think was that I would not be able to feed him his lunch.

"Dr. Bober's expecting your call," Michelle said and she led me to the nurses' station and dialed. The doctor confirmed everything the others had just told me. The pneumonia was winning; Dad's lungs were shutting down. A ventilator would breathe indefinitely for him, but that was not a blessing. He could linger for months as the leukemia slowly ravaged him.

"Nature's trying to take its course," she said. "Pneumonia is sometimes known as 'the merciful death' because it takes terminal patients quickly." The doctor knew my father's wishes as well as I did. He had made it clear he wanted to fight with everything he had as long as any chance of meaningful recovery remained. But if not, he wanted no heroic measures to keep him alive. In his religious paradigm, that would be defying God's will.

"I think today is your dad's day," the doctor said in a voice that was so gentle and so kind I nearly began to cry. "Call your brothers and sister. I'll meet you all there in an hour, okay?"

I did as I was told, then walked into Dad's room and stood at his side. He appeared to be unconscious. The whir of the machine filled the room. I could see his breath fog the mask as he exhaled and disappear as another massive gust of oxygen pushed in. Michelle came in and said, "He's been through a lot this morning. He's exhausted." She shook his shoulder vigorously and spoke in a loud voice: "Mr. Grogan, can you hear me? Mr. Grogan, wake up. Do you need anything? Mr. Grogan, your son is here."

Gradually Dad returned from his deep sleep. I touched his arm and put my lips close to his ear. "Dad, it's John," I said. "I'm here. I'm right here." He didn't open his eyes but nodded his head up and down in small, quick movements. He began to move his mouth inside the mask and was trying to lift his head and claw his hand out from beneath the blanket.

"Do you need something, Mr. Grogan?" Michelle asked in a loud voice. "Are you thirsty?" He shook his head no. "Are your lips dry?" No. "Is the mask too tight?" No. "Are you too warm?" Finally: "Are you trying to say something?" My father's head nodded vigorously in the affirmative, his eyes still closed. She unstrapped the mask and pulled it aside.

"What is it, Dad?" I asked.

"Are the kids all here?" he asked.

"It's John, Dad. The others will be here in a few minutes."

He lay there for a moment as if summoning from deep within the strength to speak. His eyes fluttered open momentarily, and he said, "I'm tired." And then, each word coming out like its own sentence: "I. Don't. Want. To. Fight. This. Anymore."

I looked at Michelle. She nodded her head that it was okay, and I looked back at my father.

"You don't need to fight anymore, Dad," I said. "You gave it everything you had. You can stop. You can just relax now." I told him what Dr. Bober had told me, that she could make sure he did not suffer. "You've been so brave, Dad," I said. "So brave. You can let go now."

Michelle replaced his mask, and he drifted back into his deep retreat. I waited in the hallway until Marijo, Tim, and Michael arrived. Their eyes were red, and I could tell they had been crying in the car on the way over. "There's something you all need to hear," I said and called Michelle over. "We took the mask off Dad and he said a few words. Michelle, I just want to make sure you heard what I heard."

"He said he was tired and didn't want to fight anymore," she said. I was so grateful for her testimony. I did not want his last words, his final wish, to rest on my shoulders alone. "Those were his words," she repeated, "'I don't want to fight this anymore.'"

By the time Dr. Bober arrived we were all in agreement that there would be no more medical intervention. Dad was ready; we had to be, too. In the ICU lounge, the doctor walked us through how the day would go. A palliative care team would take over from here, she said, and would administer adequate morphine and muscle relaxants to override his breathing impulse and eliminate any gasping reflex as his blood oxygen levels dropped. "His lungs are so compromised," the doctor said, "I don't think it will take very long."

The four of us had agreed that Mom would want to say good-bye to her husband, but when we told Dr. Bober we planned to bring her up to his bedside for a few minutes, she looked appalled. "Don't do that to your mother," she pleaded. "Please, don't. She won't be able to process all this. It will only traumatize her. Let her remember him the way he was." It was the best advice anyone could have given.

Dr. Bober said she wanted to say good-bye to the man who had been her patient and friend for twenty years. When she came out of his room a few minutes later, she was crying.

A few minutes later, a woman arrived and introduced herself as Peg Nelson. She was a nurse practitioner on the palliative care team and would be managing Dad's last hours. I instantly liked her. She was matter-of-fact without seeming blasé, sympathetic without being maudlin. She gave us a reasoned and full explanation of what the next few hours would hold. When we were ready, she would inject Dad with the morphine and muscle relaxant, then remove his breathing mask. "He will deeply relax and slip into unconsciousness and not feel any discomfort."

Like Dr. Bober, she said, "It should come very quickly."

Awkwardly, we asked about the logistics of death: When should we say our good-byes? Would he be able to hear us? She said we should say what we wanted him to hear before the injections, and that he would still be semiaware for several minutes after.

I asked when all of this was going to happen. Part of me hoped she would say we could come back tomorrow. "We can start anytime," she said. "You should eat something first. Why don't we meet back here in an hour, after you've had a chance to get some lunch." An hour. My siblings and I looked at each other. The moment was slowly sinking in. We were scheduling our father's death like we might schedule a dentist appointment. Two-thirty would work. Right after we'd had time to grab a bite to eat.

"My God," Marijo said and placed a hand over her mouth.

In the cafeteria, we picked at our food. I managed to choke down half a turkey sandwich. I knew without doubt that we were making the right decision, the decision Dad wanted, the one that Dr. Bober assured us was inevitable. He would finally be free from the pain and exhaustion and debilitation of fighting this losing battle. It was the right thing. Why then did it not feel that way?

After lunch, we stopped in the hospital chapel, and I knelt in front of the miniature altar and tried to pray. "Please take him quickly," I whispered into my hands. "Without trauma or pain. Don't let him be afraid. Let him go without doubting his beliefs." I took comfort in his certainty that eternal salvation awaited him on the other side, and that his beloved wife would join him in heaven soon enough. Before I stood up, I whispered, "Help me live my life half as well as he has lived his."

I found Tim and Mike sitting on a bench just outside the chapel. Marijo was still inside, deep in her own moment of contemplation. "I'm going to go up and sit with Dad," I said. "See you up there in a few minutes."

In his room, I found him as we had left him, eyes closed, body still, the whir of the breathing machine filling the air. I rested one hand on his shoulder and the other on his wrist beneath the blanket. "Dad, it's John," I said, and he opened his eyes. I could see he was alert and aware, though terribly weak. He began to mumble something beneath the mask, his words lost in the whirlwind of oxygen. I hushed him.

"Dad," I said, my voice quaking, "Jesus is going to take you home today. In just a little while, he's going to take you." Dad's eyes were closed again. He moved his head up and down in short, jerky motions, and I knew he understood. Whatever I had to say, now was the time. I drew in a breath.

"Dad, you know how much I love you. I love you so much." He began urgently working his mouth inside the mask, desperately trying to communicate something. "Don't try to talk. It's okay. I

know. I know you love me, too. I know that. I know you'd say it
if you could. You love me." His head jerked up and down. "And I
know you're proud of me, Dad. I never doubted that. Don't think
I ever did." More little head jerks. I told him not to worry about
Mother; we'd take good care of her. I repeated the words he had
said to me a few days earlier: "Mom's going to be okay." More
nods.

From earlier conversations, I knew he worried that the family
might crumble after he and my mother were gone, that without
their glue, the four of us kids would drift apart. I assured him we
would not. "We're going to look out for each other, Dad. We'll keep
the family together."

There was one more thing I wanted to tell him, something I
had been rehearsing for the past several days even as I denied
that the time was near to say them. "Dad, can you hear me?" I
asked, my lips close to his ear. He nodded. I paused to steady my
voice. "Dad, it has been an honor to be your son. I am so honored
and so proud." I swallowed hard, fighting to maintain composure.
"An honor."

I glanced over my shoulder, and there was Tim in the doorway. "Okay, Dad," I whispered. "Tim's here now." I ran my palm
once over his sandpapery stubble, just as I liked to do when I was
a little boy sitting in his lap. As then, I found the touch of it oddly
soothing, at once rough and warm. One more time I told him I
loved him, then kissed his temple and walked out of the room.

Chapter 35

When the others had each had their private good-byes with him, we gathered in the hallway and told Peg we were ready. The one thing we knew Dad would want was a priest to give him final absolution. Not that any of us thought he needed it. "If this man's not getting into heaven," Tim said, only half joking, "then no one is." Michael earlier had called Father Vin to ask if he would drive to the hospital from his home, more than an hour away. We thought it fitting that the priest who had married our parents and baptized all their children be there to see the first of them off, but a blizzard was threatening to sweep in off the Great Lakes, and our uncle was afraid to be caught on the interstate. We couldn't blame him. He, too, was an old man now. Michelle said she would track down the hospital chaplain.

In the room, we surrounded the bed, Marijo and I on Dad's right, Tim and Mike on his left. We each laid claim to a part of our father, a forearm or knee or shoulder, and placed our hands on him. Four children, eight hands. "We're all here, Daddy," Marijo said.

Peg was standing by with two syringes. "Are we ready?" she asked in that gentle, calm way of hers. We nodded, and she gave the injections. Almost instantly we could feel his limbs going slack beneath our hands. "We're going to let him relax for a few minutes," she said and looked at the clock. It was 2:50 P.M.

At just before 3:00, Peg removed the mask and flicked off the respirator. Without the rattling whir of the machine, the room went suddenly silent. It felt nearly serene. The four of us, and Peg and Michelle, too, kept our eyes fixed on the monitor that read Dad's blood oxygen levels. They were at 96 percent when the mask came off and began slipping almost immediately: 93 . . . 89 . . . 74. As Peg had promised, our father showed no sign of discomfort or anxiety. "We love you, Dad," the four of us said in unison.

The chaplain, a priest from Nigeria, arrived and in a clear, lilting voice administered the Last Rites, my father's second time receiving the sacrament in as many weeks. The priest dabbed sacred oil on my father's forehead and palms, using his thumb to smear it in the sign of a cross. "May the Lord who frees you from sin save you and raise you up," he prayed aloud. Then, with brief condolences to us, he was gone. Marijo suggested that Dad would find comfort in hearing us say a decade of the rosary: one Our Father and ten Hail Marys followed by a short prayer I grew up knowing only as the Glory Be to the Father. None of us had a rosary, and we used our fingers to count off each Hail Mary. With my sister and Michael leading the way, Tim and I this time were able to keep up without stumbling.

As we finished the prayers, I looked out the window and saw the first snowflakes dancing from the sky. The front edge of the storm pushing in from Canada had arrived. That's when we heard the angels sing. The voices came from far down the hall, growing louder as they neared us. A group of hospital volunteers was strolling the halls of this saddest of all wings, where battles are surrendered and life meets its inevitable end, pausing at each door to sing a Christmas carol.

Outside Dad's room, they sang "Silent Night," their soothing voices surrounding us like an embrace. I liked the idea of Dad drifting off to something so peaceful. "All is calm, all is bright . . ." We thanked them; then Tim asked, "Do you know Ave Maria? Our father was very devoted to the Blessed Mother. It would mean a lot." The lead caroler apologized; they had not rehearsed it. We thanked them again and turned back to Dad. The carolers must have reconsidered because from behind us came their voices once more, as warm and burnished as polished mahogany. As the first snowstorm of the winter swirled outside, dusting the world in white, they sang the song our father loved most. It was hard not to smile, and not to cry a little, too.

As the afternoon slipped away, the life-giving oxygen in my father's bloodstream slipped away with it. The numbers on the monitor continued to fall. 64 . . . 57 . . . 45. At 40, Peg broke the silence to say, "They don't get much lower than this." His heart, however, beat steadily on, and his blood pressure remained strong. Even in unconsciousness, he continued to draw slow, even breaths. My father was defying the predictions of a quick death.

At 6 P.M., we made a group decision. Tim and Marijo would go home and tell Mom. It was something we all dreaded, but in the end she would prove herself once again the tough old bird, accepting the news stoically. I suspect she knew before any of us that her husband would not be coming home. Mike and I would stay behind and sit with Dad. Even though he was in a deep coma now, we would not risk him dying alone. For the next two hours, the two of us sat there mostly in silence, watching Dad breathe. Finally I said, "Why don't you go home and get some rest. I'll call if anything changes." I wanted to give my brother a break; he looked exhausted. But mostly I wanted to sit alone with my father for a little while longer. Mike agreed to my offer, but first I walked to the cafeteria, ordered a bowl of soup, and called Jenny to bring her and the children up to date.

After I was done eating, I returned to the room and sent Michael home. Standing beside the bed, I let my eyes travel from my father's face to the snow outside. Now that there was no turning back, I no longer felt so helpless or inconsolable, nor did death seem so terrifying. Just the opposite. If anything, it felt peaceful. Peaceful and almost . . . beautiful. As natural a part of life's rhythm as a baby's first breath or a butterfly's inaugural ascent from the cocoon. Standing there, I thought about spring's glide into summer, and summer's march to autumn, and the reliable promise of dawn in every setting sun. I thought about the old maple tree that fell in the yard and the young garden that flourished in its footprint. Mostly I thought about Dad and the exemplary life he had led—and, for all our differences, the indelible mark he had left on me.

Michelle stuck her head in the door to say she was going home for the night. "I'm going to miss your dad," she said.

"He thought the world of you," I told her, and she hugged me.

Her replacement on the night shift was a young, extraordinarily gentle man named James. He had black hair, brown skin, a white smile, and an almost beatific presence. "Is there anything I can bring you?" he asked.

"No," I said, then reconsidered. "Actually, yes. Could I borrow a pen and a pad of paper?"

"Our father was many things," I wrote as I sat on the bed beside him, my leg touching his. Then I began to list them: son, brother, husband, father, grandfather. Engineer, mathematician, war veteran, scout leader, volunteer. Stamp collector, gardener, sailor, classical music buff. Faithful Catholic. I looked up at him lying peacefully in the netherworld between life and death, and wrote,

"Mostly he was a good guy. A good and sensitive and gentle man." Without intending to, I had begun to write the eulogy I would deliver at his funeral the next week.

I scribbled it all down on the pad, describing his itinerant childhood and the French teacher who helped him find his way to college and a future he had never dreamed possible. I mentioned his double deferment after Pearl Harbor and his decision to enlist anyway. I wrote how he returned from the war with four years of Sunday church collections in his pocket and how that serendipitously led him to my mother. I joked about his engineer's sense of precision and his quirky affection for chopsticks.

I told the story of Dad's Rube Goldberg invention for storing the *Mary Ann* during the winter, designing and building a series of braces and pulleys to haul it up into the rafters above where he parked his car. Just before the inaugural test of his boat-lifting invention, he looked over at me, his junior assistant and tool fetcher, and said brightly, "One decimal point off, Johnny boy, and there goes the Buick." He knew he had the decimal point right, but he wanted me to know that even small, innocent mistakes can lead to major consequences.

I wrote until I was out of things to say, then I folded the pages and pushed them into my pocket. "Well, Dad," I said, brushing my fingers through his white fringe of hair. "It's been quite an adventure." I let my fingers trace over his eyebrows and down the slope of his nose. "I'm going to miss you."

At eleven o'clock, Tim returned with Elizabeth, and I retreated to the lounge down the hall with a blanket and pillow. The next thing I knew Elizabeth was shaking me. "Come quick," she said. "Daddy's eyes open."

When I got to the room, his eyes were indeed open, but they were vacant. His heart rate was dropping and his breathing, which had been slow and steady all night, now came in short gasps separated by eternally long silences. Tim and I squeezed his arms and talked to him even though we knew he could not hear. He exhaled one final deep breath, and Tim and I both looked at the monitor. The green line made one last bump and then traveled flat across the screen. James the nurse must have been watching the same line from his station down the hall because he appeared behind us and said in the gentlest voice, "He's gone." A few minutes later, a doctor I had never seen before arrived and listened with a stethoscope. Time of death: 1:16 A.M., Thursday, December 23, 2004.

We walked out of the hospital and into an undisturbed snowscape that managed to make even grimy Pontiac—the city where my father was born and where, eighty-nine years and two weeks later, he had died—appear impossibly beautiful. Three inches of virgin snow covered everything, glistening in the streetlights. There were not even any tire tracks. Somehow it felt perfect, as if the heavens had conspired to wrap my father and all that he had touched in a shroud of purity and goodness and grace.

In Dad's Buick, I pulled out onto Woodward Avenue and led the way through the still-falling snow, Tim and Elizabeth following behind. I took it slow, peering through the beating wiper blades to follow the road beneath its unmarred white blanket. It was 3 A.M. when I slid beneath a comforter on the couch in the basement and fell into a deep and dream-filled sleep.

Chapter 36

———

I awoke before dawn and tiptoed into the kitchen, closing the door behind me so as not to disturb the others. I made coffee and called the airline to try to change my flight, which was scheduled to leave in a few hours. It was hard to believe that I had been so bullishly confident Dad would be fine while I skipped out for a few days. The last eighteen hours did not quite seem real, and I paused to remind myself I had not simply dreamed them. Now here I was, holding on the line, hoping to get some kind of bereavement consideration. I wanted to push the flight back one day, flying home on Christmas Eve. When the customer service agent finally came on, I explained my circumstances. "My father died five hours ago," I said. "I need to help plan his funeral today." She told me she was sorry for my loss but she couldn't rebook my flight without charging a penalty. The Christmas Eve flights were running nine hundred dollars a ticket. Supply and demand. I felt what little spirit that was left in me drain away.

Then she said: "What city are you flying out of again?"

"Detroit," I said.

"You're in luck," she told me. "That airport has declared a ground snow emergency, which means we don't expect people to make it there. I can rebook you tomorrow at the same price, no penalty."

My heart leaped, and only then did I realize how badly I missed Jenny and the kids and needed to get back to them. I looked out the window at the uninterrupted snowscape emerging in the gray light and had to smile. I did not believe in miracles, not in the literal way my parents did, but I couldn't resist the idea that my father had performed his first. I snickered at the thought that his very first order of business upon arriving at heaven's gate was to dial in a snowstorm so John could change his flight without a penalty and get home to his family for Christmas. My famously frugal father would have just hated to see a perfectly good airline ticket go to waste.

When Mom awoke, she asked, "Did Dad die?"

"Yes, Mom," I said, wrapping my arms around her. "About one-fifteen this morning."

"Oh," she said.

After breakfast, Marijo and I went into his closet and picked out a gray suit, light blue shirt, and striped tie. From the box I had made him, I pulled out his General Motors forty-year service pin with the tiny diamond and attached it to the lapel of the jacket. Marijo retrieved his grandfather's rosary, which we agreed belonged in his hands. Then with Michael we drove to the funeral home, picked out a casket that we thought fit his personality—modest but of solid hardwood—and planned the service.

Later that afternoon, we sat with Mom and paged through old photo albums for a slide show that would run at his viewing. It was therapeutic for all of us, and Mom enjoyed looking through the snapshots of their life together. I feared they might make her sad, a reminder of all that had been and was now gone, but her eyes brightened and she launched into her chestnuts. "Oh, there's Irene O'Brien. Did I tell you about the time we fell into the river?"

She had, many times, but we sat and listened intently as if it were the first telling. Then we reached the photos of us as kids and teenagers, and we managed to laugh at our bad haircuts and cringe-worthy fashion statements from the sixties and seventies.

We picked out a representative selection, starting with a photo of Dad as a toddler, then as a young boy, teen, college student, navy lieutenant, bachelor, newlywed, new father, retiree. It ended with a photo of him walking Elizabeth down the aisle at Our Lady of Refuge that summer. We marveled at how handsome he looked in his twenty-fifth-anniversary GM portrait, the young executive with the pinnacle of his career still ahead of him. And at how beautiful Mom was in her early twenties with her lustrous hair parted on the side and swept back behind one ear. As we sorted through a lifetime of memories, the passage of time was palpable. My parents' chapter was all but closed now, collapsing into the dust of memory.

Dad had wanted me to spend Christmas with my own family, and the next day that is what I did, flying home to Pennsylvania in time for Christmas Eve dinner. He had been right; it was where I belonged, and it never felt so good to be back. The day after Christmas, just as the sun was peeking over the white pines, Jenny and I packed the kids, the dog, and our best clothes into the minivan and left on the same ten-hour drive Tim and I had made not quite two weeks earlier.

Six priests and a bishop concelebrated the funeral Mass, with Father Vin giving the homily, portraying Dad in saintly terms that surely would have embarrassed him. Mom sat stoically in the front row, weeping only once. Tim read two passages from the Bible, Marijo announced a list of intentions, and Michael gave a brief history of Dad's life. Then it was my turn and I stood on the altar and gave the eulogy I had written in the hospital room. As I spoke, I looked out and saw the faces from my childhood. Old neighbors and classmates and long-forgotten acquaintances. Rock was there, and Sack, and Tommy's mother, Mrs. Cullen, herself a widow of just two months. Afterward, she told me Tommy sent his best from Arizona.

There was another group at the funeral I had not known about. A group of men, most of them about my age, who belonged to a men's prayer group my father had started. Once a month they got together for prayer and fellowship. Thirty of them had shown up in matching dark suits to serve as pallbearers, and it was instantly obvious my father had meant a great deal to them. The sight of them lined up two abreast to escort my father's casket down the center aisle to the altar was moving. For me, it was also painful, for in them I saw the son he surely wished I could have been—the kind who embraced and shared his reverence and devotion. As one by one they filed past me in the receiving line, shaking my hand and telling me how much they admired my father and what a spiritual inspiration he had been to them, I could not help feeling my failings. With each of them, he enjoyed the relationship he could only dream of with me, one that did not need to be censored or sanitized or danced around. One he could embrace openly without fear of a son's squirming rejection. Long ago, he had stopped sharing that part of himself with me, and I had been grateful that he had. We had both come to realize that religion, that grand unifying force that should have been the healing, binding balm that cemented our family, was the single most painful strain on it. When I looked at these men of certitude and shared belief, I could not help seeing the adult son my father had finally, after years of struggle, conceded I would never be.

After the funeral, and the lunch hosted by the women's altar society, and the drive to Ann Arbor to lower my father's casket into the earth beside the grave of his long-departed infant daughter, Tim and I decided to fire up the snowblower. Our longtime neighbor, Les Schoonover, had shown up unannounced the morning of Dad's death to plow out the driveway, one of countless small acts of kindness that touched us as a family and made me realize the greatest comfort to the grieving comes not from words but from actions. But more snow was threatening, and from his hospital bed Dad had urged us to start up the snowblower and make sure it was ready for the coming winter.

In the garage, we checked the oil, topped off the gasoline, and set the choke. Michael would be taking over Dad's snowblowing duties now, but he was perhaps the least mechanical person on the planet, and Tim and I knew we needed to show him how to run it. When it came time to start it, we were stumped. Somewhere was an electric ignition button, but it eluded us. We searched and searched and finally paused to scratch our heads.

"Hold on," I blurted out. "Let me go ask—" I stopped short, catching myself. We stood looking at each other, our breath vaporizing in the cold air.

"Dad," Tim said, finishing the sentence for me. "That was my first thought, too. Ask Dad."

"He's really gone," I said. "It's just now sinking in."

Tim and I had both lived independently for years, but always in the back of our minds we had known our father was there if we needed him. For a loan or career advice or handyman tips or life guidance or a place to move back to if all else failed. No longer. The paternal safety net was officially and permanently cut away. It was our turn now.

"Come on," Tim said, "we can figure this out." And we eventually did, locating the button in a hiding place beneath the carburetor. The snowblower roared to life, ready for another season.

Chapter 37

The months passed. Winter's snows surrendered to spring's trumpet call. The forsythia bloomed with exceptional vigor that year, followed by the cherry trees and azaleas and redbuds. Our backyard hens hatched out a clutch of chicks, and the wild rabbits emerged from the woods with their babies to stage nightly raids on the vegetable garden. The Canada geese again flew north in V-formation. Like I knew it would, life marched on.

Three days after my father's death, as we prepared to bury him, a human tragedy of unimaginable proportions struck halfway around the world. A tsunami off the coast of Sumatra sent a giant wall of water cascading across the Indian Ocean at the speed of a jet plane, claiming an estimated 150,000 lives and displacing millions. And yet my siblings and I barely registered it at the time. Enmeshed in our own grief and personal loss, we somehow did not even notice this indiscriminate extinction of human life. Now, months later, it offered a valuable contrast to our own experience. People die every minute of every day; sometimes they die in vast numbers without warning, sometimes in horrific and terrifying ways, sometimes decades before their time. My father had lived a long and healthy life. He had remained vital and physically strong until the final few months, and mentally sharp until the end. As deaths go, his was a gentle and peaceful one, surrounded by his children. He had had time to put his affairs in order without too much time to linger, and he left this world believing it was just the warm-up act, that the true journey, the real reward, still awaited him. Not such a bad way to exit a full and worthy life.

In the months following my father's death, a new friend came unexpectedly onto my horizon. His name was Michael Murray, and he was a regular reader of my newspaper column who one day took the time to send an e-mail commenting on one of my pieces. His words reflected an intelligence and sensitivity I admired. I wrote back, and soon we were corresponding. I liked him right away. He was smart and thoughtful; funny and self-deprecating; direct and plainspoken. Only gradually did I figure out that my new e-mail pal was a Roman Catholic priest. He did not hide his religious faith, but he did not wear it on his sleeve, either. He insisted I skip the "Father" business and just call him Michael. I was so comfortable being candid with him that sometimes I had to remind myself I was talking with a clergyman.

He was a fan of what I did for a living, of using words to reach out to the larger community. As he put it in one e-mail, "Just remember: Jesus's favorite and most frequent way of teaching was telling stories. Is it any surprise that as things have come and gone with the passage of time, storytelling remains? It is part and parcel of what makes us human—and puts us in touch with our humanity." He called writing my "ministry" and added, "In your own way, John, you are doing God's work."

One day in May we met at a pub near my office for bratwursts and beer. Michael was my age, broad-shouldered and bearded, a guy's guy who looked more likely to be running a lumber mill than a retreat center. His father had died six years earlier, and his mother now lived alone on the family homestead. He was trying to balance his vocation with his care for her. Trying to be a good son but feeling guilty that his best was not quite enough. We had a lot to talk about.

As I drove home afterward, I had to laugh. Was Dad meddling again? It seemed oddly coincidental that this likeable, nonjudgmental, wise priest had just happened to pop into my life. I enjoyed the image of Dad somewhere in a cloud-ensconced heaven, white robes flowing just like in the cartoons, hard at work to find the perfect moral adviser to parachute into my life. I could almost hear him ruminating: "That John's a piece of work. Whoever I send can't be too conservative; can't be preachy; can't be overly dogmatic or holier than thou; can't come on too strong. Has to be a regular kind of guy. Someone who can curse a little and enjoy beer. Should be about his age, too. Hmmm, let's see. Ah, what do we have here? Father Michael Murray at the Oblates of Saint Francis de Sales down in Wilmington. A little liberal for my taste, but John would like that. This looks like a good fit." I found something comforting in the fantasy of my father busy at the switch, minding the details, like the Wizard of Oz furiously working the levers behind the giant curtain.

Summer turned to fall and fall to winter. As Christmas neared, I brought home a tree and strung lights. But mostly I thought about how to mark the first anniversary of my father's death. I couldn't visit his grave; it was three states away. I couldn't get together with my siblings or my mother; we were scattered across an even wider swath of geography. I didn't want to drag Jenny and the kids through some kind of schmaltzy family ceremony. Maybe I would just take a hike in the woods, like I did so often with him as a kid.

On December 22, I wrote Father Michael a brief e-mail: "Tomorrow's the anniversary of my dad's death. I'd appreciate you keeping him in your prayers." Over his lifetime, Dad had spent a fortune making prayer offerings for others; I knew if anyone would appreciate having a priest say a prayer for him, it was Dad. A few minutes later came Michael's response: "I'll do your dad one better. I'll say Mass for him. And for you. Merry Christmas, John." Why this meant so much to me I still do not know. I had spent a lifetime avoiding Mass, ridiculing it, daydreaming through it, trying to get out of it at every turn. Yet Michael's gesture touched me deeply. In my reply, I thanked him and added this postscript: "Who knows, this prodigal son just might get up a little early tomorrow and stop by a church on the way to work."

The next morning I did exactly that. Saint Joseph's Catholic Church was just down the hill from my house, but in five years I had never once walked through its doors. I arrived as the nuns were shepherding in scores of exuberant students from the parish elementary school, positioning them in the pews with a full arm's length between each child to discourage horseplay. It was the last day of school before their Christmas break, and the kids bubbled with excitement. The girls wore blue plaid jumpers with knee socks and the boys dress shirts with navy ties and slacks, just as we had back at Our Lady of Refuge. Some things did not change. The altar was decorated with a life-size crèche scene and scores of potted poinsettias, another throwback to my past, and the altar servers wore the same ill-fitting, wax-spattered cassocks. I slipped into the empty back row, not quite sure why I had come or whether I would stay. Out of habit, I knelt and crossed myself. As kids, we were taught to say a silent prayer as we waited for the Mass to start, but no prayers came to me, and I spent the time watching the children fidgeting in the pews, thinking it was an experience my own children had never known.

The organist launched into a hymn, signaling us that the priest and altar servers—boys *and* girls now—had begun their way up the center aisle. Father was a tall, graying man with a folksy manner. He was good with the kids, and geared the liturgy to them. During his sermon, he walked up and down the aisle, talking to them about the true meaning of Christmas and coaxing them into a dialogue. During the Offertory, a boy and girl nervously carried the vessels of wine and communion wafers down the aisle, and I remembered the thrill of being picked for that special task—the excitement tinged with terror over the imminent possibility of stumbling and sending the sacraments flying.

After the priest consecrated the hosts and wine, it was time for the kiss of peace, that part of the Mass where congregants are encouraged to turn to those around them and offer a greeting. I had always dreaded the stilted handshakes and forced pleasantries with strangers, and I was grateful that I was sitting alone in the last row. I watched as the children exchanged gleeful greetings, their one opportunity to bridge the dead zones between them and touch. Three pews in front of me, a freckle-faced girl about nine greeted the children on either side of her. Then she turned around and smiled at me. I nodded at her, and she knelt on the seat and stretched far over the back of the pew, so far I thought she might tumble into the empty row behind her. She extended her arm out to me. It took me a second to realize she wanted to shake my hand. I reached forward over the empty pew in front of me and met her halfway, letting her hand slip into mine. "Peace of the Lord be with you," I mumbled woodenly, the words that had been drilled into me decades earlier.

"Merry Christmas, mister," the little girl said. And her face and voice and bright eyes were filled with such innocence, such beauty and voice and bright eyes were filled with such innocence, such beauty and wonderment and unbridled joy, I could not help but feel a rush of holiday warmth. For just a moment I wanted to scoop her up and hug her.

"Merry Christmas," I said.

The children filed to the altar for Holy Communion, and when it was my turn I filed up behind them. Except for the wafer I had accepted at my father's funeral Mass, it was the first time I had received the sacrament in many, many years. I knew I was no doubt violating some ironclad Church rule—I had not been to confession in decades—but I didn't care. It was the anniversary of my father's death and something I wanted to do, for reasons I could not quite pinpoint. As I made my way back to the pew, the organist began "Silent Night," and all the children sang along in their squeaky sweet voices. I flashed back to my father's deathbed and the hospital carolers who had gathered in the doorway. In my pew, I knelt and rested my face in my cupped hands. I closed my eyes and let the music carry me to a serene and safe place.

"Hey, Dad," I whispered. "Bet you didn't think you'd find me here, huh?" It had been a year; there was much to catch him up on. I told him about the kids and how fast they were growing up. "You should hear Patrick on the trumpet," I said. "He's really getting the hang of it. And Conor's quite the little writer now. The teacher asks for ten sentences; he turns in ten pages. You wouldn't even recognize Colleen; she's a foot taller than when you saw her last and reading chapter books now."

I told him about my own book, the one he had known about but never gotten the chance to read. "It's on the bestseller list, Dad, and each week it moves a little higher. I know how proud you'd be." I told him how Mom was doing and how Michael was getting along alone at the house. "You're not going to believe this, but he's mastered both the lawn mower *and* the snowblower." I assured him the Buick was still going strong, and we'd gotten the gutters cleaned out before the first freeze. I told him how much everyone missed him. "I can't believe a whole year has gone by," I said.

From somewhere far outside our private conversation I heard the priest's voice boom out: "The Mass is over. Now go in peace to love and serve the Lord." Then everyone was singing "Joy to the World," and I could hear the squealing, happy children filing out past me. That's when I realized I was crying. I was not sure for how long or why. Maybe it was the children's sweet angel voices or the season's celebration of birth and how for me it would now always be tinged with loss as well. Maybe it was the girl who offered me her hand, and with it a reminder of all life's promises and broken dreams. I had fought back tears at the hospital a year earlier and again at the funeral, but nothing like this. I was a mess, a snot-nosed, blubbering mess. I kept my head down and let the tears soak my sweater sleeve. "For Christ's sake, John," I whispered. "You're acting like Mom." Now I could see more clearly why she cried her eyes out each time she received the Eucharist. Part of it, no doubt, was her belief that she quite literally was taking Christ's body into her own, but maybe another part was that it helped her feel closer to those she had loved and lost. Maybe it was her portal into a place where she could commune with her parents and lost siblings and the infant daughter she would never hold. I thought of the lay definition of communion: the sharing or exchanging of intimate thoughts and feelings, especially on a mental or spiritual level. Maybe that was what all her tears were about.

When I looked up, the church was empty and silent again. I wiped my face on my sleeve and told Dad to take it easy and not worry too much about the rest of us left behind. "We're going to be okay, Dad," I said, and I knew we would. I knew I would. It was my life, for better or worse. He had laid the groundwork; the rest was up to me. The only expectations I had to meet now were my own.

I walked out into the wan December sunlight, the cold morning air a welcome slap to my face. Rummaging through my pockets, I found a tissue and gave my nose a good blow. Then I started the car and drove off to begin a new day.

Epilogue

At the front desk I signed in, then made my way down the polished linoleum floors to the last door on the right. To the corner suite we had briefly, hopefully, considered the place where my mother and father could live out their days together, and where Mom now stayed alone. Peering in the door, I spotted her cane against the couch, but her wheelchair was gone and so was she.

At the nurses' station, I said, "I'm Ruth Grogan's son. Is she around?" It was a ridiculous question. This was a nursing home. Of course she was around. All the patients were always around.

"Ruth's at Mass right now," the nurse said and pointed toward the chapel.

I walked down the hall past a row of wizened women lined up along one wall in their wheelchairs. A few looked up at me; most stared at the floor. One called out, "Take me with you."

At the chapel entrance, I peered through the glass doors to see an ancient priest, himself a resident, saying Mass before a handful of nuns and about three dozen women in wheelchairs. From behind, the residents all looked alike—crowns of fine white hair bowed between slumped shoulders. At first I thought their heads were lowered in prayer but quickly realized every one of them was sound asleep. Among them, I spotted Mom, a sweater over her shoulders, her chin resting on her chest, eyes closed.

"Wake up, Ruthie," I whispered, sidling up beside her and kissing her on top of the head. "It's your number three son."

Her eyes opened and she smiled up at me with wonderment as if she were seeing me for the first time, even though I had visited the previous evening with Jenny and the children. After a few seconds, a glimmer of recognition spread across her face. "Oh, hi, John," she whispered.

I sank down on one knee and rubbed her shoulders, looking up at Father as he soldiered through the profession of faith for the sleeping residents. When I looked back, Mom's eyes were closed again, too. At communion, the priest walked down the rows of wheelchairs, waking each resident long enough to press a wheat wafer on her tongue. Mom opened her mouth without opening her eyes and murmured, "Amen." The instant the host was inside her, she pressed a fist to her heart and began moving her lips in silent prayer, even though she still appeared asleep. Some things were not easily lost.

After Mass, I wheeled her into the courtyard, where she tilted her head toward the sun and smiled. Deep furrows crossed her face now, and her hair was as snowy as an egret, but it was a child's face basking in the warmth, lost in innocence. She began to hum and then sing, her fingers dancing on an imaginary key-board. It was a song I had never heard before, a children's ditty about a brash child swallowed by an alligator she thought she could tame. Mom had no idea what she had eaten for breakfast that morning or why I had miraculously materialized beside her at Mass, but she reeled effortlessly through the stanzas, not missing a beat.

"Where did you learn that?" I asked.

"Girl Scouts," she said.

"Girl Scouts?" I exclaimed with a laugh. "That was eighty years ago! It's about time you got around to singing it to me."

That was all the invitation she needed to sing it all over again.

I wheeled her back to her room and positioned her in front of the window where she could look out on the lawn and gardens. "I'll be back this evening with Jenny and the kids," I told her. "We're here all week."

"I'll count on it, dear," she said, but I knew better.

"Love you, Mom," I said, pressing my lips to her temple.

"Love you, too, sweetheart," Mom said. Then she added something I was not expecting.

"Once they leave home, that's it," she said. "They come back to visit, but it's never the same."

I wanted to protest, but she was right. It never is. It never was.

Outside on the sidewalk, I glanced back through the window where I had left her. She was gazing up at something far away as if her eyes had locked on an airplane or flock of geese in the distant sky. I waved and caught her eye, and she flashed me the same startled look of pleasant surprise she had given me in the chapel.

"Aw, Mom," I whispered.

She blew me a kiss, and I blew her one, too.

Acknowledgments

Writing is a solitary act, and yet a book like this one cannot happen without the help and support of many people.

I would like to start by thanking my literary agent, Laurie Abkemeier, for the indispensable role she played in developing this story from a seed of an idea to a finished manuscript. She served as my sounding board, brainstorming partner, cheerleader, therapist, and first line reader and editor, and her suggestions proved invaluable. I owe a big debt of gratitude to my entire publishing team at William Morrow for believing in this book and making it a reality, including Michael Morrison, Lisa Gallagher, Lynn Grady, Seale Ballenger, Michael Brennan, Jennifer Schulkind, Ben Bruton, and especially my editor, Mauro DiPreta.

I want to thank Anna Quindlen, Doris Kearns Goodwin, Brian DeFiore, Jim Tolpin, Dan Sullivan, JoAnn Burke, Susan and Peter Brown, and Sara and Dave Pandl for their listening ears, encouraging words, and wise counsel. Ray Albertson took a dilapidated shack and turned it into a beautiful writing studio for me that exceeded my wildest dreams. Nice work, Ray! Thanks also are due to Lehigh University in Bethlehem, Pennsylvania, in whose elegant Linderman Library I wrote much of this book while my studio was under construction.

My siblings, Marijo Grogan, Timothy Grogan, and Michael Grogan, trusted me to tell this story accurately, honestly, and sensitively, even while recognizing that each of us sees our shared past through a unique prism; I appreciate the faith they put in me. My siblings also helped me reconstruct many of the scenes in this book, sharing their own insights and memories, and Michael dedicated hours to helping me find and catalog a half century of family photographs, movies, memorabilia, and documents. My mother, Ruth Marie Howard Grogan, even in advanced age, continues to inspire me with her wit, spirit, and boundless sense of humor, and her lifelong gift of storytelling is reflected in these pages. My late father, Richard, remains a strong presence in my life, guiding me by his past example, and I often find myself asking the W.W.D.D. question—what would Dad do? My eternal debt of gratitude to both my parents for a happy childhood, and for a love so deep and unconditional it defines the word.

Finally, a big affectionate thank-you to my loving wife, Jenny, and children, Patrick, Conor, and Colleen, for once again allowing me to mine our family experience and their lives for my inspiration. Thank you for your support and understanding and for always being there for me at the start and end of each day. This book is about family, and I am so grateful for mine. I love each of you beyond words.

The Longest Trip Home
by John Grogan

1. John Grogan's parents were devout Catholics. How did their faith impact John? How did his struggle with his parents' Catholicism shape his way of dealing with life and death, most notably when his father was dying?

2. What kind of household were you raised in? How did your parents' faith, or lack of it, influence your life?

3. Discuss John's relationship with his parents. Could you have been as accepting as his parents were during his adolescence? If you are a parent, talk about your relationship with your own children. If not, what kind of parent do you think you'd be?

4. What is the role of parents in children's lives? Do you think this role has changed from what it was in the 1960s and 1970s, when John Grogan was a boy?

5. In your opinion, what were the most important lessons John learned from his parents?

6. Grogan had to depart from his parents to find his way back to them and back home. Do you think his is a common experience?

7. What role did meeting Jenny play in John's transformation? How did John and Jenny's relationship compare to that of John's parents?

8. Becoming a parent himself was a motivating element in John's journey. Can someone truly understand their parents if they remain childless?

9. It is often said that we "become" our parents as we age. How does John resemble his parents? How have his experiences made him different?

10. At the end of the book, when John is visiting his mother, she tells him, "Once they leave home, that's it. They come back to visit, but it's never the same." John wants to protest but acknowledges that she is right. Do you agree? Why is it "never the same"?

11. Doris Kearns Goodwin praises *The Longest Trip Home*: "Every now and then a memoir is so well written that readers are able to find elements of their own life story in the chronicle of the writer's life." Do you agree with her? If so, what elements of your own life did you discover while reading?

12. A baby boomer born into a solidly middle-class midwestern household, John Grogan came from a very traditional American family. How might his story compare to others from different backgrounds? Can someone from another background—say the child of a single mother growing up in a large city—relate to his story? Why or why not?

13. Consider John at the various stages of his life. How are you similar and different from your younger self?

14. Did *The Longest Trip Home* affect the way you see your own childhood and family?

15. John Grogan writes openly and guilelessly about some very painful and deeply personal moments in his life. He also speaks freely of the mischievous and sometimes devious adolescent that he was. If you were to write your own memoir, how honest could you be? Do you think you could face and expose your weaknesses and strengths the way he did?

16. Do you think writers like John Grogan see the world differently, or more clearly, than other people?

17. John meets a Catholic priest: "a fan of what I did for a living, of using words to reach out to a larger community. As he put it in one e-mail, 'Just remember: Jesus' favorite and most frequent way of teaching was telling stories. Is it any surprise that as things have come and gone with the passage of time, storytelling remains? It is part and parcel of what makes us human—and puts us in touch with our humanity.' He called my writing my 'ministry' and added, 'In your own way, John, you are doing God's work.'" What do you think about this?

18. In his memoir, John Grogan touches on the themes of morality and grace, spirit and faith, and the powerful love of family. How are these demonstrated? Give some examples of each.

19. Speaking of the themes above, how does a memoir differ from fiction in conveying universal truths about the human condition? Do you think the message is stronger or more indelible when it is transmitted through a memoir rather than a novel?

20. If you've read John Grogan's previous book, *Marley & Me,* how does it compare to *The Longest Trip Home*? Are the tales similar? Do you see a connection between the two?

ALSO BY JOHN GROGAN

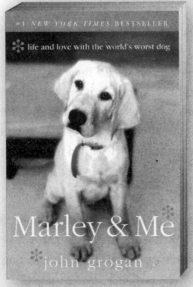

ISBN 978-0-06-081709-1 (paperback)

MARLEY & ME
Life and Love with the World's Worst Dog

When John and Jenny brought home Marley, a yellow Labrador retriever puppy, they realized their lives would never be the same. He crashed through screen doors, flung drool on guests, and ate everything in sight. And yet, his love and loyalty were boundless. Marley shared the couple's joy at their first pregnancy and their heartbreak over a miscarriage. He was there to protect and play with their children, and when the screams of a seventeen-year-old stabbing victim pierced the night. Even as he made a mess of things, Marley won the hearts of those around him and proved that unconditional love comes in many forms.

"It would take a heart of stone to resist *Marley & Me*."

—*New York Times*

"Heartfelt and frequently hilarious . . . [*Marley & Me*] gets at the heart of the animal-human bond, with humor and with pathos, in a deeply personal manner."

—*Philadelphia Inquirer*